The Violent World of
Broadus Miller

The Violent World of Broadus Miller
A Story of Murder, Lynch Mobs, and Judicial Punishment in the Carolinas

Kevin W. Young

The University of North Carolina Press CHAPEL HILL

This book was published with the assistance of the Authors Fund of the University of North Carolina Press.

© 2024 Kevin W. Young
All rights reserved
Set in Merope Basic by Westchester Publishing Services
Manufactured in the United States of America

Library of Congress Cataloging-in-Publication Data
Names: Young, Kevin W., author.
Title: The violent world of Broadus Miller : a story of murder, lynch mobs, and judicial punishment in the Carolinas / Kevin W. Young.
Description: Chapel Hill : The University of North Carolina Press, 2024. | Includes bibliographical references and index.
Identifiers: LCCN 2024005602 | ISBN 9781469679006 (cloth) | ISBN 9781469679013 (paperback) | ISBN 9781469679020 (epub) | ISBN 9798890887627 (pdf)
Subjects: LCSH: Miller, Broadus, -1927. | African Americans—North Carolina—Social conditions—To 1964. | African Americans—South Carolina—Social conditions—To 1964. | Murder—North Carolina—Morganton—History—20th century. | Lynching—North Carolina—History—20th century. | North Carolina—Race relations. | South Carolina—Race relations. | BISAC: SOCIAL SCIENCE / Ethnic Studies / American / African American & Black Studies | HISTORY / United States / State & Local / South (AL, AR, FL, GA, KY, LA, MS, NC, SC, TN, VA, WV)
Classification: LCC E185.93.N6 Y68 2024 | DDC 305.896/0730756— dc23/eng/20240229
LC record available at https://lccn.loc.gov/2024005602

Cover art: The Burke County courthouse and Confederate monument, Morganton, NC, in 1928. (History Museum of Burke County, Eugene Willard Collection, submitted to Picture Burke, a digital photograph collection of the Burke County Public Library, Morganton, NC.)

If we were not something more than unique human beings, if each one of us could really be done away with once and for all by a single bullet, storytelling would lose all purpose. But every man is more than just himself; he also represents the unique, the very special and always significant and remarkable point at which the world's phenomena intersect, only once in this way and never again.

—HERMANN HESSE, *Demian*

Contents

List of Illustrations, Maps, and Table ix

Prologue 1

CHAPTER ONE
Greenwood Boyhood 6

CHAPTER TWO
Alcohol, Guns, and Brute Force 16

CHAPTER THREE
Lynching and Foul Murder 25

CHAPTER FOUR
Mobs and Lone Killers 34

CHAPTER FIVE
Bloody Anderson 42

CHAPTER SIX
Calculating the Wages of Death 51

CHAPTER SEVEN
South Carolina State Penitentiary 59

CHAPTER EIGHT
The Chains of the Skyway 71

CHAPTER NINE
Law and Order in a White Supremacist State 77

CHAPTER TEN
Asheville's "Sordid Saturnalia" 86

CHAPTER ELEVEN
Morganton — Natives and Outsiders 95

CHAPTER TWELVE
The Convergence of the Twain 107

CHAPTER THIRTEEN
Outlawed 113

CHAPTER FOURTEEN
Mountain Manhunt 121

CHAPTER FIFTEEN
A Killing and a Celebration 131

CHAPTER SIXTEEN
Reverberations and Patterns 142

Epilogue 151

Acknowledgments 161
Notes 165
Bibliography 209
Index 231

Illustrations, Maps, and Table

ILLUSTRATIONS

1.1 Reverend James Selden Maddox (1857–1944) 11

4.1 Anthony Crawford (c. 1865–1916) 35

4.2 Reverend James Walker and the Briar Hollow school 40

5.1 Judge George E. Prince (1856–1923) 45

8.1 Signatures of Broadus Miller and his bride, 1924 76

9.1 Ku Klux Klan in Asheville, 1924 84

10.1 Alvin Mansel 87

10.2 Chain gang in upstate South Carolina, 1917 93

11.1 Franklin Pierce Tate House, Morganton, NC 97

11.2 Burke County courthouse and Confederate monument, Morganton, NC 98

11.3 Morganton editor Beatrice Cobb (1888–1959) 101

12.1 Garrou Knitting Mill, Morganton, NC 109

12.2 Gladys Kincaid and family 111

14.1 Reward notice for Broadus Miller 125

15.1 Bear hunters in Linville Falls 132

15.2 Morganton courthouse square, July 3, 1927 137

15.3 Commodore Vanderbilt Burleson 140

E.1 Gravestone of Gladys Kincaid 159

MAPS

  1.1 Shoals Junction and surrounding region, 1910 7

14.1 Western North Carolina in the Broadus Miller manhunt, 1927 127

TABLE

  6.1 Legal executions in South Carolina, 1892–1921 57

The Violent World of
Broadus Miller

Prologue

Morganton, North Carolina, lies at the western edge of the Piedmont in the foothills of the Appalachians. The town dates to the early 1780s, when officials chose a stretch of high ground near the Catawba River to serve as the site of a county seat for recently created Burke County. There a log-cabin courthouse was erected. In the 1830s this primitive wooden building gave way to a stately new courthouse, two stories tall and made of stone. During the antebellum era, the North Carolina supreme court held its annual summer sessions in Morganton, allowing the justices a respite from Raleigh's sweltering heat. With close political ties to the state capital but sitting in the shadow of the mountains, Morganton was a figurative as well as a literal middle ground, at the edge of the established judicial system but only a short journey from the rough justice of the frontier.[1]

In the early twentieth century, as furniture factories and textile mills sprang up across the Piedmont, Morganton rapidly grew into a thriving town with the historic stone courthouse at its center. On East Union Street, less than two blocks from the courthouse, stood Garrou Knitting Mill, which produced artificial silk hosiery for women and mercerized dress socks for men. In the spring of 1927, a fifteen-year-old girl named Gladys Kincaid began working at Garrou Knitting Mill. Kincaid lived with her widowed mother and several siblings on a farm next to the Catawba River, about a mile and a half from the mill. On her daily walk to and from work, she traveled along Bouchelle Street, which began a few hundred yards from the family's farmhouse and led up a gently sloping hill to the middle of town. Around the lower end of Bouchelle resided a handful of other white families, including the Foxes and Whisenants, but further up the hill and closer to downtown the street passed through an African American neighborhood. Among the Black families living on Bouchelle were Will and Annie Berry. Will Berry worked as a delivery driver for a furniture factory, his wife Annie taught school, and the couple supplemented their income by renting out rooms in their two-story house.[2]

On Tuesday, June 21, 1927, Gladys Kincaid's shift at Garrou Knitting Mill ended at five thirty in the afternoon. A dark sky threatened rain as Kincaid began her long walk down Bouchelle Street toward home. Nearing the end of the street, she briefly stopped to speak with Ida Whisenant, who was outside with her young children. The two of them discussed going to a show one evening the following week, when the American Legion would host a musical comedy called "Cupid-Up-to-Date" at the local high school. Kincaid mentioned that she was hungry after her ten-hour day in the mill and Whisenant invited her to stay and have something to eat. "No, I must go on home," the girl replied. "I am very tired." More work awaited her, for she had to prepare supper for the rest of her family and have it ready when they came in from laboring in the fields. Saying goodbye to Whisenant, the young mill worker resumed her journey home.[3]

Around seven o'clock Kincaid's mother finished working outdoors and returned to the house to discover that her daughter had not arrived, so the entire family began looking for her. Gladys's twenty-two-year-old brother Harvey went to the home of John Fox and enlisted the help of Fox's son Virgil. As Harvey Kincaid and Virgil Fox searched the area around the lower end of Bouchelle Street, they "heard a groan and discovered her body in a clump of bushes a few yards off the road, evidently carried up the embankment and pitched there." She was unconscious and bleeding profusely. Her skull behind her right ear had been "crushed like an egg shell" by one or more blows from a blunt instrument, and according to some accounts, her "clothes were torn to shreds." A section of iron pipe, stained with blood, lay near her body. The young men flagged down a passing car and rushed Kincaid to Morganton's Grace Hospital, but she never regained consciousness, dying around three thirty the next morning.[4]

Gladys Kincaid had been fatally attacked about 500 yards beyond the Whisenants' house and almost in sight of her own home. In an adjacent field stood several large haystacks, leading to speculation that her assailant may have hidden behind one of them and ambushed the girl. Led by Burke County sheriff Julius "Jules" Hallyburton, law enforcement officials quickly converged on the scene, and when they spoke with Ida Whisenant, she told them that around the time of her conversation with Kincaid, she had seen a Black man in a yellow raincoat walking down the street with an iron pipe in his hand. Police soon identified the man as an itinerant laborer who boarded at Will Berry's. His name was Broadus Miller.[5]

Accompanied by his wife, Miller had arrived in Morganton a few weeks earlier to work at a local construction site, and the couple had taken up residence in Berry's house. On that fateful Tuesday afternoon, Miller had finished work about four thirty and returned to his lodgings and eaten supper around five o'clock. After the meal, he chatted with a couple of coworkers who came to visit; he then left the house and walked off down the street. When police arrived at Will Berry's, Miller was nowhere to be found, but a few articles of clothing had been taken from his room. His wife said she had not seen him since supper, but that he may have returned and left again without her knowledge. Searching the house, police discovered Miller's yellow raincoat hidden behind a door. The raincoat was spattered with fresh bloodstains.[6]

That evening, as news of the attack on Kincaid spread, mobs of enraged white men gathered in downtown Morganton and fanned out to search for Broadus Miller. Journalists from across the state rushed to the scene. A correspondent for the Raleigh *News and Observer* arrived to find the town's residents in a frenzy: "Two thousand men went wild. Armed with every sort of weapon from ancient squirrel rifles to the latest automatic, they beat about the streets here, pried the alleys, backyards and every conceivable hiding place, and then lay a dragnet far out into the hills. A rain around 10 o'clock offered no check. All night the hunt was on in determined fashion. One citizen of Valdese who refused to stop his car at the command to halt had a bullet fired through his automobile top. Every available man, every available firearm was in service." All freight trains passing through Morganton and the nearby town of Hickory were stopped and searched, while rumored sightings of the suspect sent men racing to locations in the nearby countryside. The sixty men of the local National Guard company had been conducting their weekly drill that Tuesday evening. The company included Corporal Willie Kincaid, Gladys's older brother. Acting on their own initiative, Kincaid and the other guardsmen began searching for his sister's accused killer. By midnight, several hundred residents of Catawba and Caldwell Counties had arrived to join the manhunt, and the Caldwell County sheriff deployed a hastily assembled posse along the Burke County border. A Morganton resident later marveled that "many an innocent person" was not shot, for "about everyone who could carry a gun was out searching."[7]

In the hours following the discovery of Gladys Kincaid's body, racial tensions in Morganton were at a fever pitch, and every young Black man in town ran the risk of being mistaken for Broadus Miller. Initial accounts emphasized the accused killer had worn a raincoat. On the southern edge of town, a Black man in a raincoat was walking home from his job at Burke Tannery when a mob seized him. As they prepared to lynch him from a railway bridge, one of his white coworkers happened to pass by. Vouching for the man's identity and insisting that he had been present at the tannery all day, the coworker persuaded them to release their intended victim. Police arrested and jailed Broadus Miller's wife and Will Berry, both as material witnesses and for their own protection. The African American families living on Bouchelle Street stayed up throughout the night, armed with knives and makeshift weapons, anxiously looking out their windows as carloads of white men drove by yelling racial epithets. Some residents took up positions on their roofs with shotguns, ready to defend their homes against any onslaught of a mob.[8]

Early on Wednesday morning, a policeman found a pair of trousers and a work shirt in the woods where the Catawba and Johns Rivers converged, apparently discarded by Broadus Miller when he changed clothes after the previous night's downpour. However, an intensive search along the riverbanks proved futile. Throughout the morning "the roving, restless bands who scoured the town and country" gradually returned to the courthouse square. After the previous night's uproar, Morganton was eerily silent. Business in the town had come to a standstill, with many employers giving their workers time off to join the manhunt. Groups of white men clustered together on the courthouse lawn and surrounding streets, taciturn and grim, exhausted from the sleepless night and awaiting any news that Broadus Miller had been sighted. Around ten thirty that morning, word came that Miller had allegedly been seen near Lake James, about a dozen miles west of Morganton. The news electrified the crowd: "The scattered groups instantly became hundreds dashing madly across the streets and into automobiles. . . . There appeared to be no speed limits, no thoughts for safety of men or machines. The first rush for position having been settled on the score of survival of the fittest machine and the fastest driver, the long line of automobiles stretched out over the hills. . . . A few cars dropped out of the way; the occupants were picked up by others." A reporter overheard one man begging for a ride. "Here, let me go," the man pleaded. "I got a hell of a good gun."[9]

By noon, an estimated 2,500 people had swarmed to the scene of the alleged sighting, a wooded area between the communities of Nebo and Bridgewater. "Backwoodsmen from the hills, armed with squirrel rifles and shotguns," searched the woods alongside mill hands and factory workers. "Bewhiskered farmers with long nosed pistols sticking from their pockets strolled along the highway as solemn as so many judges," one journalist noted. "Every now and then a false alarm would come from one section of the wood and in a minute a crushing mob was there." The Associated Press reported that the "roads from Bridgewater to Nebo are choked with automobiles carrying men and even some women to the scene," and police officers on site admitted that they "could not control the crowd if the negro was captured." The prospect of a lynching proved a boon for local merchants. In Bridgewater, "cold drinks were sold out in the three main stores by noon," and all the "filling stations and country merchants from Bridgewater to Nebo did a land office business." But the alleged sighting turned out to be merely a rumor, and after hours of fruitless searching, the large mob slowly dispersed, with many people heading back to Morganton to resume their vigil on the courthouse square.[10]

In the coming days, the search for Gladys Kincaid's accused killer would expand into the largest manhunt that had ever taken place in western North Carolina, involving several thousand men and covering numerous counties. Yet Broadus Miller remained an elusive figure. An itinerant laborer of obscure origins, he had arrived in Morganton around the same time Kincaid began working in the hosiery mill. A couple of press reports mentioned that Miller was a native of South Carolina, but only when speculating on which direction he might flee. Journalists considered the accused Black man's background and personal history irrelevant. He had apparently killed a young white woman, and nothing he had previously done could add to or detract from the infamy of such a deed. Newspapers across North Carolina offered extensive coverage of the ongoing manhunt, but only the *Winston-Salem Journal* noted what Burke County authorities had learned about the accused killer's past. Sheriff Hallyburton had spoken with officials in Broadus Miller's native state who confirmed what one of Miller's acquaintances in Morganton had told the sheriff: the man wanted in connection with Gladys Kincaid's death "had once killed a woman in South Carolina."[11]

CHAPTER ONE

Greenwood Boyhood

At the western edge of South Carolina, along the Savannah River that forms the state's border with Georgia, are Abbeville and Edgefield Counties. For most of the nineteenth century the two counties adjoined one another and covered a vast territory, from the Savannah eastward to the Saluda, but in the 1890s the counties' large size became a cause for complaint. Landowners far from the county seats received little funding for roads and bridges, so they petitioned the state legislature to carve out a new county with the town of Greenwood at its center. In 1897 legislators granted the request and created Greenwood County from Abbeville and Edgefield. The new county had a population of nearly 30,000 people, two-thirds of whom were former slaves and their descendants.[1]

The northern end of Greenwood County consisted of a large rural township called Walnut Grove, and the main railway line running north from the town of Greenwood passed through a small depot in the middle of the township. Located fourteen miles from the county seat and just below the Abbeville County border, the depot became a focal point for the rural community, a place where people came to receive freight shipments or ride racially segregated train cars to town. In 1906 workers completed five miles of track from the depot eastward to the newly established textile mill at Ware Shoals on the Saluda River, connecting the mill town with the main railway line. The depot at Shoals Junction, as the place came to be known, quickly grew into a busy transit point with a general store and post office (see map 1.1). By the 1910s, trains ran from Shoals Junction to Ware Shoals some two dozen times a day, and the Southern Railway and Piedmont & Northern made Shoals Junction a regularly scheduled stop on their routes in and out of Greenwood.[2]

At the beginning of the twentieth century, a Black tenant farmer named Tom Walker lived in the countryside east of Shoals Junction, between the depot and Ware Shoals. In his late twenties, widowed and with a small son, Walker had resided in the area his entire life. Around 1908 the young widower remarried. His new wife, Alpha Williams, was about ten years younger than her husband. She too had been previously married and had a son of her own. In addition to these two sons, the newly married couple took four

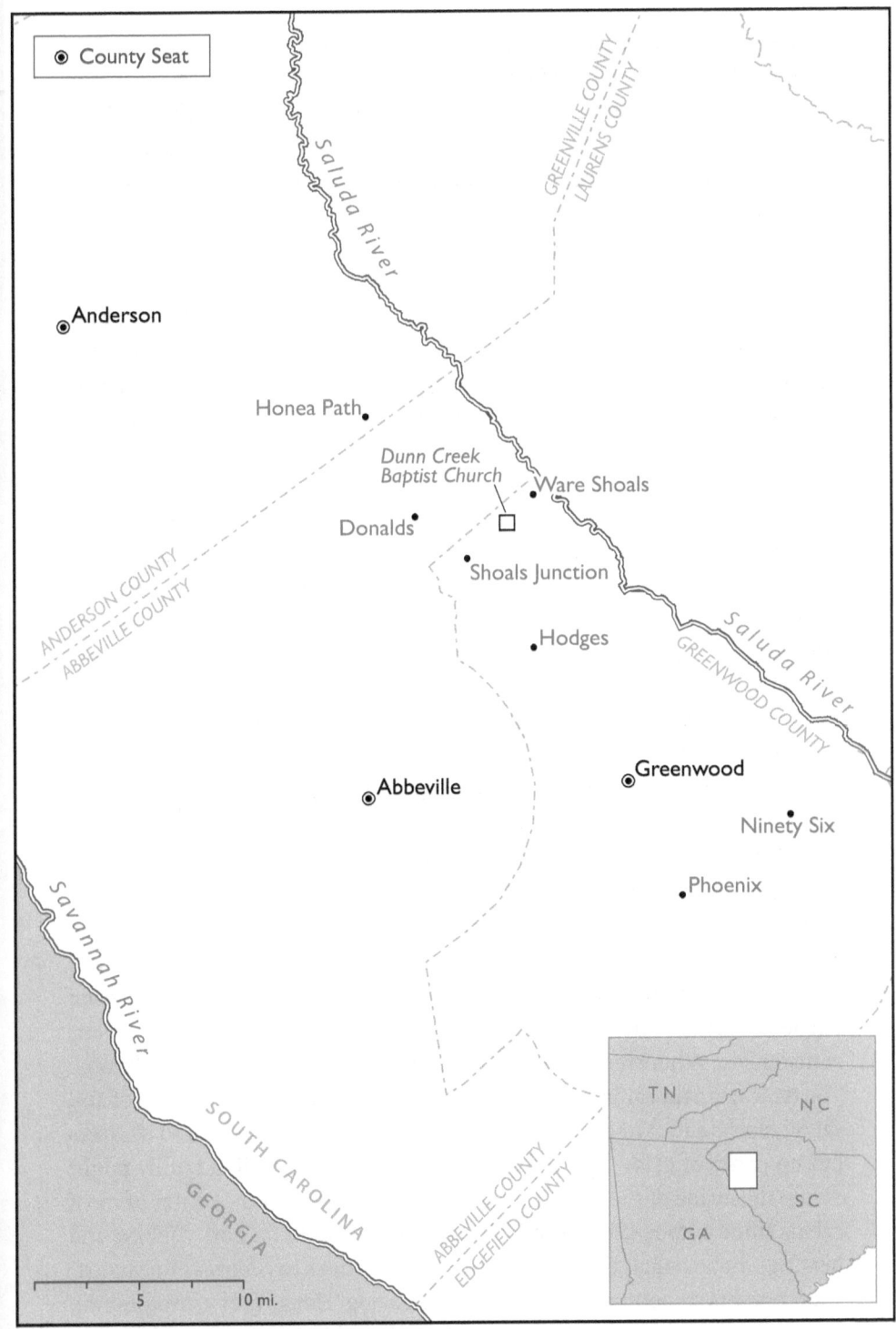

MAP 1.1 Shoals Junction, South Carolina, and surrounding region in 1910. (Map by Josh Platt.)

orphaned children into their home—a girl and three boys who had the surname Miller and were listed on census records as the Walkers' niece and nephews. The youngest child had been born the same year as the Walkers' marriage; the eldest, ten years earlier. There is no record of when or how their parents died. One of these children, a boy born about 1904, was Broadus Miller.[3]

The Walkers lived in the eastern half of Walnut Grove township, within a census district bounded by Turkey Creek and Long Cane Creek. Between these streams lay two dozen square miles of rolling fields and scattered farms. In 1910, the district contained 133 households and had a population of 735 people, nearly 60 percent of whom were Black. Almost all these residents, both white and Black, had lived in upstate South Carolina for several generations, but only one-quarter of the district's families owned land. The majority—including the Walkers and nearly 90 percent of other African Americans—either rented or sharecropped the farms on which they lived. Nominally free laborers, farm tenants were contractually bound to their landlords, usually by oral agreements that would be remembered and interpreted as the landlord wished. Under the provisions of an 1897 South Carolina labor law, if a landlord furnished cotton seed and fertilizer in the spring, then sharecroppers and contracted wage laborers had to work on the farm until the crop was fully harvested in the fall; if they did not fulfill this obligation, they could be sent to a chain gang. In 1907 a federal court declared the law unconstitutional, ruling that it created "a system of peonage or involuntary servitude," but for years afterward many farm owners and local officials flagrantly ignored the court decision and kept Black sharecroppers and farmhands in virtual slavery.[4]

As tenant farmers, Tom and Alpha Walker left little trace in any written records. Every decade, a census taker noted their presence in Walnut Grove township, but at the end of each year tenant families sometimes moved from one local farm to another, asserting a limited freedom to change their circumstances. Wherever they went, a family found similar living conditions. The typical tenant cabin had rough plank walls and a corrugated tin roof and sat on blocks a foot or two off the ground. Windows had clapboard shutters but no panes of glass. By putting up an interior plank wall, a family might divide the inside of the cabin into two or more rooms. In the center of most cabins stood a stone-chimneyed fireplace that was used for both cooking and heating, for although the temperature hovered near 100 degrees in August, winter nights sometimes dropped below freezing. House fires were common in winter, with young children especially vulnerable to dying in such blazes.

Without indoor plumbing, buckets of water had to be hauled from a spring or nearby creek. The slow grind of abject poverty and unsanitary living conditions fostered disease. Pellagra and dysentery were widespread, and infants occasionally died of malnutrition.[5]

Like Broadus Miller, the prominent civil rights activist Benjamin Mays grew up in Greenwood County, the son of tenant farmers. Born in 1894—about ten years before Miller—Mays eventually overcame his origins through determination and a lifetime of dogged struggle, becoming president of Morehouse College and a mentor to Martin Luther King Jr. When looking back on his childhood, Mays emphasized the crucial role that strong family ties had played in his personal success. Most African Americans in the county came from a family background similar to Mays's. In 1910, only five of the seventy-eight Black households in the Walkers' district included children who had neither a father nor mother. In each of these cases, the children lived with grandparents or uncles and aunts. Yet, even among these five households, the Walkers were unique. In addition to Tom Walker's son by his first wife, Alpha Walker's son to whom she had given birth as a teenager, and the four Miller children, a few years after the Walkers' marriage another child joined the household—an illegitimate daughter whom Tom Walker had fathered by another woman. The Walkers thus raised a total of seven children, the sons and daughters of at least three different fathers and four different mothers. No other household in the district had such a tangled web of family ties.[6]

About two miles east of the Shoals Junction depot, along the dirt road leading to Ware Shoals, lived a prominent white landowner named W. E. Algary. The site of his home became known as Algary and served as the headquarters for the local school district. In the countryside around Algary resided a handful of extended families of white landowning cotton farmers who frequently intermarried and had close kinship ties with each other. Two of these families were the Rasors and the Agnews. They had settled in the area during the late eighteenth century, and by 1850, several members of the two families had become wealthy slaveholders. The planter James Agnew owned twenty-eight slaves, while his neighbor Ezekiel Rasor held forty men, women, and children in bondage. Over half a century later, the grandchildren of these two men would be the labor lords of Tom and Alpha Walker. The Walkers seem to have periodically moved between various farms owned by the Rasors and Agnews. The 1910 census listed them next to the home of landowner William E. Agnew. A few years later, they were tenants on the farm of Agnew's brother-in-law, Harrison Latimer "Lat" Rasor, and by 1920 they resided beside an elderly widowed farm owner named Orlena Agnew, who was a cousin of both Lat Rasor and William Agnew—and whose son would marry Lat Rasor's daughter.[7]

For several generations, the Rasors and Agnews had been members of Turkey Creek Baptist Church. Following emancipation, Ezekiel Rasor had donated a small tract of land on Dunn Creek, a little over a mile from the Turkey Creek church, for the newly freed people to establish a church of their own. Originally a crude brush arbor made of tree limbs and scraps of wood, and later replaced by a more substantial wooden building, Dunn Creek Baptist Church became a center for the Black community, a place to congregate for both spiritual and secular affairs. Though Black tenant farmers owned no land and had no legal claim to a permanent home, and though they might drift from tenancy on one farm to another, the church provided a place they could call their own, a common ground that belonged to them and to which they belonged. In 1901, Reverend James Selden Maddox became the pastor of Dunn Creek, a position he would hold for nearly four decades (see figure 1.1). The middle-aged Maddox was the son of a local white plantation owner and a Black female slave. His father had recognized him as a son and deeded him several hundred acres of farmland, making him one of the region's largest African American landowners. Maddox's congregation at Dunn Creek included the family of Tom Walker, who served as a deacon in the church.[8]

As a child, Broadus Miller undoubtedly did various farm chores, but he had not yet been consigned to full-time labor in the fields. In 1910, a census taker noted that the six-year-old Miller had attended school the previous year. The South Carolina constitution mandated racially segregated schools, and Miller went to a one-room schoolhouse within a mile or two of his home, where a young Black woman in her early twenties taught a few dozen children of various ages. Throughout South Carolina, communities funded and operated their own schools. Greenwood County had a total of forty-eight separate school districts. The chairman of the Algary district was Harrison "Lat" Rasor, one of the landlords of Miller's family. Rasor oversaw four primary schools, two for white pupils and two for Blacks, each of them taught by a single female teacher. These four schools operated on an annual budget of around $460. Some of this money came from a poll tax and a tax on dog ownership, but around 80 percent came from local property taxes. White landowners paid most of these taxes, and the distribution of school funding was overwhelmingly weighted in their favor. In 1911, the two white schools served a total enrollment of 62 pupils; the two Black schools, 117. A

FIGURE 1.1 Reverend James Selden Maddox (1857–1944), the pastor of Dunn Creek Baptist Church. (A. B. Caldwell, ed., *History of the American Negro: South Carolina Edition* [Atlanta: A. B. Caldwell, 1919], 24.)

white teacher received an annual salary of $167.70; a Black teacher, $60. The white schools were valued at $450; the Black schools, $100. Most Greenwood County school districts had even greater inequality in funding. On average, the county's schools spent $11.23 annually on each white pupil and only $1.22 for each Black child.[9]

Statistics alone cannot convey the stark difference in quality between the racially segregated facilities. In 1911, the state superintendent of education J. E. Swearingen surveyed African American schools throughout South Carolina. "The negro schoolhouses are miserable beyond all description," Swearingen reported. "They are usually without comfort, equipment, proper lighting, or sanitation." For a few months each year, Black children "crowded into these miserable structures" to learn from teachers who usually had little experience and no formal training. Despite the wretched conditions, most African American parents were determined for their children to receive an education. On average, 74 percent of Black children in the Algary district attended school, compared with a 60 percent attendance rate for whites. Noting a much higher countywide enrollment rate among school-age Blacks than among whites, the head of Greenwood County's schools lamented that

Greenwood Boyhood

"white people do not take the same interest in the education of their children."[10]

Highly critical of the schools provided for African Americans, the state superintendent of education wanted South Carolina's Black population to receive a good education—in agricultural skills that would benefit the ruling white elite. "The negro is now, and will be for years to come, the tenant farmer of South Carolina," argued Swearingen. "His welfare and the prosperity of the white race depend largely upon his efficiency as a farmer." For the education secretary, "a better existence" for African Americans meant "a more constant labor supply" for white landowners. Such sentiments represented a comparatively enlightened progressivism. Many South Carolina political leaders opposed funding any education for African Americans. As Ben Tillman noted, a literacy test served as a primary means of preventing Blacks from voting, and education would thus undermine the test's purpose. As governor in the 1890s, Tillman had led the campaign to disfranchise African Americans; on becoming a US senator, he called for repealing the Fifteenth Amendment so disfranchisement could be based explicitly on race. Until the amendment was repealed, he argued, there should be no attempt to uplift the Black population through education. Tillman's one-time protégé Coleman Blease scornfully dismissed public funding for African American schools as a waste of white taxpayers' money. "When a good cotton hand gets a smattering of education, he has got to be a preacher with a long-tailed coat and a beaver hat, or a doctor or something, and he won't work," asserted Blease.[11]

By the time he entered his teen years, Broadus Miller's smattering of formal education had ended and he had become a full-time farmhand. The agricultural economy in Greenwood County revolved around cotton. It had been the region's most important crop during the antebellum era, but residents had also cultivated grain and raised livestock. In the decades following the Civil War, however, farm owners increasingly focused on growing cotton "almost to the exclusion of other crops." By the early twentieth century, the county's cotton fields covered over 70,000 acres—more than half the available farmland—and annually produced over 30,000 bales. Rural merchants often made raising cotton a condition for extending credit, but in many cases farmers themselves chose to concentrate on the potentially lucrative cash crop. When reminiscing about his childhood, Benjamin Mays recalled that his family and their neighbors never produced enough food to last the entire year, and he found this lack of agricultural self-sufficiency puzzling. "The curse was cotton," Mays concluded. "It was difficult to make farmers see that more corn, grain, hogs, and cows meant less cash but more profit in the end. Cotton sold instantly, and that was *cash* money."[12]

Cotton agriculture was labor intensive, and from late winter through the following fall, tenant farmers such as the Walkers spent long days working in the fields. In March they began preparing the ground, beating down the remnants of the previous year's plants and gathering and burning the stalks. They then tilled and harrowed and spread barnyard manure over the freshly upturned dirt. After plowing up long rows of elevated beds about four feet apart, they cut a shallow furrow down the middle of each bed and sprinkled fertilizer along the furrows. In early April the cotton seed was planted, either by hand or with a mule-drawn mechanical planter. Within days, the plants began sprouting, shooting forth in thick bunches that impeded each other's growth. Throughout May, farmhands with hoes chopped the cotton, cutting away about four young stalks for each one left standing, and in the following weeks they regularly hoed grass and weeds from around the plants. Work came to a sudden halt in early July, with the cotton left untended—or "laid by"—until the ground dried out and the plants came to fruition. After about six weeks, the swollen bolls began bursting open, revealing the white-fibered crop. Throughout the early twentieth century, cotton was still picked by hand, as it had been under slavery. As soon as the morning dew evaporated, field hands began moving down the rows, picking the cotton and placing it in a cloth sack, then emptying the filled sack into a basket or large bag. At sundown the basket or bag was weighed; an experienced and physically fit worker could pick over 400 pounds a day.[13]

The 1920 census listed sixteen-year-old Broadus Miller as a wage-earning farm laborer, but he probably worked primarily at home on the Walkers' tenant farm and then, whenever the workload slackened, hired himself out as a day laborer. A hired hand typically earned thirty-five to fifty cents a day for chopping or hoeing cotton. But from late August to October, with a limited window of time for harvesting the crop and farm owners eager to get it to market, the demand for workers dramatically increased. Pickers usually received around forty or fifty cents per hundred pounds and could thus earn up to a couple of dollars a day, so many cooks and other domestic servants—both men and women—would temporarily leave their regular employers for a few weeks to pick cotton.[14]

At best, toiling in the cotton fields allowed families such as the Walkers to survive from one year to the next. Under ideal conditions, a typical two-mule farm of forty acres could produce sixteen bales of cotton, each weighing around 500 pounds. If a family sharecropped the farm, with the landlord furnishing the mules and equipment, then theoretically the crop would be equitably divided and the tenants would keep eight bales, but unscrupulous landlords often cheated sharecroppers out of their fair share. A tenant family's profits could be significantly higher if they owned their own mules and could rent instead of sharecrop. In upstate South Carolina, renters typically paid one bale of cotton annually for every ten acres of land, though some landlords calculated rent according to "the age and earning capacity" of a tenant's children and increased it as the children grew older. If a family renting a forty-acre farm paid their landlord four bales, they could sell the remaining twelve bales for around $500 to $700, depending on the price of cotton. After they repaid a merchant for any supplies taken on credit—a bill that was frequently falsified and padded—then whatever money remained would have to tide the family over to the next spring and the planting of a new year's crop.[15]

The financial situation of tenants was always precarious, and any unexpected event could spell disaster. With a hailstorm or a flood, a drought or a pestilence, a family's entire yearly income might suddenly vanish. Reporting the news from Algary in the spring of 1919, a correspondent for the Greenwood *Index-Journal* briefly noted that "Tom Walker, a colored man, living on Mr. H. L. Rasor's place, lost a good mule last week." A single line in a gossip column, but the consequences of the loss for Broadus Miller's family can only be imagined. Mules were prized work animals, more expensive than horses. Three years earlier, the South Carolina State Agricultural Society had estimated the average value of a mule at $150, approximately one-quarter of the gross annual income of a tenant family renting a farm. But in order to rent instead of sharecrop, a family had to own a mule. In 1919, the same year as Tom Walker's misfortune, a creditor seized the mule of an Abbeville County tenant family. The family had struggled to claw their way up from sharecropping to renting; the loss of their mule reduced them to sharecropping once again.[16]

Tenant families such as the Walkers had no possibility of improving their economic condition through political means. Though Blacks comprised a majority of South Carolina's population, in 1895 a new state constitution established a poll tax and property and literacy requirements for voting. During the November 1898 election, this new constitution was baptized in blood, with the rural community of Phoenix in Greenwood County becoming an epicenter of electoral violence. When African Americans who met the ostensible voting requirements attempted to cast ballots in Phoenix, a clash at the polls sparked a four-day reign of terror in which armed mobs of white men rode through the southern half of the county and killed at least eight Blacks. "The negroes have had a severe lesson and a forcible turn from a fancied road to power," rejoiced the *Greenwood Index*. In an editorial titled "No Negro Domination," the newspaper set forth the ideology sanctioning such violence:

> It is a basic principle in our unwritten law that the white man must rule. . . . Everything that pertains to citizenship, to property and the pursuit of happiness must conform to this law. . . . It is a painful fact, however, that in order to enforce this law, harsh measures are sometimes necessary, but whether the measures are right or wrong, the higher law which brings about these measures is always right. . . . No, our civilization won't allow us to entertain any thought of the negro taking a part in a white man's realm and any steps from him in this direction will result to the detriment of those who aid him and to his own destruction. It is better for the negro to keep out of politics.[17]

Occurring the same week as a much larger massacre of African Americans in Wilmington, North Carolina, the violence at Phoenix would loom large in the collective memory of Greenwood County residents for decades to come. Underneath a veil of supposedly color-blind constitutional measures, Blacks had been disfranchised at gunpoint. Two weeks after the bloody November 1898 election, the Atlanta editorialist Wallace Putnam Reed reflected on what had happened. "It is nonsense to indulge in any gush about the New South," Reed concluded. "That masked figure may be very conspicuous at banquets and reunions, but the Old South is behind the mask, ready at a moment's notice to strike a blow with the iron hand, which is as heavy as of yore, despite its velvet glove."[18]

CHAPTER TWO

Alcohol, Guns, and Brute Force

In the early twentieth century, white supremacy seemed a permanent feature of political and social life in South Carolina, but in other respects the region around Shoals Junction was rapidly changing. By 1912, six textile mills had opened in Greenwood County, including the one at Ware Shoals, about three miles from Broadus Miller's home. The white mill workers who toiled in wage-labor subservience could at least take comfort in having jobs inaccessible to African Americans. In 1915 the South Carolina legislature decreed that all textile mill operations be racially segregated, and though Blacks would be hired for menial tasks such as sorting raw cotton or loading trucks, only whites were allowed to work inside the mills running the machinery. With the growth of the mills came railway expansion and local short lines that connected even small rural communities to the regional rail network. Yet there were already signs hinting at the railroads' eventual obsolescence. In 1916, a new highway was completed between Shoals Junction and Ware Shoals, with a celebratory procession of automobiles marking its opening. The following year, in a sign of both the massive growth of the automotive industry and the increasing regulatory power of the state, South Carolina began mandating state registration of automobiles.[1]

During this era of material and technological change, churches such as Dunn Creek helped African Americans maintain a sense of continuity and community, with the rhythms of church life following the same well-worn grooves as cotton agriculture. Sunday was a day of rest from hard labor. When the cotton was laid by during July and early August, revivals and camp meetings lasted for several days or even weeks and attracted hundreds of people. In winter, after the crop had been harvested, church associations held weeklong meetings. The cycles of cotton farming influenced the church calendar, but the activities of African American churches could force white residents to alter their own schedules. In December 1915, when Abbeville hosted the annual state conference of the Negro Methodist Church, the local newspaper noted that the town's white residents would have to adjust their plans for the week accordingly. "Most of the cooks of the town have given notice that they want a holiday . . . and light housekeeping and short meals are going to be the style around town," the paper reported.[2]

African American churches hosted a wide variety of social events, and such gatherings sometimes resulted in conflict instead of communion. As Benjamin Mays later recalled, "Fighting and heavy drinking on church property were common practices in many churches." When rural Black residents came together after laboring through the week on isolated farms, then any long-standing grievances could come to a head, often with fatal consequences. The white press delighted in reporting such deadly encounters between Black churchgoers. In 1906, a brawl at a church social in Greenwood County left one man dead and others injured. "All of the negroes seemed to have been drinking and rows and fusses were very common around this particular church," a journalist noted. At a church supper in 1910, one African American shot and killed another in retaliation for an earlier assault, and in 1918 an argument between two men at another church in the county culminated in one of them drawing a pistol and killing the other. In the spring of 1920, a fatal shootout between two Black men occurred at a church in neighboring McCormick County. According to a press account, "The two negroes had not been on good terms for some time, and when they met at the church decided to settle once and for all time, while services were being held in the building." After a deadly gunfight erupted at a 1916 church picnic in Edgefield County, the *Edgefield Advertiser* offered an acerbic appraisal of what had occurred: "Saturday afternoon about five miles north of Edgefield the negroes of the community held a Sunday school picnic. It appears however that the Ruler of the Lower Regions directed the affairs of the occasion."[3]

In addition to church-sponsored events, African Americans in rural South Carolina held social gatherings known as "hot suppers." Beginning in October, as work in the cotton fields ended and farm families had a bit of spending money from selling their crop, and continuing through the winter, these suppers were enormously popular. The organizers of such events sometimes used them as a means of raising money, either by charging admission or by having food and drink for sale. The meal usually consisted of a fish fry, a roasted beef, or a large tub of stew or hash, with cakes and pies for dessert. For some men, such gatherings served as an opportunity to play cards and shoot craps, but the primary entertainment at a hot supper was music, usually provided by a fiddle player accompanied by someone on banjo or guitar. Dancing lasted late into the night and occasionally into the following morning. Men sometimes paid women a small amount of money to be their partners for a dance or treated a dance partner to one of the desserts offered for sale.[4]

Throughout the early twentieth century, the South Carolina press regularly reported news of shootings, stabbings, and razor-slashings at hot suppers. Undoubtedly motivated in part by suspicion of Black social gatherings, the media coverage highlighted the depressing frequency of such violence. In 1901, seeking to curtail "the troubles that grow out of negro entertainments," a state legislator from Abbeville introduced a bill that would have required anyone planning a hot supper to obtain a license from the clerk of court. Later that year, after a man was shot and killed at a hot supper in Greenwood County, the local newspaper described hot suppers as "fatal entertainments among the colored people." On a Sunday night in October 1911, a large crowd attended a hot supper in the community of Donalds, about three miles from Broadus Miller's home. "Grub and fighting fluid were in abundance," a journalist reported. As the whiskey flowed and passions rose, one man ended up cutting another's throat and nearly killing him. In 1914, the Greenwood County sheriff lobbied state lawmakers to pass "a bill prohibiting the hot supper and kindred frolics." His efforts were unsuccessful, but that spring, after yet another fatal shooting at a supper, the Greenwood *Daily Journal* editorialized in favor of banning them. "We think it right to prohibit anything that is inimical to life, and that is likely to cause murder and bloodshed. In this class is to be found the negro hot supper," the paper argued. "It seems to be the place for drinking, carousing, and slashing with razors, and brandishing shooting irons in general."[5]

Most contemporary observers cited the combination of alcohol and firearms as the primary cause of lethal violence in upstate South Carolina. At first through local referendums, and after 1916 by state-wide prohibition, Greenwood was officially a dry county, but bootleggers known as "blind tigers" plied their trade throughout the region, distilling the liquor themselves or importing it from thriving bootlegging centers such as Augusta, Georgia. In May 1913, the *Greenwood Index* noted that sixty gallons of whiskey had been seized over the previous ten days and the county jail was full of blind tigers. Moreover, all South Carolina residents could legally order alcohol from out of state and have it shipped to their home county. In 1915, state lawmakers limited such orders to one gallon a month per person; two years later, the limit was further reduced to one quart. The chronically thirsty found their way around such restrictions by placing orders in other people's names, and shipments of booze regularly poured into railroad depots such as Shoals Junction. "Anybody who has seen the great crowds, especially negro women, around the express offices must know that the gallon-a-month law serves no good end," a local judge complained.[6]

One of the main arguments for prohibiting alcohol was its role in fueling gun violence. Many rural families owned shotguns, which were widely used for hunting, but pistols did not have such a clearly benign purpose. "The pistol toting habit goes most generally with that of drinking and the two make a deadly combination," a Greenwood journalist noted. "Put a flask of whiskey and a pistol in a man's pocket and he is ready for ugly work." In 1900, a South Carolina judge delivered an impassioned sermon from the bench, decrying "the deplorable custom of carrying pistols." The following year, Representative Robert Cooper—a future governor of the state—introduced a bill prohibiting the manufacture, sale, or carrying of "any pistol less than twenty inches long and three pounds in weight." In the words of one of the bill's sponsors, "A pistol is a disgraceful thing, and no man ought to be allowed to carry one whether concealed or not." State lawmakers eventually approved the legislation and the pistol ban went into effect, with violations punishable by fines of up to $100 and thirty days in jail.[7]

Even more than the prohibition of alcohol, South Carolina's ban on pistols would be widely flouted and seldom enforced. In the years following the ban, young men in Greenwood County—whites and African Americans alike—routinely carried pistols, either in their pockets or in holsters beneath their shirts. Years later, Benjamin Mays recalled that most Black men in the county took their pistols with them wherever they went. In 1905, a Greenwood editor deplored "the evil and pernicious habit of pistol carrying" that prevailed throughout the county. If the prohibition on pistols had any effect, then perhaps it caused them to be less openly displayed, but the same legislative session that produced the pistol ban also passed a law prohibiting concealed weapons of any sort, including knives, metal knuckles, and razors. The ban on concealed weapons proved largely unenforceable; if weapons remained truly hidden, then possession of them could not be prosecuted, but their presence was generally assumed. In 1908, a Greenwood County grand jury lamented this state of affairs. "We believe the cowardly and unlawful practice of carrying concealed weapons is too common, even prevalent, pistol toting particularly," the grand jury declared. "In this twentieth century it is a shame and a disgrace for men to act as barbarians."[8]

Around the same time that the South Carolina legislature banned pistols, lawmakers in other Southern states passed similar measures. In 1901, the Florida legislature prohibited the possession of pistols. But as a Florida supreme court justice explained years later, "The statute was never intended to be applied to the white population and in practice has never been so applied." Instead, the law had been adopted "for the purpose of disarming the

Alcohol, Guns, and Brute Force

negro laborers." The reasons for South Carolina's pistol ban were more complex, with many contemporary observers expressing alarm at the high rate of intraracial homicides among whites, but white South Carolinians also worried about Blacks with guns. In September 1908, an African American minister from Ninety Six—a small community in eastern Greenwood—claimed that some local Blacks were stockpiling guns and planning to assassinate prominent white residents. Though the minister's accusations were widely dismissed as "a scheme hatched up by one negro to get revenge on other negroes," the county sheriff arrested and briefly jailed a dozen alleged ringleaders of the plot.[9]

Writing for the *Edgefield Advertiser* in 1916, an editorialist called on law enforcement officials to make a greater effort to fight intraracial crime within Black communities so that African Americans would feel more secure—and thus "have practically no cause for arming themselves." Such an argument willfully ignored one of the main reasons Black South Carolinians felt a need to be armed: to deter potential white supremacist violence. In the wake of African American disfranchisement and the bloodshed of 1898, the boundary drawn by Jim Crow served as an armistice line, its contested contours running through the middle ground between full equality and complete subjugation. African Americans had been forced into a separate and unequal place, but they were armed and would stand their ground to protect their homes and defend themselves when attacked. In 1910, in the first legal case ever taken on by the newly formed National Association for the Advancement of Colored People (NAACP), the organization's attorneys represented Pink Franklin, a tenant farmer from Orangeburg County. Three years earlier, Franklin had broken his work contract with a white landowner. Seeking to enforce the state's unconstitutional labor contract law, police officers invaded Franklin's home in the middle of the night, attempting to arrest him. He shot and killed one of the officers, which led to his conviction for murder and a death sentence. The NAACP could not get Franklin's conviction overturned, but they succeeded in securing a commutation of his sentence and eventually he was paroled.[10]

Over 20,000 Black South Carolinians served in uniform during the World War, with several thousand deployed to Europe. In the war's aftermath, as African American soldiers who had fought to make the world safe for democracy returned home to a state governed by white supremacist ideology, South Carolina officials viewed these men as a dangerous menace. In July 1919, Governor Robert Cooper—who two decades earlier had authored the pistol-toting ban—organized a state conference of law enforcement officers. One of the primary items on the agenda was the question of how to deal with "the negro soldier who has come back from France with altered views as to social equality." But despite alarmist fears of increased Black militancy, other observers identified other, all-too-familiar causes for criminality. In 1919, the Abbeville County solicitor convened a meeting of local officials to discuss crime prevention. "I believe that blind-tiger liquor and pistol toting are the chief causes of crime not only in Abbeville county, but in every county in the State," the solicitor argued. "Crime is more noticeable among the negroes because we have more negroes, but in the last analysis the white people are to blame because they are the ones who form public sentiment."[11]

Throughout the early twentieth century, South Carolina's political leaders set quite an example for the state's citizens. On the Fourth of July in 1918, two Democratic candidates for governor came to Greenwood and held a debate at the county fairgrounds. On a podium in front of 3,000 spectators, John Duncan and former US senator John McLaurin exchanged heated words that degenerated into a physical brawl, leaving both men battered and bruised. But such scuffles between politicians were little more than a crudely entertaining sideshow. A more insidious violence permeated the state's entire legal and judicial systems. When Black South Carolinians looked at the world in which they lived, they saw an all-white police force and judiciary enforcing a state constitution and legal code explicitly designed to guarantee the supremacy of the white minority, and they saw their own tenuous place within that world, defended by barely concealed weapons. How could they not conclude that beneath the mask of formal law, brute force was the ultimate arbiter?[12]

In 1915, South Carolina counties began keeping vital statistics and issuing death certificates. From 1915 through 1920, thirty-two homicides were recorded in Greenwood County. In nearly all these cases, whites and Blacks died as they had lived—in segregated realms, killed by same-race perpetrators. Seven of the thirty-two homicide victims were white, all seven of them killed by other whites with guns. In October 1916, a drunk chain gang guard drew a pistol and killed the supervisor of the county work farm and the supervisor's father-in-law, seriously wounded the captain of the guards, and then turned the gun on himself. In at least two other cases, white men were shot and killed in drunken quarrels. Though alcohol played a prominent role in most homicides among whites, notions of masculine authority and family honor also proved deadly. In the summer of 1917, a young mill worker killed his seventeen-year-old wife and gravely wounded her mother "because his wife had left him to visit her parents after he had told her she should not do so." In December 1920, a magistrate in Ware Shoals learned that his unwed daughter was pregnant, so he confronted the girl's lover at the local post office and at gunpoint demanded that he marry her. When the man refused, the magistrate shot him in the head; a coroner's jury quickly convened and ruled the killing a justifiable homicide.[13]

In the six years from 1915 through 1920, twenty-five African Americans—sixteen men and nine women—were shot, stabbed, or beaten to death in Greenwood County. Three of the male victims were shot by white men, and in another case the killer was unidentified, but at least twenty-one Black victims died at the hands of Black assailants. The violence affected both men and women, young and old. In June 1919, a teenager bludgeoned to death an elderly farmer. The following month, an irate husband shot and killed a seventy-year-old wagon driver whom his estranged wife had hired to pack up and move her belongings. Six weeks later, a woman fought with her sister-in-law and fatally stabbed her with a knife. In the spring of 1920, after a twenty-three-year-old washerwoman was shot and killed, a local official recorded her cause of death as "a scrap between two negro women." Judicial punishment for such killings sometimes seemed as arbitrary as the crimes themselves. On March 4, 1915, a twenty-year-old farmhand was gunned down in Hodges, about six miles south of Shoals Junction; a seventeen-year-old boy would be convicted of murdering him and sentenced to the chain gang for life. Just two days later, on March 6, a man cut the throat of a twenty-year-old woman in Ware Shoals; convicted of manslaughter, the killer received a five-year sentence.[14]

Approximately one-third of African American homicides in the county resulted from lovers' quarrels and marital disputes; in such cases, the murder weapon was frequently a shotgun. In January 1915, a farm laborer named David Jeter took a shotgun and confronted his wife and her alleged lover, George Robinson. "After shooting Robinson, Jeter broke the shot gun over his wife's head, then attempted to reload it and shoot her as she ran away," a journalist reported. On surrendering to police, Jeter "expressed only one regret, that he did not kill his wife in addition to killing Robinson." Two months later, at a Saturday evening hot supper in Ninety Six, a young man became jealous of a woman and used a shotgun to kill her. In January 1917, a tenant farmer shot and gravely wounded his sixteen-year-old wife; the next week, as her condition worsened, he fled the county before he could be charged with murder when she died. Nine months later, a man in Hodges killed his estranged wife with a shotgun, shooting her at such close range that her clothes caught fire from the muzzle blast. In November 1919, a farmer in Ninety Six discovered that his wife was with another man. Armed with a shotgun, the betrayed husband stormed into the cabin where the couple were clandestinely meeting. After shooting and killing his wife's lover, he turned the gun on her, but she managed to wrest it from his hands. He then "grabbed an iron poker from the fire place and beat his wife over the head," crushing her skull.[15]

Gambling on games of chance frequently provoked deadly disputes. The most popular forms of gambling included a card game known as "skin," in which each player drew a single card and placed bets on whose would be the first to be matched as the remaining cards in the deck were turned over one by one. In November 1915, two young men in Hodges quarreled over five cents that had been lost in a "skin game" the day before. When one of the men pulled a knife, the other responded by hitting him with a rock and breaking his neck. The following February, a card game in Ninety Six led to the death of a farmhand, Ernest Teague. According to the *Greenwood Journal*, "Several negroes were in Teague's room playing 'skin,' a game dear to the heart of the negro gambler." When Teague won a hand, one of the other players angrily objected and "shot him through the head." In November 1916, two men had a fatal argument during "a gambling game in Briar Hollow" (an African American neighborhood in Ware Shoals). One of the men struck the other "above the ear with [a] piece of steel, three or four inches long, and crushed his skull," then jumped aboard a railway boxcar and escaped.[16]

Greenwood County and the surrounding region had a long history of high homicide rates. When the county was formed in 1897, its southern half had been carved out of Edgefield, which during the antebellum era had a notorious reputation for violence. However, early twentieth-century Black residents of Greenwood lived in a world that was even more deadly than antebellum Edgefield. In the two decades immediately preceding the Civil War, Edgefield had an annual rate of eighteen homicides per 100,000 inhabitants. From 1915 through 1920, Greenwood County's Black population suffered from an annual rate of more than nineteen homicides per 100,000 persons. Greenwood was by no means exceptional; the homicide rate for African Americans in adjacent counties was as high or even higher. In November 1919, the Abbeville *Press and Banner* reported that a shootout between two African Americans had left one man dead and the other seriously wounded. "This is the first killing that has taken place in Abbeville County since August," the paper noted. "During the summer there were many negro killings, the average being about two a week." The front page of the *Press and Banner*'s very next issue featured an article headlined "Negro Killing," describing yet another intraracial homicide.[17]

During the early twentieth century, violence was a bloody thread running throughout the cultural and social fabric of upstate South Carolina. Often fueled by liquor and facilitated by firearms, this violence affected all segments of the population, but the region's Black residents suffered disproportionately. In 1903, only a few months before Broadus Miller was born, the scholar W. E. B. Du Bois published his groundbreaking work *The Souls of Black Folk*. Surveying the living conditions of African Americans in the South, Du Bois concluded that environmental influences—dire poverty, lack of education, and pervasive violence—played a profoundly detrimental role in shaping children's future behavior. In communities plagued by violent crime, Du Bois warned, the most intractable problem was "not the punishment of the criminals, but the preventing of the young from being trained to crime."[18]

CHAPTER THREE

Lynching and Foul Murder

Most homicides in upstate South Carolina were unpremeditated, arising from drunken quarrels and domestic disputes between same-race perpetrators and victims. However, some killings had a more deliberate intent. In a region where African Americans comprised a majority of the population, the white minority maintained supremacy by force, and the targeted killing of Blacks sent a stark message to all African Americans, reminding them of their designated place within the local hierarchy. According to the NAACP, in the years after its formation, Greenwood County would witness more lynching deaths—sixteen—than any other county in the state. Half of these deaths occurred at Phoenix in 1898. In the following years, mobs lynched Blacks accused of committing crimes or behaving in ways that seemed to challenge white supremacy. No whites were ever lynched in twentieth-century upstate South Carolina; all lynching victims were African Americans. From Broadus Miller's birth in 1904 until the time he left Greenwood County in 1921, at least six recorded lynchings took place within a twenty-mile radius of Shoals Junction, while additional lynching victims may have vanished without a trace, their deaths unreported and their names unknown.[1]

In September 1904—around the time Broadus Miller was born—the body of James "Babe" Stuart was discovered near the Saluda River, his hands tied behind his back and a gunshot wound in his chest. Stuart had been serving time on a Laurens County chain gang when a white farmer paid his court fines and then apparently kept him in involuntary servitude for the next two years. One afternoon, the farmer left to visit a cotton gin, leaving his two teenage daughters picking cotton alongside Stuart and the other field hands. When the farmer returned, his daughters claimed Stuart had attempted to rape one of them but had been scared off by her sister. That evening, several dozen of the farmer's relatives and neighbors seized the accused field hand, then argued among themselves about whether to turn him over to the local sheriff. A few of the men decided to take matters into their own hands and marched Stuart over a river bridge into Greenwood County, where they executed him with a single shot to the heart. In response to the killing, *The State*—one of South Carolina's leading newspapers—published an editorial denouncing white farm owners whose "wives and daughters were made to work side by side with negroes in the fields" and calling on these farmers to "keep the negro in his place and maintain their own proper position."[2]

During the early 1900s, African Americans inhabited a precarious place in upstate South Carolina, forced to navigate a treacherous terrain between variously positioned segments of the white population, and any misstep could prove fatal. The region's white residents consisted of town elites, mill workers and other wage laborers, landowning farmers, and tenant farming families. Many of the town elites—businessmen, lawyers, and other urban professionals—employed Black domestic servants and manual laborers, and though these elites ascribed to white supremacy, they feared the specter of a mob of working-class whites, unruly and ungoverned. For white tenant farmers and wage laborers, any resentment of these town elites could be directed with near impunity at the African Americans whom the elites employed. Kinship ties connected many white tenant families to local landowning farmers, and though some of these landowners provided Black tenants with feudal protection, others kept African Americans in virtual slavery. Tacitly supported by many people, a few white families played a leading role in much of the mob violence against Blacks.[3]

About eight miles north of Shoals Junction was the town of Honea Path. At the turn of the twentieth century, in the countryside around Honea Path lived the Ashleys, an extended white family of cotton farmers. At their forefront stood Joshua "Citizen Josh" Ashley, the local representative to the state legislature. A short, stocky man with red hair and moustache, Citizen Josh was frequently mocked by journalists for his homely diction and lack of formal education, yet he possessed a keen financial shrewdness and astute political skills. He had grown up in modest circumstances, the son of a nonslaveholding farmer, but in the decades following the Civil War he amassed considerable wealth, becoming one of the largest landowners in upstate South Carolina. From his plantation just outside Honea Path he wielded great influence and power. The middle-aged Ashley had entered politics in the turbulent 1890s as a protégé of Ben Tillman. Quick-tempered and pugnacious, he never shied away from physically confronting those with whom he disagreed. "Josh Ashley is regarded as a formidable proposition in a fisticuff," observed one reporter. "He is chiefly feared since when he has a fight on his hands he manifests an alarming tendency to bite."[4]

In the 1880s and 1890s, the Ashley clan "had their own wild way in Honea Path." Dozens of male family members would come into town on Saturday afternoons to congregate "along Main Street, heavily armed, and shoot up the town in true Western style." But the coming of the twentieth century heralded a new era in this Carolina-style Wild West frontier. In 1902, the establishment of the Chiquola Mills textile factory transformed Honea Path into a thriving mill town, with more than 400 men and women working in the mill and over 1,000 people living in company-provided housing. Honea Path's rapid growth stimulated the rise of a well-heeled business and professional class. Josh Ashley and his rural white supporters did nothing to conceal their enormous contempt for these town-based elites. As one press account noted, Ashley "despises the well-dressed man, and a gentleman wearing cuffs and a necktie cannot secure his aid." This sense of resentment toward town elites was shared by many mill hands, and though white landowning farmers often looked on the wage-laboring mill workers with disdain, Citizen Josh succeeded in attracting political support from both farmers and mill hands.[5]

In 1905, Ashley's twenty-one-year-old nephew Jim Moore instigated a fatal fight that highlighted the local divisions of race and class. Despite his uncle's wealth and political power, Moore's parents were tenant farmers, not landowners, with only their influential kinship ties distinguishing them from other poor rural whites. As one journalist noted, Moore and his father and several brothers had a reputation as "rowdies, and have been in numerous brawls." On a Sunday in September 1905, while traveling on the road in a horse-drawn buggy, the drunken Moore scraped wheels with a buggy driven by an African American named Allen Pendleton, who worked as a manual laborer for a white merchant in Honea Path. Later that evening, around seven o'clock, Moore and a companion accosted Pendleton about five miles north of Shoals Junction. Moore seized the reins of Pendleton's buggy and pulled him to the ground, lashed him with a whip, and began beating him with the whip's butt end. In self-defense Pendleton drew a knife and slashed Moore, fatally severing an artery, then climbed back into the buggy and fled. News of the incident quickly spread, and a small mob of about a dozen men—including the dead man's father and brothers—set out in pursuit and caught Pendleton on the outskirts of Honea Path.[6]

Soon after the mob captured Pendleton, John Marion Ashley appeared on the scene. A cousin of Citizen Josh's, John Marion was a towering, barrel-chested man with a reputation as a violent drunk; once, in an alcohol-fueled brawl, he had allegedly bitten off his own brother's ear. Ashley immediately stepped to the forefront of the mob and began savagely beating Pendleton with a wooden plank. He and the other men then put Pendleton in a buggy and drove him back to the scene of his fatal encounter with Moore. It was around ten o'clock in the evening and a crowd had gathered, but many of

Lynching and Foul Murder 27

them were reluctant to convene a session of Judge Lynch's court. Eyewitnesses insisted Jim Moore had drunkenly attacked Pendleton without provocation, and several bystanders urged the men to wait and turn over their captive to the sheriff, who had been summoned and was on his way. John Marion Ashley angrily responded that local Blacks "were getting damned biggity and some of them would have to be killed." He and a few other men dragged their captive into the nearby woods. A subsequent coroner's report would give a grisly postmortem of Allen Pendleton's fate: neck broken with a chain tied around it, skull crushed, multiple gunshot wounds in the torso, shotgun blast at close range.[7]

The brutal killing was an act of terror, reminding Blacks how precarious their position was within the local community. Pendleton's killers had left his body by the roadside. His family apparently feared that any attempt to recover it would provoke further violence; a day or two later, county officials buried him where he lay, in a hastily dug and shallow grave. Observing the reaction of African Americans in the area, a journalist noted that "the negroes are greatly excited." White elites in Honea Path and other upstate towns were appalled by what had happened. Jim Moore had been widely known as a hotheaded young man with a tendency for violence, while Allen Pendleton had a starkly different reputation. In the words of the Newberry *Herald and News*, Pendleton had been "a very humble negro" who was "inoffensive" and "peaceable," making it "inconceivable that he should have sought a row with white men." According to the newspaper, since Pendleton had acted in self-defense, his death should not be considered a "lynching." As implicitly defined by the newspaper, lynching referred to the extrajudicial execution of someone who had committed a heinous act—in other words, someone who deserved to be punished. Based on the circumstances of Pendleton's death, the *Herald and News* argued that "instead of being a lynching it was a foul murder."[8]

Though eyewitnesses and press accounts publicly identified John Marion Ashley and the other killers, a coroner's inquest concluded Pendleton died at the hands of "persons unknown." In response, Governor Duncan Heyward notified the state solicitor that "a murder has taken place in Honea Path" and ordered him to investigate, which led to John Marion and six other men being indicted on murder charges. The press in South Carolina and neighboring states applauded the indictments. "There is no doubt but that there is a growing sentiment against lynching," a journalist noted. However, he quickly added, this growing sentiment did not yet translate to criminal convictions for lynch mob members. "Mob violence is more generally condemned than ever before," he explained, "but the trouble is that when a certain community is touched with the affliction, local sentiment and influence are set to work to clear those accused." The reporter's words proved prescient. Citizen Josh declared he would shun anyone who cooperated with the prosecution, and the attempt to hold Pendleton's killers legally accountable dragged on for several months and ultimately ended in an acquittal.[9]

John Marion Ashley did not live long enough to learn of the verdict. Just six months after killing Pendleton, a drunk and belligerent Ashley accosted an African American on the street in Honea Path. The man retreated and summoned the local police chief, who confronted Ashley and ordered him to go home. A heated argument ensued. Both Ashley and the police chief drew pistols and fired, but the lawman emerged unscathed while John Marion ended up dead. Other members of the Ashley family quickly gathered into a mob, headed by Citizen Josh himself, and set out to avenge their kinsman. Only the timely arrival of a militia company from Anderson kept the mob from killing the chief of police, who had to be rushed by train to the safety of the Anderson County jail. Surveying the reaction of town elites in Honea Path to John Marion's death, a journalist concluded that "everybody is thankful for the riddance of Ashley."[10]

The death of John Marion did not rid the region of the most notoriously violent member of Citizen Josh's extended family. This dubious distinction belonged to John T. McGaha, a nephew of Citizen Josh's who had been adopted by his uncle and raised in Ashley's home. McGaha had been arrested numerous times, bore the scars of multiple bullet wounds, and had been implicated in the deaths of several people, both Black and white, but his family's political influence helped him avoid any judicial reckoning. As a journalist later recalled, "He was feared throughout this whole section and, because of this fear, exercised great power over negroes and a certain class of whites." Once, after a drunken brawl with another white man, McGaha walked a mile to his home to get a shotgun, then returned and gunned the man down. He pled self-defense and was acquitted. A few years later, in the spring of 1908, McGaha shot and killed an unarmed African American in cold blood. He fled to Georgia after the shooting, but was arrested and brought back to South Carolina to stand trial. Securing the services of a prominent defense attorney—the brother of a South Carolina supreme court justice—McGaha claimed he had meant no harm in firing the gun and that the killing had been accidental. Some witnesses changed their testimony, others refused to appear in court, and once again, the legal system's attempt to hold McGaha accountable ended in an acquittal.[11]

Lynching and Foul Murder

Following the verdict, journalists warned it was only a matter of time before McGaha committed further acts of violence. "It does not require a seer or a prophet to predict that sooner or later John McGaha will kill somebody else, or will force somebody to kill him," remarked the editor of the *Anderson Daily Mail*. Less than a month later, McGaha traveled to Greenville County to seize some African Americans who had previously worked for him. He claimed they had broken their work contract, and he intended to bring them back at gunpoint and force them to continue laboring in his cotton fields. The attempt at armed kidnapping went awry, resulting in a shootout and McGaha's death. His demise elicited little sympathy from the South Carolina press. "A Bully Killed," proclaimed a headline in the Abbeville *Press and Banner*. Three African Americans were indicted and put on trial for killing the adopted son of one of South Carolina's most powerful lawmakers. But given the dead man's infamous reputation, his influential family ties could not guarantee harsh legal punishment for the Black men accused of killing him. Two and a half years later, following an extended legal process and at least one mistrial, two of the defendants were acquitted and the third convicted on a lesser charge of manslaughter.[12]

In 1909, less than four months after McGaha's death, a federal grand jury indicted Citizen Josh Ashley for peonage, charging him with holding "negro farm hands in involuntary servitude on his farm," where they were "guarded day and night with shotguns and rifles." Ashley claimed the men were working off their debts, both to him and to the deceased McGaha. One of the laborers had ended up on the farm after a judge fined him twenty-six dollars for a bootlegging conviction; Ashley paid the fine—and then held the man in involuntary servitude for four and a half years. Though federal officials made a serious effort to prosecute the case, local juries proved reluctant to convict the influential lawmaker. A first trial ended with the jurors hopelessly deadlocked. The following year, after deliberating for only thirty minutes, a second jury acquitted the powerful labor lord.[13]

While town elites deplored the behavior of the Ashley clan and African Americans bore the brunt of this behavior, Citizen Josh remained immensely popular among white farmers and mill workers, who repeatedly reelected him to represent them in the state legislature. The region's rural white farmers were Ashley's natural constituency, and early in his political career he had won the support of mill workers by sponsoring legislation limiting the workday in the mills to ten hours. The mill owners had retaliated by charging rent for company housing that they had previously provided for free, leading the workers to conclude that the costs of any government regulation would eventually come out of their own pockets. In the following years, when fighting against child labor legislation and opposing any increase in mill owners' liability for workplace accidents, Ashley had the support of both owners and workers. The mill workers may have had rational reasons for endorsing these positions, but their economic interests were not the same as those of rural farmers. A shared sense of racial solidarity and resentment unified the disparate elements within Citizen Josh's coalition of supporters. Coleman Blease drew from this same well of support to become South Carolina's governor, with Josh Ashley serving as one of Blease's closest political allies. In September 1911, Governor Blease visited Ashley's plantation and addressed a large gathering. "When a negro touches the person of a white woman," the governor declared, "the sooner the negro is swung to a limb of a tree the better." Six weeks later, Citizen Josh would put Blease's words into action.[14]

On the morning of October 10, 1911, while herding a cow to pasture about a quarter mile outside Honea Path, an eleven-year-old white girl was apparently assaulted. According to newspaper accounts, a young Black man seized her and dragged her into a nearby clump of woods, where he "accomplished his devilish purpose" and then fled. A passerby saw the girl as she came stumbling out of the woods, her clothes disheveled and muddy, and took her back to her home. Within the next hour, police apprehended a series of suspects and brought them before her, and she identified one of them as her assailant—a teenager named Willis Jackson, who worked as a delivery boy for a Honea Path meat market. Press accounts described Jackson as seventeen years old; census records suggest he may have been a year or two younger. One of eight children, he had grown up on a farm in the small community of Donalds, near Broadus Miller's family. His father had died when Jackson was still a child. At the turn of the century, his family had lived next to—and almost certainly had been the tenants of—a landowner named Larkin Agnew, the brother-in-law of Tom and Alpha Walker's landlord, Harrison "Lat" Rasor.[15]

News of the rape accusation against Jackson quickly spread. Fearing a potential lynch mob, law enforcement officials rushed him to the jail in Anderson, but word soon came that scores of armed men were on their way from Honea Path. What followed would be, in the words of a press account, "one of the most sensational man chases" in the region's history. Leading the pursuit was Citizen Josh Ashley, who sat in a large touring car clutching a Winchester rifle. The Anderson police hurriedly sent Jackson on to Greenville, where the sheriff declared his jail could not withstand attack from a mob. The sheriff transferred Jackson to an automobile and departed for Spartanburg. About six miles outside Greenville, he ordered the car's driver to stop, disembarked with his prisoner and one deputy, and set off on foot into the nearby woods while the car returned to town. The sheriff later claimed that he had worried about being overtaken on the muddy dirt road by men in more powerful automobiles. But if his intent had been to turn Jackson over to the mob, then he could not have arranged it any better, for after interrogating the driver when he arrived back in Greenville, Ashley and some two dozen followers drove to the woods and seized the prisoner. According to eyewitnesses, Willis Jackson was visibly trembling in fear as he got into Citizen Josh's car for what would be his final journey.[16]

The rape accusation and day-long pursuit had stirred white residents of the upstate into a frenzy. By the time Jackson's captors made it back to Honea Path late that evening, several thousand people had gathered. They first brought Jackson to the home of the young girl whom he was accused of assaulting. After she again identified him as the culprit, they took him a few hundred yards down the road to the scene of the apparent assault. Members of the mob tied a rope around one of the boy's feet, tossed the rope over the top of a nearby telephone pole, and hoisted him up about twenty feet off the ground. As he dangled upside down, crying and pleading for mercy, the mob took aim and let loose with rifles, pistols, and shotguns. "The body hangs tonight covered with blood and shot full of holes," reported the *Greenwood Index*. At sunrise the dead boy still swung from the pole, but during the night trophy hunters and souvenir collectors had cut off his fingers. Throughout the morning spectators came to gaze at the "horribly mutilated body." Among the onlookers were several African Americans. "The negroes have maintained a quiet and awed demeanor," one observer asserted. Other accounts, however, indicate the public exhibition of the bloody dead boy engendered very bitter feelings. "One negro man was dealt with for making an insulting remark to a gentleman looking on the body this morning," a press report airily noted. "The negro was not injured, being subjected merely to a light whipping."[17]

By participating in the lynching of Willis Jackson, several thousand people had reinforced their communal solidarity—a solidarity based on a sense of shared racial identity and white supremacy. "Mob Riddled Coon's Body," a headline in the *Bamberg Herald* proclaimed. Governor Blease praised Ashley and the mob for what they had done, and he announced that if prosecutors tried to convict anyone for taking part in the lynching, then he would use his power as governor and immediately issue a pardon. Safe from prosecution and enjoying widespread support for his actions as mob boss, Citizen Josh proposed that the state legislature legalize lynching in cases where "the preponderance of the testimony" indicated a person was guilty of rape or attempted rape.[18]

Whereas the killing of Allen Pendleton had prompted outrage among town elites and editorial condemnation, the general consensus among white South Carolinians was that Willis Jackson deserved to die. Jackson had apparently assaulted a white girl, and the Newberry *Herald and News* declared that "such human brutes should be dealt with as you would deal with a wild animal or a rattlesnake." However, the newspaper drew the line at the posthumous desecration of Jackson's corpse. "We can not understand," the *Herald and News* confessed, "how any member of the mob should want a toe or a finger of the brute as a reminder of the horrible deed."[19]

CHAPTER FOUR

Mobs and Lone Killers

Though political leaders such as Coleman Blease and Josh Ashley championed mob rule, some South Carolina officials recognized that lynch mobs posed a serious threat to law and order. Five years before the killing of Willis Jackson, a similar lynching spectacle had occurred a few miles south of the town of Greenwood. In August 1906, a young Black man named Bob "Snowball" Davis—the "mentally deficient" son of tenant farmers—had attacked a white woman as she worked alone in a country store. During the struggle he slashed her with a carving knife, then fled when he heard an approaching buggy; later that afternoon he assaulted a sixteen-year-old African American girl on a nearby farm. Over the next two days, hundreds of men scoured the countryside searching for Davis. The press reported that "no earthly power could prevent a lynching," but Governor Duncan Heyward decided to go to Greenwood County and make a personal appeal for the rule of law. By the time the governor arrived, Davis had been captured and a large crowd had gathered. Addressing the crowd, Governor Heyward denounced Davis as a "black devil and fiend of hell," but he begged them to let the accused be tried and punished by the state. "Shall the people be allowed to be ruled by their passions and prejudices or shall the supremacy and the majesty of the law be upheld?" the governor implored. Refusing to heed the governor's plea, the mob tied Davis to the trunk of a pine tree and killed him in a hail of gunfire.[1]

In the fall of 1916, events in Abbeville vividly demonstrated the danger of letting mobs reign supreme. Only a half-hour train ride southwest of Shoals Junction, Abbeville was a scenic historic town of nearly 5,000 residents, with elegant antebellum homes and a large public square at its center. A few miles outside town lived Anthony Crawford, one of the wealthiest African Americans in upstate South Carolina, who owned over 400 acres of cotton fields (see figure 4.1). Many of his children were also landowning farmers and resided near their father. On a Saturday morning in October 1916, Crawford came into Abbeville to transact business, but after a heated argument with a cottonseed buyer, he was arrested and jailed. Released on bail, he emerged from the jailhouse only to be chased down the street by a group of local roughnecks headed by McKinney Cann, who worked

FIGURE 4.1 Anthony Crawford, a prosperous cotton farmer who was killed by an Abbeville lynch mob in October 1916. (Library of Congress Prints and Photographs Division, Reproduction Number: LC-USZC2–6302.)

as a salesman at a downtown livery stable and had a reputation as a "rough chap." The men pursued Crawford into the boiler room of a cotton gin, where he defended himself by hitting Cann in the head with a hammer and knocking him unconscious. The rest of the men quickly overpowered Crawford and began beating him until the Abbeville sheriff arrived and intervened, carrying the seriously injured Crawford back to jail. Later that afternoon, McKinney Cann's brothers were at the forefront of a mob of about 200 men who stormed the jailhouse and hauled their victim outside. They bashed him with rocks and beat him with wooden boards and then dragged him through the streets to a public fairground, where they hanged his dead body and riddled it with gunfire.[2]

In the following days, the inflamed anger of Abbeville's mob continued unabated. The threat of violence kept Black-owned businesses closed, and there was heated talk of driving Crawford's entire family out of the county at gunpoint. On a Saturday evening two weeks after the murder, police arrested McKinney Cann's brother Will and four other men for "whipping some negroes out near the fair grounds." Released on bail, Will Cann was arrested again later that same evening, this time for roughing up a Black teenager who worked as a delivery boy for the post office. The prospect of mob rule by working-class whites alarmed both African Americans and white elites. "If the lives and property of negroes in Abbeville may be taken at the pleasure of a mob," an editorialist warned, "the lives and property of white men who happen not to be in sympathy with the acts of the mob are scarcely in less danger." Cotton agriculture served as the cornerstone of the region's economy, and if mob violence drove away Black farmworkers, then Abbeville's white residents might discover they "had lynched their own pocketbooks."[3]

In response to the threat that mob violence posed to African Americans' lives and white elites' pocketbooks, a group of Abbeville's leading businessmen formed a committee to restore order in the town. The committee included James S. Stark, owner of the livery stable where McKinney Cann worked. Stark was one of Abbeville's most prominent residents, a cotton planter and businessman in his mid-fifties who dressed in coat and tie and sported a well-groomed goatee. His commercial and agricultural interests had earned him great wealth, and his home—a large antebellum mansion on North Main Street—was the most famous house in town, the place where the fleeing Jefferson Davis had held one of the last meetings of the Confederate government. In early November, Stark and the rest of the committee organized a public meeting at the county courthouse that was attended by "practically every business man of Abbeville." At the meeting, the business leaders adopted resolutions deploring the "spirit of lawlessness that seems rife in the county" and demanding that the sheriff and town police "use every effort to enforce the law and to protect the citizens of the town and county regardless of condition or color." And in a dramatic step that directly contradicted white South Carolinians' long history of resistance to any outside interference in local race relations, the business leaders declared that if necessary, they would call on assistance from the federal government to ensure "that every citizen may enjoy his rights under the constitution."[4]

Despite town elites' efforts to reassure Black residents of their continued place in the community, over the next few months several hundred African Americans left the county and headed north, with the murder of Anthony Crawford and the subsequent reign of terror precipitating their departure. Crawford had committed no crime, but his economic success, instead of providing greater security, had made him a target for an angry mob. Reflecting on the exodus of African Americans from Abbeville, the *Charlotte Observer* claimed lynching in upstate South Carolina had previously "never affected the industrious, property-acquiring Negro." In contrast to earlier lynching victims, Crawford had been "killed not because he was a law-breaker," but because "he had become a rich Negro and was an enviously prosperous figure in the community." State prosecutors attempted to pursue a murder case against the Cann brothers and other leaders of the lynch mob, but no one would agree to testify against them and a grand jury refused to issue any indictments.[5]

About two years after participating in the murder of Anthony Crawford, McKinney Cann's brother Lester was appointed deputy sheriff of Abbeville County. In February 1919, Lester Cann led two other white men on a nighttime raid of the home of Mark Smith, a "mulatto" tenant farmer who lived a few miles outside Abbeville. The men claimed to suspect him of bootlegging, but Cann had no warrant and his two companions were undeputized, and when they burst into Smith's house during the night, he responded by grabbing a shotgun and exchanging fire with the deputy. Both Smith and Cann were wounded, but Smith escaped and fled by train to Washington, D.C. Two weeks later he was arrested and sent back to South Carolina to face charges of assault and battery. At his trial, Mark Smith argued that any man, white or Black, had an inviolable right to use "such force as necessary for the purpose of ejecting" unlawful intruders in his home. An all-white Abbeville jury agreed, acquitting the African American who had shot a white deputy sheriff.[6]

James Stark served as the foreman of the jury that acquitted Smith. Town elites such as Stark did not question the basic tenets of white supremacy, but many of them also believed in offering paternalistic protection to the resident Black population. The 1895 South Carolina constitution had effectively stripped African Americans of the right to vote, but that same constitution also enshrined the sanctity of one's own home as an inviolable right regardless of race. From the perspective of Stark and others like him, if African Americans remained in their designated place, then they had the right to be left in peace, unmolested by unwarranted raids or unprovoked acts of violence. When deliberating Smith's case, Stark and the other jurors undoubtedly took pragmatic considerations into account as well. Unlike the local roughnecks who delighted in racial bullying, the jurors were acutely conscious of Black laborers' vital role in the regional economy. In a month's time the annual cycle of cotton agriculture would begin anew. Abbeville County's fields would need to be plowed and sown and the cotton would eventually need to be picked, and if African Americans had no guarantee of security in their designated place and began leaving in large numbers, then who would do the labor?[7]

Though a tenant farmer, Mark Smith was relatively prosperous and owned an automobile. In the weeks following his acquittal, white men sometimes tried to hire him and his car for various trips, but Smith was wary of their intentions and always refused. On Saturday, June 7, 1919, he drove into Abbeville with his mother, his young son, and two other passengers. They spent the day shopping, then headed back home around nine o'clock that evening. About three miles outside town, a car with four or five white men overtook them, so Smith pulled his automobile over to the side of the road to let them pass. The other car stopped beside him and two men jumped out with pistols drawn and opened fire. Smith got out and ran into an adjacent field, but as his mother and the other passengers watched in horror, his assailants followed, firing until he fell, then standing over him and shooting him several more times. The men carried his body back to the road, where they laid him down for a moment to confirm he was dead, then loaded him in their car and drove away. Four days later, fishermen discovered a Black man's corpse on the bank of the Savannah River. After they reported their discovery, but before law enforcement officials arrived on the scene, the body was dragged ashore and butchered in an attempt to render it unidentifiable. However, the badly mutilated remains included a hand with a distinctive scar—the gunshot wound Mark Smith had suffered in his recent shootout with Deputy Sheriff Cann.[8]

The murder sparked an angry response from the state press, which emphasized that Smith's acquittal "by a jury of white men" should have definitively settled the case against him. "This killing seems to have been a murderous assault on the courts," declared an editorial in *The State*. In the editorialist's words, "the important fact" was "not that the negro was killed, but that the killing was repudiation of the white government." The Abbeville *Press and Banner* denounced the murder as "an insult to the citizens of Abbeville County, a blow at our laws, an affront to the jury that freed Smith, [and] a blot upon civilization." But though the press reacted with outrage, most local white residents seemed unperturbed by what had occurred. "There have been no arrests and nobody seems to be very greatly concerned about it," concluded a visiting reporter. Smith's mother and the other eyewitnesses stated they had not recognized his attackers, and though law enforcement officials questioned and briefly jailed a young white tenant farmer, no one would ever be charged in connection with the killing. The lack of success in solving the case was perhaps unsurprising: Deputy Sheriff Lester Cann helped lead the investigation. Three months after the murder, a coroner's jury delivered its verdict, concluding Smith had met his death "at the hands of unknown parties."[9]

Whereas "unknown parties" killed Mark Smith, there was never any doubt about who murdered Reverend James H. Walker, a minister and educator in the mill town of Ware Shoals. Reverend Walker shared the same surname as Broadus Miller's relatives and adoptive family, who lived on a tenant farm about three miles west of Ware Shoals, but he was apparently unrelated to them. However, though Miller and his family attended Dunn Creek Baptist Church and were not members of Reverend Walker's congregation, they undoubtedly knew the distinguished minister, at least by reputation. Born in 1868, he had grown up in Laurens County, the eldest child of tenant farmers. Like Benjamin Mays, the young Walker saw education as a way out of the cotton fields, and he continued attending school long after most African Americans his age were full-time field hands. He enrolled in Benedict Institute, an academy in Columbia that had been established by a Baptist mission society to provide "education to the colored people." There he met and married a fellow student named Emma Mouldin, with whom he would have eight children. For several years they lived in her hometown of Greenville, where Reverend Walker pastored a church. In 1917, the Walkers moved to Ware Shoals to take charge of an African American school in Briar Hollow, the town's Black neighborhood. The minister served as the school's principal and his wife as the teacher (see figure 4.2).[10]

On the afternoon of June 21, 1920—exactly seven years before the murder of a young mill worker in Morganton—Reverend Walker entered the company store in Ware Shoals to buy groceries. Inside the store were a few white mill hands, including forty-year-old Pope McCarty. McCarty apparently became enraged at the very sight of the well-dressed minister. A white store clerk later testified that as he waited on Reverend Walker, McCarty walked up and, without provocation or warning, snarled that Walker "looked like a damned lawyer" and slapped him in the face. The blow stunned the minister and sent his glasses flying to the floor. He hurriedly picked them up and fled out of the store, closely pursued by McCarty, who had pulled out a concealed pistol and had it in hand. Rushing into the mill's office seeking protection, Walker jumped over a railing and attempted to take shelter beneath a desk. The pistol-wielding mill hand entered and leaned over the railing with his gun, firing three times and mortally wounding the most prominent African American in Ware Shoals.[11]

The next day's Greenwood *Index-Journal* ran a brief article presenting McCarty's version of the incident. The mill hand claimed Walker had "stepped on his foot," leading to a scuffle that culminated in the shooting.

FIGURE 4.2 Reverend James Walker (back row, on right) and his wife, Emma Mouldin Walker (back row, on left), with the students of the Briar Hollow school in Ware Shoals, South Carolina, in 1919. (Town of Ware Shoals, *From Hill to Dale to Hollow: Ware Shoals, South Carolina* [Ware Shoals, SC: R. L. Bryan, 1983], 38.)

This falsehood was reprinted in newspapers throughout the country. The African American press found the story credible, for it seemed to exemplify white Southerners' disproportionate response to any minor misstep by a Black man. "Pope McCarty, white, shot and killed James H. Walker, colored, because the Negro stepped on his foot," read a short news item in *The Crisis*, the monthly magazine of the NAACP. Yet according to the white store clerk, Walker had done nothing to provoke the murderous assault. One week after the killing, the *Index-Journal* mentioned in passing that prosecutors would "make an effort to bring up the case of Pope McCarty." But the judicial process moved extraordinarily slowly, suggesting significant local resistance to punishing the white mill worker. While most criminal court cases in upstate South Carolina commenced within weeks of the alleged offense, Pope McCarty did not go on trial until June 1921 — one year after Reverend Walker's death.[12]

Press accounts of the trial portrayed McCarty as the quintessential mill hand, ill bred and poorly educated. "McCarty is a small, sharp featured man, hardly weighing over a hundred pounds," a journalist reported. "He appears almost emaciated, with deep sunk, close set, shifty eyes, mouth somewhat shrunken by loss of teeth and a slightly receding chin." Around the turn of the century, he had married a woman some fifteen years his senior; both he and his wife began working in the Ware Shoals mill soon after it opened. Census records show the couple drifting from one rented lodging to another, from boardinghouse to mill village cabin, and moving so frequently that the 1910 census had listed them twice, recording them in one spot and then another. At trial, McCarty claimed Reverend Walker had first stepped on his foot and had then donned brass knuckles and punched him in the belly. The mill worker's brother and another mill hand had been present in the store during the confrontation; both men testified under oath in support of his implausible tale. Under cross-examination, McCarty lost his temper and refused to answer any questions. "I don't know nothing," he snapped repeatedly. "I tell you I don't remember nothin'." After his disastrous attempt to testify concluded, defense attorneys hurriedly entered a plea of temporary insanity. The all-white jury deliberated for nearly three hours and convicted the mill worker of manslaughter; the judge then sentenced him to seven years in the state penitentiary.[13]

Pope McCarty had acted alone in shooting Reverend Walker, but racially motivated murders that would never be categorized as "lynchings" could have just as profound an effect on Black communities as the actions of a mob. Before the fatal confrontation, McCarty had not even known the minister, but the sight of a Black man wearing glasses had provoked a murderous blind rage. When the lowly mill hand gunned down one of the leaders of the local Black community, then the extent of white mill workers' animosity for Blacks was made manifest, and every member of that community must have felt threatened. But the minister's widow, Emma Walker, decided to remain in Ware Shoals after her husband was killed, assuming the roles of both principal and teacher at the school in Briar Hollow. Eight years after Reverend Walker's death she remarried, becoming the wife of Reverend James Selden Maddox of Dunn Creek Baptist Church.[14]

CHAPTER FIVE
Bloody Anderson

In 1917, the United States entered the World War. For South Carolina cotton farmers, the war proved a financial windfall. Wartime demand fueled record high profits, and this sudden prosperity led farmers to invest even more heavily in growing cotton. But though prices remained high in the war's immediate aftermath, they soon proved unsustainable. "South Carolina entered the year 1920 buoyant," the state agriculture commissioner later ruminated. "Our hopes were running high, our credit freely pledged, for we confidently expected to have a good crop year and the whole world was our market." That summer, as demand evaporated, the price of cotton plummeted and the fickle cash crop lost two-thirds of its value; it was, in the words of one historian, "the most drastic price collapse in cotton history."[1]

During the spring of 1921, as the agricultural depression worsened, thousands of African Americans began departing rural areas in desperate search of work. "When the Negro leaves the farm," observed the sociologist Arthur Raper in the 1920s, "he must of necessity go to the urban community. He leaves a community where everybody knew each other; he goes to a place where no one seems to know anyone else or gives a continental what happens." Among the displaced South Carolina farmworkers was the teenage Broadus Miller, who left Shoals Junction and headed for the town of Anderson, about thirty miles away. He most likely went by train. The Piedmont & Northern Railway ran from Greenwood to Anderson, stopping at the Shoals Junction depot along the way. Either purchasing a ticket for a segregated, second-class passenger car, or surreptitiously hopping aboard a freight train boxcar, Miller would have arrived in the town about an hour later. On disembarking, he would have emerged into a hectic hive of social interaction and potential friction far removed from life on a farm. The growth of the regional textile mills had turned Anderson into a booming town. At the turn of the century, it had been home to some 5,500 residents; by 1920 the population had almost doubled. At the center of town, in the middle of a large open plaza, stood an elegant brick courthouse with a tall bell tower and a gabled roof, while a hydroelectric dam in the nearby countryside supplied electric lights and powered the streetcars that circled the downtown streets.[2]

Beginning in the late nineteenth century, a vibrant African American community had formed in Anderson, but Blacks were continually reminded of their designated place within the larger society. In 1919, some of Anderson's most prominent Black residents created one of the first chapters of the NAACP in upstate South Carolina—only to be driven out of town by angry whites who accused them of promoting "social equality." Barred from most jobs in the region's textile mills, many working-age African Americans—especially men—began heading north to pursue a better life elsewhere. From 1910 to 1920, the Black population of Anderson declined by several hundred people, and African Americans went from comprising 35 percent of the town's residents to less than 30 percent. However, aggregate population figures mask the full extent of the outward migration. At the same time as many Black men were departing town, others were arriving. Like Broadus Miller, most of these newcomers had grown up laboring in the cotton fields and had little formal education and no occupational training. Entering a strange new urban environment, they faced a precarious struggle to survive. Some found work in a local cottonseed mill, grinding the seeds into cattle feed and extracting the oil to use in margarine, soap, and lard. Others were hired as municipal workers to clean and maintain the town streets, or as service workers in hotels and restaurants.[3]

On arriving in Anderson, African Americans found lodging with local Black families or in one of the downtown boardinghouses. One such boardinghouse was at 122 West Market Street, half a block off Main Street and a couple of blocks south of the courthouse square. A two-story wooden building, it stood directly across the street from a freight train station. The keeper of the boardinghouse was a middle-aged African American widow named Essie Walker. She and her husband Frank had been tenant farmers on the outskirts of Anderson, but in the early 1900s they obtained a mortgage for a home in a Black neighborhood in town, where Essie Walker opened a small restaurant and her husband began working as a shoemaker; together they raised a young grandson, the child of an absentee daughter. After Frank Walker's premature death, his widow leased the West Market Street boardinghouse, living there with her grandson and renting out some half dozen rooms to itinerant laborers. On the evening of Sunday, May 1, 1921, the grandson stumbled over something in a pitch-dark hallway in the house. After fetching a light, he discovered a horrific scene. The walls of the hallway "were spattered with blood" and on the floor lay Essie Walker's body, with a bullet wound in her chest and her head crushed by multiple blows from a baseball bat.[4]

Violent deaths were not uncommon in Anderson. In 1921 town residents burned to death in house fires, were fatally kicked by mules, and fell victim to automobile and industrial accidents. Despondent businessmen shot themselves or swallowed strychnine. But the leading cause of violent death was neither accidents nor suicides. With its rapid growth and ever-changing population, Anderson had the second-highest homicide rate of any town in South Carolina—higher than any major city in the United States. In the months following the collapse of cotton prices, the number of homicides spiked throughout the state. From 1920 to 1924, more South Carolinians were killed at home than had died abroad on the battlefields of the World War. The deadliest year was 1921, when officials recorded nearly 300 homicides throughout the state, including seventeen in Anderson County. Essie Walker was the third African American woman killed in Anderson that year. In January, a thirty-year-old maid had been murdered at her home, while on April 24—exactly one week before Walker's death—an assailant shot and killed a middle-aged widow.[5]

But though homicides occurred with depressing regularity in Anderson during the early 1920s, the killing of Essie Walker stood out as especially vicious. In the words of one press report, the dead woman "had been beaten so that she was hardly recognizable." A journalist later described her death as "one of the most brutal killings" in the county's history. Within a few hours of the discovery of Walker's body, police arrested an African American named James Mattison, for whom they had an outstanding warrant stemming from an incident the previous year. On a Friday evening in January 1920, a group of Black men had driven to a hot supper on the outskirts of Anderson. There they had been accosted by Mattison, who drew a pistol and ordered them to leave, firing several shots at their car as they drove away. The men notified the police and a warrant had been issued, but over a year had passed and nothing had been done about the incident. Only after Walker's death did police arrest Mattison, and under interrogation, he told them the boardinghouse keeper had been killed by Broadus Miller.[6]

Police picked up Miller at a boardinghouse at 404½ South Main Street, several blocks from the crime scene. According to press accounts, when taken into custody, he "had bloodstains all over his clothes," but "denied having killed the woman." Apparently the discovery of additional evidence further implicated him in the killing: "When later an inside pocket of a coat was found near where the woman lay, the officers carried it to the jail, and it fitted the coat which Miller had on." The police interrogation then turned physically coercive, and after being "put through the third degree," he "broke

FIGURE 5.1 Judge George E. Prince (1856–1923). Prominent in Anderson County civic affairs for several decades, Judge Prince oversaw the 1921 murder trial of Broadus Miller. (Yates Snowden and Harry Gardner, eds., *History of South Carolina* [Columbia, SC: Lewis, 1920], 3:14.)

down and confessed his guilt," stating "that the woman hit him with a baseball bat and he shot her." Prior to confessing, Miller "first asked another prisoner if he thought they would kill him if it was found that he had killed the old woman." None of the press accounts indicate whether Miller had found some type of employment in Anderson or if he had been residing in Walker's boardinghouse. Though the press identified Broadus Miller as the sole killer of Essie Walker, on Monday, May 9, a grand jury indicted both Miller and James Mattison for murder. In addition, police resurrected the year-old accusations against Mattison, leading to a separate indictment against him for assault and battery with intent to kill and for carrying a concealed weapon. When the case came to trial, Mattison would testify against Miller—and in exchange, all charges against him were dropped.[7]

Only two weeks after Essie Walker's death, Broadus Miller went on trial for murder. Presiding over the May session of Anderson County criminal court was Judge George E. Prince, who would play a decisive role in determining Miller's fate (see figure 5.1). A portly bald man in his mid-sixties, with a jovial smile half hidden beneath a large walrus moustache, Judge Prince exemplified the town-based ruling class in upstate South Carolina. He had been prominent in Anderson County civic affairs for several decades, first as an attorney and state legislator, then as a judge. While serving in the legislature during the 1890s, he had been the managing director of one Anderson County textile mill and the acting legal counsel for several others. Prince used his position as a lawmaker to further the mills' interests, combining his advocacy of the mills with a strong sense of noblesse oblige and unstinting work as a community booster. He had led the fight to create a public school system in the county, and when Ben Tillman governed South Carolina as a virtual one-man state, Prince had openly defied the governor by advocating a strong and independent judiciary.[8]

As a longtime court observer noted, Judge Prince had a reputation for "doing and saying what he thinks is right, and he doesn't care one whit whether anybody approves of his course or not." In the courtroom, the judge displayed a Victorian fustiness enlivened by occasional flashes of anger. On one occasion, after a courtroom outburst from a safecracker whom he had just given a ten-year sentence, Prince impetuously tacked on another five years. "I gave this man a sentence entirely too severe," he later confessed, writing multiple letters to the governor urging him to issue a pardon. A stickler for formalities, he had a penchant for delivering long moralizing sermons from the bench. When attorneys appeared in his courtroom wearing light-colored suits, he demanded they conform "to the rules governing the court" and don black clothing. Imbued with early twentieth-century notions of manliness, Prince once preached to a grand jury about the need to hire male schoolteachers. Only men could control the mischievous behavior of boys, the judge informed the jury, adding that "if your boy has no mischief about him, he is a sissy, and a sissy is no good."[9]

In the eyes of Judge Prince, African Americans had a clearly defined and legally enshrined place in South Carolina. There would be harsh consequences for any Black who transgressed the boundaries of this assigned place, but the judge believed that within these boundaries, African Americans were entitled to the full protection of the law. In an era when many politicians condoned lynching, he vocally denounced it. At the 1895 state constitutional convention, he had advocated anti-lynching legislation, arguing that lynching undermined judicial authority. "Every man ought to feel that once in the hands of the officers of the law he is safe," Prince declared. "A man should not be punished unless he is tried by law." The judge saw African Americans as social inferiors, to be treated with a supposedly benign paternalism. In 1907, while opening a court session in Clarendon County, Prince lectured a grand jury about "the crime of a certain intercourse between the two races." Like most of his peers, he found the idea of a consensual relationship between a Black man and a white woman inconceivable; the "crime" consisted of white men taking Black mistresses. Prince ordered the grand jury "not to bother with the colored people, who knew no better, but to get after the white folks who did know better," and he declared that "if there were any rusty or crusty old bachelors in the County guilty of this crime, no matter how broad his acres or big his bank account, those were the ones he wanted to try."[10]

Prince had close ties to Greenwood County, where his father-in-law had been the founding president of Lander College. His wife's brother now served as the college president, the judge himself sat on the school's board of trustees, and the Princes frequently visited the county and had a wide circle of friends and acquaintances there. On Saturday, May 14, Judge Prince issued a brief court order concerning the seventeen-year-old Greenwood County boy whose upcoming murder trial he would oversee. Noting it had "been brought to my attention that there is some doubt as to the sanity" of Broadus Miller, the judge appointed Dr. Anne Young to examine the defendant. A graduate of the Woman's Medical College of Pennsylvania, the twenty-nine-year-old Young specialized in mental health and had worked for three years at the South Carolina State Hospital for the Insane, where her duties included unmasking patients who feigned mental illness. On moving to Anderson in 1918, she was the only professionally trained psychiatrist in upstate South Carolina. The federal government regularly employed her to examine mentally disabled war veterans, while state courts appointed her to determine the legal competency of criminal defendants. Called on to examine the accused killer of Essie Walker, Dr. Young concluded Broadus Miller "was not normal mentally."[11]

Judge Prince's court order and Dr. Young's diagnosis cast a stark new light on Miller's character and actions. They also raise numerous questions. Who had brought the issue of his sanity to the judge's attention, and what had prompted this concern? What did the phrase "not normal" mean in Miller's case? Was he psychotic? Developmentally challenged? The court records are fragmentary, the questions unanswerable. But these two brief and enigmatic phrases—*some doubt as to the sanity, not normal mentally*—echo over time, an ominous warning of tragedies yet to come.

ON MONDAY, MAY 16, 1921, Broadus Miller went on trial in the Anderson County courthouse for the murder of Essie Walker. As the sociologist Guy Johnson later noted, the US judicial system was an alien and hostile environment for any Black defendant. "When a Negro goes into court," wrote Johnson, "he goes with the consciousness that the whole courtroom process is in the hands of 'the opposite race'—white judge, white jurors, white attorneys, white guards, white everything, except perhaps some of the witnesses and spectators." On the bench sat Judge George Prince, while the prosecution would be conducted by Leon W. Harris, who had been elected solicitor of the Tenth Circuit the previous year. Only twenty-nine years old, Harris had previously served as private secretary to Senator Ben Tillman. The right to counsel in capital cases would not be nationally recognized until 1932, with the US Supreme Court's decision in the Scottsboro case, but South Carolina had a history of guaranteeing this right dating back to the colonial era, and a local attorney—twenty-six-year-old John Alexander Neely Jr.—had been appointed to represent the defendant.[12]

During a physically coercive police interrogation, Miller had confessed to killing the boardinghouse keeper, but the murder trial began with the defense entering a plea of "not guilty," apparently based either on a claim of mental incompetence or a lack of premeditation. Throughout the first day of the trial, the prosecution and defense presented their various witnesses. The first person called by the prosecution was the county physician Dr. Halbert H. Acker Jr., who had examined Essie Walker's body and signed her death certificate. Following the doctor's testimony, nine other men—both Black and white—took the stand for the prosecution. These witnesses included residents of the West Market Street boardinghouse and James Mattison, who had first directed the police to Miller, as well as the mayor of Anderson, Foster Fant. The mayor's appearance on the witness stand and the nature of his testimony are a mystery. What did he personally know that was relevant to the case? There is no transcript of the trial, and the question cannot be answered.[13]

Whereas all the prosecution's witnesses were Anderson residents, the defense relied solely on character witnesses who had no firsthand knowledge of Essie Walker's death, but were well acquainted with the accused killer. As the scholar Albert Bushnell Hart had noted a decade earlier, a Black criminal defendant in the South enjoyed "a special protection whenever he can call in a respectable white man to vouch for him," for "the Court is then likely to impose a light sentence." Farm owners Harrison "Lat" Rasor and Clarence Agnew both traveled from Shoals Junction to Anderson to testify on Miller's behalf, while W. E. Algary sent a written statement of support. One can only speculate why Rasor and Agnew agreed to make the journey to Anderson, but as the social scientist John Dollard later noted in his landmark study of Southern race relations, white employers often appeared as character witnesses for Black laborers accused of violent crimes against other Blacks. "Very probably from the white standpoint these actions seem benevolent, since the whites know the accused Negroes as good servants or field hands," wrote Dollard. "From the white standpoint it is a feudal protectoral relationship, an extension of family ties to 'their' Negroes."[14]

Such feudal protectoral relationships were common throughout upstate South Carolina. A few years earlier, after one African American shot and killed another at an Anderson County church, the accused's white landlord immediately announced he would provide bond for the man, whom he described as "an honest, hard-working negro." However, seemingly benign acts could come at a heavy price, for white employers sometimes expected more work for less pay in exchange for feudal protection. In 1919, Abbeville officials complained that some Black laborers "had few scruples against committing crime" because of "the willingness of the white employer to pay the fines of the negroes arrested and convicted"; the white employer "could easily afford to pay these fines because in many cases the negroes were being paid half wages and some of them not even that." More ominously, as John Dollard noted, African Americans who belonged to "the feudal group of some influential white man" might "have extraordinary liberty to do violent things to other Negroes."[15]

Instead of a single influential white man, a tightly knit group of white landowners acted as feudal protectors for Broadus Miller's family. Harrison "Lat" Rasor, Clarence Agnew, and W. E. Algary were relatives and close neighbors of one another, as well as three of the most prominent and well-respected residents of the region around Shoals Junction. All three men were active members of Turkey Creek Baptist Church, where Rasor served as church clerk and Algary as treasurer, and Rasor had been the local school superintendent when Miller was a child. The motives for their testimony may have been benevolent, but even generous acts carried an implicit expectation of gratitude. In addition to these white witnesses, Tom Walker came to Anderson to testify on behalf of his nephew and adopted son, as did the family's minister, Reverend James Selden Maddox of Dunn Creek Baptist Church. After the testimony of the witnesses from Shoals Junction, Broadus Miller himself took the stand. Perhaps he asserted his innocence or claimed the killing had been an unpremeditated act of passion—in other words, manslaughter instead of murder—or perhaps the defense called him as a witness merely to demonstrate a lack of mental competence. The last person to testify was the court-appointed psychiatrist, Dr. Anne Young, who stated that Miller's mental condition made him "irresponsible for the crime."[16]

Following Dr. Young's testimony, the court adjourned for the day. When the trial reconvened the following morning, the solicitor and defense attorney delivered their closing arguments and Judge Prince turned the case over to a jury of twelve white men. A couple of the jurors were tenant farmers, and at least one worked in a cotton mill, but the majority were middle-aged landowning farmers from rural Anderson County, coming from backgrounds similar to those of the white men who had testified on the defendant's behalf. The jury deliberated for several hours before the foreman — a fifty-nine-year-old farmer named Thomas Webb — informed the court they could not reach a verdict. Judge Prince ordered them to reconsider the case, but after further deliberations "the foreman again stated that they could not agree," so the judge declared a mistrial. The jury apparently could not come to a consensus concerning Miller's mental competence and whether the killing should be punished as premeditated murder. For the next week and a half Broadus Miller sat in the Anderson jail awaiting a new murder trial, but on Thursday, May 26, he agreed to plead guilty to a lesser charge of manslaughter. Judge Prince then sentenced him to "hard labor in the State Penitentiary for a period of three years."[17]

CHAPTER SIX

Calculating the Wages of Death

When charged with killing a middle-aged Black woman, Broadus Miller had been well defended, with a professional psychiatrist testifying on his behalf, and he had ultimately been sentenced to only three years in prison. Six years later, accused of killing a white girl, Miller would be relentlessly pursued by thousands of armed manhunters, and if he were to escape lynching and be captured and tried, then he would almost certainly be convicted and executed. The contrast between the two cases is striking, but hardly surprising. In the early twentieth century, no crime provoked greater fury among Southern whites than an alleged assault on a white female by a Black man. On the other hand, at least at first glance, the judicial response to Essie Walker's death seems an example of disproportionately lenient sentencing for Black-on-Black crime. But is this first impression correct? In early twentieth-century South Carolina, how extensive was racial disparity in judicial punishment for homicide, and how typical was Miller's three-year sentence?[1]

The South Carolina legal system classified homicide as either murder or manslaughter; murder entailed acting with "premeditation or malice," while manslaughter meant the culprit had reacted to "reasonable provocation." The distinction between these two categories was inconsistently applied, and defendants indicted for murder often plea-bargained for the charge to be reduced to manslaughter. A murder conviction carried a mandatory death sentence unless—as frequently occurred—a jury recommended mercy; such a recommendation meant the convicted murderer would not be executed, but would instead be sentenced to life imprisonment in the state penitentiary or on a county chain gang. For manslaughter convictions, judges had enormous discretion in sentencing. According to law, individuals convicted of manslaughter could be sent to the penitentiary or chain gang for up to thirty years, but sentences of more than a few years were not common.[2]

Black South Carolinians accused of killing whites were almost always tried and convicted of murder, regardless of the circumstances. (The judicial outcome in the killing of John McGaha, the adopted son of Citizen Josh Ashley, had been an extremely rare exception.) In two separate cases in 1921, Governor Robert Cooper paroled African Americans serving life sentences in the state penitentiary for murdering white men. One of the parolees, James

Sanders, had confronted three white men who "made improper approaches to Sanders' wife on the street." After the men drew knives and began throwing bricks, Sanders pulled a pistol and shot one of them, which led to a murder conviction. The second man whom Governor Cooper paroled—Charles Campbell—had shot and killed a "very vicious" white assailant. "I am a white man, and Campbell is a negro, but I want to be fair," a witness to the killing wrote to the governor. If not for the racially charged atmosphere of the trial, the witness asserted, then Campbell "could have gone before a jury and been acquitted on plea of self defense." Instead, he had been convicted on a murder charge with a recommendation of mercy, leading to an informal deal between the judge and the prosecutor; the judge imposed the mandatory life sentence, "but upon agreement on the part of the Solicitor that he would see that Campbell was paroled after serving a few years." By the time Governor Cooper paroled Sanders and Campbell, both men had spent five years in prison.[3]

Trial by jury entailed behind-closed-door negotiations and tacit compromises. If jurors were not fully convinced of a defendant's guilt, then African Americans charged with murdering white men did not automatically receive death sentences. Instead of acquitting an accused Black man outright, an all-white jury would convict him and recommend mercy, thus ensuring he received a life sentence instead of death. Jurors saw themselves as saving the Black man's life, not as condemning him to a life in prison. They did not want to face the potential backlash from the white community that an acquittal might provoke, and they assumed that if a defendant were indeed innocent, then at some point in the future someone else would shoulder the responsibility of ensuring the prisoner was pardoned or paroled. If indicted and tried for killing a white victim, an accused Black man was usually guilty until proven innocent, with mercy often recommended if a jury had doubts about his guilt.

In 1913, Judge Prince had presided over the trial of Will Goggans, an African American charged with murdering a white man in Newberry County. Goggans steadfastly maintained his innocence, and the only evidence against him was the highly dubious testimony of two other African Americans who had also been accused in the case. But a jury convicted him and did not recommend mercy, so Prince therefore handed down the mandatory death sentence. Within weeks, both judge and jury joined several other white citizens in petitioning Governor Coleman Blease to commute the sentence to life imprisonment. The jurors explained that they had grave doubts about Goggans's guilt and had wanted to recommend mercy, but they had been waiting for Judge Prince to suggest it. The judge insisted he had expected the jury to make such a recommendation, but the decision had been entirely theirs and out of his hands. As one anguished petitioner hastened to assure the governor, "I naturally believe in white supremacy, and not social equality." However, the outcome of the trial had left him deeply troubled. "Fact is, the trial was like that of a white man, *except* the *verdict*." Seeking to placate the various white constituents in his native county, Governor Blease granted Goggans a series of extended reprieves, and in 1915, newly elected Governor Richard Manning commuted the death sentence to life imprisonment.[4]

When the evidence against African Americans accused of killing white men was flimsy, prosecutors often displayed more eagerness for a death sentence than juries did. In 1915, three African Americans in Laurens County went on trial for murder. They had allegedly killed a white farmer and burned down his house, and all three men received life sentences after the jury convicted them but recommended mercy. The solicitor had wanted the death penalty for the trio's alleged ringleader, so he then charged the man with arson, which, though rarely prosecuted as such, was on the books as a capital crime. Following a second conviction, the solicitor succeeded in securing the desired death sentence, but state officials objected to his attempted end run around the original jury decision. "If the negroes are guilty they are equally guilty," the state pardon board reported to Governor Manning, who commuted the sentence to life imprisonment.[5]

Whereas any African American who killed a white man was almost certain to be convicted of murder, whites who killed African Americans usually did so with impunity. In 1921, an editorialist for *The State* admitted that the South Carolina judicial system was "often too lenient to white men when they are indicted for criminal offenses against negroes." However, the writer argued, it would be wrong to conclude that whites who killed Blacks never received judicial punishment. "While convictions of white men who kill negroes are not numerous, they are not unheard of," he asserted. And indeed, by the late 1910s, all-white juries in upstate South Carolina occasionally convicted white men for killing African Americans—but very rarely, and always for manslaughter and not for murder. In comparison with the sentences typically levied in such cases, the mill worker Pope McCarty's seven-year sentence for killing Reverend James Walker was exceptionally severe. On Christmas Day, 1915, a white overseer on an Anderson County farm got drunk and led two Black farmhands in "raising rough houses" through an African American neighborhood. They stormed into several homes, beating and pistol-whipping the occupants, and in one household the overseer fatally struck a forty-year-old man with an axe. A local jury convicted all three "rough housers" for manslaughter, with the overseer and one of the farmhands receiving five-year sentences, while the other farmhand got three years.[6]

White farmworkers and mill hands were potentially vulnerable to prosecution for interracial manslaughter, but town elites and landowning farmers had much less reason to fear any judicial punishment for killing African Americans. In 1921, an Anderson County farm owner went on trial for killing his Black tenant. The tenant's stepdaughter had recently moved away, but the landlord had wanted her to stay and continue laboring on the farm, so he confronted her stepfather and shot him. In a marked departure from the judicial apathy typical in such cases, the solicitor Leon Harris vigorously prosecuted the killing and—based "almost totally on negro testimony"—secured a manslaughter conviction and two-year sentence. Harris celebrated the outcome in a letter to the *New York Herald*. The farm owner was "as prominent as any man of the county," he "had some of the best white men of the county to testify as to his character," and he had been "represented by as able attorneys as the State of South Carolina affords." Nevertheless, the solicitor had won the case, which he trumpeted as proof "that Southern white juries will give a man justice regardless of his color."[7]

The press heralded the conviction and two-year sentence as a victory for the legal system. As *The State*'s editorialist approvingly noted, it was "becoming increasingly dangerous for a white man to kill a negro." However, initial convictions were usually a preliminary step in a long process. Like many white men found guilty in criminal cases, the Anderson County farm owner immediately posted bail and announced he would appeal his conviction to the South Carolina supreme court, and it is unclear if he ever served any of his sentence. For a white defendant with sufficient money, the judicial process could be expensive and time-consuming, but it was usually winnable. And if convictions were not overturned on appeal, then a parole, pardon, or commutation by the governor meant that most defendants served far less time than their original sentence. In the case of the Anderson "rough housers," the white overseer who committed homicide was paroled less than two years later, while his Black accomplices remained in prison.[8]

African Americans accused of killing whites were almost always convicted of murder, while whites who killed African Americans received either no judicial punishment or, at most, a manslaughter conviction. However, most homicides were intraracial killings, with same-race perpetrators and victims, and in the 1920s the South Carolina judicial system typically treated same-race homicides among both whites and African Americans in a cavalier fashion. Coroner juries sometimes ruled such killings justifiable. Grand juries refused to indict accused killers, regardless of the evidence, or issued indictments only for lesser charges, such as carrying a concealed weapon or "disorderly conduct." When homicide cases went to trial, the state's all-white juries acquitted over one-third of Black defendants, while more than two-thirds of white defendants were freed. In the mid-1920s, the newspaper publisher Walter E. Duncan surveyed the state and counted 150 pending murder trials, most of which would end in acquittal or conviction on lesser charges. "Human life is cheap in South Carolina," Duncan concluded.[9]

On May 14, 1921, less than two weeks before Broadus Miller's plea bargain, Judge Prince passed sentence in three separate intraracial homicide cases. The defendants—two white, one Black—had all been charged with murder, but the trials of all three men had ended in hung juries. One of the white defendants, Sloan Jones, had quarreled with someone and then tried to gun him down on a residential street in Anderson on a Sunday afternoon, but the only person Jones killed was a passing white pedestrian whom he accidentally shot in the back. After one mistrial, a second jury convicted Jones of manslaughter. "I have to consider not just how much punishment will do you, but what will be sufficient to set an example to other people not to go around shooting people," Judge Prince explained to Jones during sentencing. "I have got to punish you." The judge then ordered him to be confined for three years in the state penitentiary. After the mistrials in the murder cases against them, the defendants in the other two cases—one white, one Black—both accepted plea bargains and received two-year terms, the minimum sentence for manslaughter convictions.[10]

If given a sentence of ten years or less, an individual convicted of manslaughter could post bail and remain free pending appeal, and though judges occasionally handed down sentences of more than ten years, such punishment was rare. On the same day he sentenced Broadus Miller, Judge Prince held a sentencing hearing for Ernest Ashley, a member of Honea Path's notorious Ashley clan. At a political rally in Honea Path the previous fall, a policeman had "walked into a crowd where several men were scuffling." One of the men tried to engage the lawman in a wrestling match, but the officer refused, at which point Ashley stepped up and accused the policeman of acting "huffy." A heated argument ensued, and it culminated in Ashley drawing a pistol and killing the officer. The subsequent trial turned into "one of the hardest contested legal battles in the criminal court of Anderson." A team of prominent attorneys represented the defendant, who claimed self-defense, but a jury convicted him of manslaughter and Judge Prince then imposed an eleven-year sentence, deliberately preventing Ashley from remaining free pending an appeal. After defense counsel "implored Judge Prince to temper justice with mercy," the judge relented and reduced the sentence to ten years, thus allowing him to post bail.[11]

African Americans were just as likely as white offenders to receive long sentences for intraracial manslaughter. In March 1921, an Abbeville court sentenced two African Americans convicted of manslaughter for killing other Black men; one of the killers received a ten-year sentence, the other twelve years. As in the death of Essie Walker, the killing of African American women by Black men sometimes resulted in convictions for manslaughter instead of murder; such an outcome seems to have occurred less frequently when white men killed white women. However, in intraracial homicide cases among both whites and Blacks, jurors generally showed a greater willingness to convict the killer for murder instead of manslaughter if the victim was a woman. Six weeks before Essie Walker's death, a Black man in Laurens County was convicted of murder and sentenced to life imprisonment for "killing a negro woman," and the day after Walker died, an African American in Spartanburg received a life sentence for murdering his former girlfriend.[12]

Whereas punishment for interracial killings was profoundly unequal, in the early 1920s the South Carolina judicial system punished intraracial homicide with rough parity for white and Black offenders. Regardless of their race, intraracial killers were more likely to be convicted of manslaughter than murder, and convictions for either murder or manslaughter usually resulted in comparable sentences for whites and Blacks. This approximate equality in punishment was a relatively recent development. At the beginning of the twentieth century, the state's judicial system had punished Black-on-Black homicide *more harshly* than white-on-white killings. On average, two or three Black men had been hanged every year for committing intraracial murder. For three straight years, from 1907 through 1909, Greenwood County had carried out one hanging a year—the only legal executions in the county's history; in all three cases, Black men were hanged for murdering Black victims. In December 1911, two convicted African American murderers were hanged in Lancaster, the first executions to take place there in twenty years; in both cases, the murder victim had been a Black man. After South Carolina adopted the electric chair in 1912, all prisoners sentenced to death were transported to Columbia, housed on death row, and electrocuted within the

TABLE 6.1 Legal executions in South Carolina, 1892–1921

	1892–1901	1902–1911	1912–1921
Total executions	70	62	55
Whites executed for intraracial murder	5	4	3
Blacks executed for arson	3	0	0
Blacks executed for interracial murder	30	22	28
Blacks executed for rape	5	7	5
Blacks executed for attempted rape	0	5	14
Blacks executed for intraracial murder	27	24	5

Sources: Daniel Allen Hearn, *Legal Executions in North Carolina and South Carolina: A Comprehensive Registry, 1866–1962* (Jefferson, NC: McFarland, 2015), 142–175; M. Watt Espy and John Ortiz Smykla, *Executions in the United States, 1608–2002: The ESPY File*, 4th ICPSR ed. (Ann Arbor, MI: Inter-university Consortium for Political and Social Research, 2004).

walls of the state penitentiary. The frequency of executions remained roughly the same, and African Americans continued to comprise a vast majority of the condemned men. But after 1912, lethal punishment for Black-on-Black homicides suddenly and sharply declined (see table 6.1).[13]

For two decades prior to 1912, African Americans convicted of same-race murder had been executed at a steady pace, accounting for nearly 40 percent of all hangings in South Carolina. But in the decade after the adoption of the electric chair, only five Black men were put to death for committing intraracial murder, less than 9 percent of all executions. Due largely to a 1909 state law making attempted rape a capital crime, the overall number of executions did not significantly change; in the decade following 1912, fourteen Black men would be executed after being convicted of attempting to rape white women. Because overall executions occurred at the same rate as before, and because the racial demographics of capital punishment remained the same, the subtle change in how officials implemented the death penalty went unnoticed by observers. Removed from the local level and veiled by "the majesty of the law," the machinery of the state dramatically increased the disparity in capital punishment for Black-on-white versus Black-on-Black offenders.[14]

Various factors contributed to this change. Until 1912, county law enforcement officials were responsible for hanging persons sentenced to death. By the beginning of the twentieth century, South Carolina had officially abandoned the practice of public executions, but conditions varied widely from county to county, and large crowds—sometimes numbering a few hundred spectators—could be present at a hanging in a jailhouse or behind a jail yard wall. Like lynching, the legal hanging of African Americans sent a visible message to Black communities, reminding them who held the reins of power and had the authority to decide whether a person lived or died. The transition from county hangings to state electrocutions occurred during the tenure of Governor Coleman Blease, who shrilly denounced alleged Black criminality while indiscriminately dispensing pardons and commutations for intraracial homicide convictions to whites and Blacks alike. Capital punishment for intraracial homicide among African Americans plummeted during his reign as governor, and it never returned to pre-Blease levels after he was gone.[15]

Yet, even after 1912, African Americans convicted of intraracial murder ran a risk of being put to death by the state. The risk had dramatically decreased and was statistically small, but for those unlucky few who ended up sitting in the electric chair, the unlikelihood of their fate provided no consolation. In 1921, the year Broadus Miller went on trial, South Carolina executed eight men. All were Black. Seven of the men had been convicted of murdering or raping white victims. The eighth was a Greenville County resident named Will Lomax, who had killed his wife. In August 1919, a local court had delivered murder convictions against Lomax and three other African Americans; in all four cases, the men had killed Black victims, and all four of the men were sentenced to death. But through legal appeal or commutation, the lives of the other three men were spared. Influential Greenville County citizens wrote to the governor on behalf of Will Lomax. He had a "low grade of intelligence," "his mother was feeble-minded," and the wife whom he had killed "was also idiotic." Only hours before a scheduled execution, Lomax received a reprieve, and his advocates successfully petitioned twice more to postpone his death. A board of physicians ultimately sealed the condemned man's fate, examining him and concluding he was "below normal intelligence but not insane."[16]

Unlike the teenage Broadus Miller, Lomax was an adult and the victim had been his wife, but the contrast in the outcomes of the two cases is nonetheless striking: on February 4, 1921, less than three months before the slaying of Essie Walker, the state of South Carolina executed a mentally impaired Black man for killing a Black woman.[17]

CHAPTER SEVEN

South Carolina State Penitentiary

On Tuesday, May 31, 1921, Broadus Miller arrived at the South Carolina State Penitentiary in Columbia. Only one other convict, an African American named Bob Russell, entered the prison that day. Convicted of housebreaking and larceny, Russell had been sentenced to six years—double the term given Miller, who had pled guilty to killing a woman. Russell came from Greenville County, adjacent to Anderson, and police officers probably brought both men to Columbia together. On arrival, they were escorted through the massive arched gate of the administrative building—a forbidding granite fortress, topped by crenelated towers—and taken to the bath house, where they were stripped naked, inspected for vermin, given a bath, and issued prison clothing. New prisoners were neither fingerprinted nor photographed, for state officials refused to allocate the $300 such a system would cost. However, a clerk recorded the men's physical descriptions: the seventeen-year-old Miller stood five feet, eight inches tall and had a dark brown complexion and scars on both knees. Within a day or two of their arrival, the men were checked by the prison doctor, who vaccinated them against smallpox and decided whether they were physically able to work.[1]

Located only a few blocks from the state capitol, the South Carolina penitentiary had been constructed in the immediate aftermath of the Civil War, in part to administer punishment previously meted out by individual slaveholders. The penitentiary covered eighteen acres on the eastern bank of the Columbia Canal, near the point where the Broad and Saluda Rivers joined to form the Congaree. Brick walls from fifteen to forty-five feet high surrounded the grounds and its various buildings, some of them badly dilapidated. The main cellblock was a large cavernous structure dating from the late 1860s and containing five tiers of dank and narrow cells. In the shadow of the cellblock stood the squat, rectangular "death house," erected in 1912 to house half a dozen death row inmates and the state's electric chair. At the other end of the prison complex, a large brick building served as a factory where inmates made wooden chairs. Between the factory and the main cellblock, set off to the side and standing by itself, was a prison hospital; the dozen or so other buildings included a commissary and a tuberculosis ward.[2]

Miller entered the penitentiary at a time when its population was rapidly growing. At the beginning of the 1920s the prison had contained around 120 inmates, but over the next few years, due in large part to the agricultural depression, South Carolina's crime rate soared and the number of prisoners dramatically increased. By 1923 the penitentiary held more than 400 persons. Nearly 90 percent were men—both Black and white—who were housed in the main cellblock, while the ramshackle second floor of the commissary served as a dormitory for a few dozen Black women and a handful of white female prisoners, all of whom shared a single lavatory. In 1921, Governor Robert Cooper declared that the commissary was "not a fit place for incarceration of human beings, either white or black," and he commuted the sentences of two white women on condition that they leave South Carolina "and engage in respectable lives elsewhere."[3]

Throughout the late nineteenth and early twentieth centuries the male inmate population had been overwhelmingly Black, but the demographics rapidly changed after the World War. In 1919, for the first time, white men comprised a majority of male inmates, and in the following years they accounted for nearly 60 percent of the prison's male population. Nationwide, rapid postwar demobilization and the enforcement of prohibition laws caused a significant increase in white male convicts. In the South Carolina penitentiary, however, the demographic transformation was largely the unintended consequence of changes in state law. In 1912 the legislature mandated that able-bodied male convicts be assigned to local chain gangs, unless—as in the case of Broadus Miller—a judge explicitly sentenced someone to the penitentiary. At the same time, lawmakers decreed that counties must racially segregate the chain gangs, while allowing local officials to send unwanted prisoners to the penitentiary. As state inspectors began strictly enforcing the segregation requirements, some counties ended up transferring their long-term white prisoners to Columbia and maintaining all-Black chain gangs.[4]

Other factors also influenced the transfer of convicts from county to state. Able to choose which prisoners they wished to keep, counties held on to able-bodied laborers while getting rid of the disabled and the incorrigibly violent. Consequently, the state penitentiary became—in the words of one official—a "dumping ground." Throughout the entire South Carolina penal system many prisoners were mentally ill, including nearly one-quarter of county jail inmates, but the transfer of unwanted prisoners to Columbia meant there was an especially high percentage of mentally ill individuals in the penitentiary. In 1921, the year Miller arrived, social workers examined the inmates and concluded that only one in five had "normal" intelligence. Many had learning disabilities, while some 40 percent of the Black inmates—and 51 percent of white inmates—were diagnosed as having a "mental defect," a "psychopathic personality," or a "mental disease." A prisoner with exceptionally severe mental illness might eventually be transferred to the State Hospital for the Insane; Bob Russell, who entered prison the same day as Miller, would be transferred to the State Hospital the following year. However, during their time in the penitentiary, all inmates—the coldly calculating and the feebleminded, the psychotic and the sane—were thrown together into the general prison population.[5]

The rapid increase in the number of inmates exacerbated the already poor living conditions in the prison. The top three floors of the main cellblock lacked electricity, so most cells had only a small unscreened window for light. Each cell measured five feet by eight feet, with a six-and-a-half-foot-high ceiling, and contained one small bunk. Because of overcrowding, sometimes two men were housed together in a single cell. As one prisoner recalled, the bed consisted of "just a pair of springs and a frame and the springs were broken and the blankets stunk." In summer, when Columbia sweltered in humid heat, bedbugs infested the cells. A bucket in the corner served as a toilet and was emptied once a day. "You have to use the bucket and it stays in there all night, with the smell," complained an inmate. Once a week the prisoners were allowed to bathe and were given a clean change of underwear. Male prisoners ate in a single mess hall, a dozen men to a table, with segregated sections for Blacks and whites. On special occasions—Christmas and Thanksgiving—they might receive pork. Otherwise, the mess hall served the same meals every day of the week. Breakfast—bread, molasses, hominy, gravy, bacon, a piece of meat, coffee. Lunch—bread, molasses, vegetable of the day. Supper—bread, molasses, hominy, gravy. The monotonous menu caused frequent complaints, as did the wretched quality of the food. In the words of one inmate, it contained "bugs and worms," and "you can see the bugs and stuff in it and you can't hardly eat it at all."[6]

When decreeing the racial segregation of convict laborers, the South Carolina legislature had explicitly exempted the state penitentiary, and all the prison's inmates, both Black and white, were assigned jobs in the facility. A few dozen worked in the mess hall and kitchen, the laundry, and other prison facilities, but most were employed in the chair factory, where male inmates manufactured the wooden frames and, in a separate workroom, Black female inmates wove the fiber seats. Though only lightly supervised, inmates were prohibited from speaking to one another during working hours. Unlike other jobs in the penitentiary, those in the factory provided a nominal wage—called a "bonus"—to anyone who exceeded a production quota. A typical worker might receive two or three dollars a month, with the most productive potentially earning double that amount. The prison doctor examined prisoners who claimed to be too sick to work; if he thought they were malingering, he allegedly punished them with hypodermic injections that caused extreme nausea and vomiting.[7]

Life in the penitentiary followed two different schedules, depending on the season. On the summer schedule, male inmates were let out of their cells at six in the morning and had thirty minutes for breakfast. They worked until noon, when they had an hour-and-a-half break. After eating lunch, they could sit in the prison yard, smoking and talking, before returning to work at one thirty and remaining there until five o'clock. Dinner lasted half an hour, then the inmates were locked up at five thirty. During winter, the day began an hour later and the lunch break lasted only thirty minutes; work ended at a quarter after four and the prisoners were back in their cells by a quarter to five. As a prison inspector noted, the men were locked up "for twelve hours a day in the summer and fourteen hours in winter," which was "a long time to sleep and look at the four walls of a cell." After working nine-hour days Monday through Friday and half a day on Saturdays, the male inmates were allowed to spend Saturday afternoons in the prison yard playing baseball. Three Sundays a month the prison chaplain held morning and afternoon services; attendance at morning services was compulsory, but inmates could decide whether to return to the chapel in the afternoon.[8]

In the early 1920s, a former state legislator named Arthur K. Sanders served as prison superintendent. An honorifically titled "colonel," Sanders had been involved with the administration of the penitentiary for over twenty years, first as a member of the board of directors and then as superintendent—a position to which he had been appointed thanks to his extensive political connections. By the time Broadus Miller arrived at the penitentiary, discipline had allegedly become lax, with guards allowing some inmates to don civilian clothes and spend evenings in the bars of downtown Columbia. Tales of such escapades led to the resignation of the captain of the guards, and in December 1921, Colonel Sanders hired Clay Roberts to replace him. "Captain Roberts is an experienced man in prison work," the superintendent noted. Indeed, Roberts had served as the guards' captain once before. Born in 1875, he had grown up on a farm in Lexington County, just outside Columbia, and began working as a guard at the penitentiary in the late 1890s. Within a few years he had risen to the rank of sergeant; soon thereafter, he received his first appointment as captain and assistant warden. In 1913, Roberts had quit working at the prison, but it is unclear if he left voluntarily or was forced to resign.[9]

Returning to his former job as prison captain, Clay Roberts quickly established dictatorial command over inmates and staff alike, alienating many of the guards under his command. "At first I had guards come to me complaining to me about what the captain had done," recounted Colonel Sanders. But the prison superintendent was glad to have the captain assume full control of day-to-day affairs, leaving Sanders to focus exclusively on the prison's finances, and he peremptorily dismissed all complaints. "I told them out and out that if you can't please the captain you can't please me," the superintendent explained. "The captain has absolute management of them. I try to look after the business end." Roberts had even greater authority, unconstrained by any formal guidelines, over the prisoners themselves. In 1923, a state legislative committee was stunned to learn the prison had no written rules or regulations. "How do you suppose the prisoners know what to do if you haven't any rules for them to see?" a lawmaker asked the prison superintendent. "I suppose a man knows what the general rules are," Colonel Sanders responded. "What are the general rules?" the legislator persisted. "Behave yourself," replied the colonel.[10]

In the absence of any formal rules and regulations, Captain Roberts arbitrarily decided what constituted acceptable behavior and how to punish transgressions. An investigation by the State Board of Public Welfare concluded "that the discipline of the penitentiary is largely based upon the personal likes and dislikes of the captain of the guards and is extremely severe." Prisoners were sometimes placed in solitary confinement for fifteen days and given only bread and water, or were chained to a cell door for hours at a time. The most dreaded form of punishment was flogging. Using a thick leather strap about two inches wide and attached to a round wooden handle, a guard—usually Captain Roberts himself—would lash an inmate's naked back, raising welts and bringing blood. Both men and women were whipped, even for seemingly trivial offenses; on one occasion, a Black woman was flogged for stepping out of line on the prison grounds to pick a flower. Women were taken to the lavatory in the female dormitory, stripped to the waist, and placed in stocks; they then received up to twenty-five lashes across their bare backs. The women's screams could be heard throughout the building; afterward, they often spat up blood. Men sometimes received more than forty lashes. To whip male inmates, guards occasionally took them to the autopsy room inside the "death house," where they were stripped naked and held face-down on "the table where they lay the dead prisoners after they are executed." Usually, however, male prisoners were taken to the basement beneath the prison hospital, to a place known as "the leather room," and handcuffed to an iron ring high on the wall. Even inmates in the main cellblock could hear the screams coming from the hospital basement.[11]

Appearing before a legislative committee in February 1923, Colonel Sanders defended the flogging of prisoners by pointing to penal systems elsewhere in the South. "Nearly all of the Southern States have the strap and punish them by whipping them," the colonel argued. However, a year and a half earlier, in a court ruling penitentiary officials flagrantly ignored, a South Carolina judge had decreed that "there is no authority for corporal punishment in this state." The judge's action had come in response to the case of Tom Keelan, a white man whom police in Spartanburg County arrested in August 1921 for hoboing aboard a freight train. Sentenced to thirty days on the local chain gang, Keelan was whipped to death by a guard after he became too ill to work. The dead man's New Jersey relatives pressed the US Department of Justice to investigate, which prompted South Carolina officials to conduct an inquiry and prosecute the guard. Just four months after Keelan's death, in a similar case that garnered much greater publicity, a hobo named Martin Tabert was arrested in Florida and flogged to death in a labor camp; extensive press coverage of his death led Florida lawmakers to declare a moratorium on flogging. Nor was Florida alone in banning the practice. In 1922, the governor of Alabama forbade the whipping of prisoners and ordered the leather straps destroyed, warning prison administrators they would be fired for any violation of the new policy. The same week that Colonel Sanders appeared before the committee in South Carolina, the Georgia governor issued an executive order prohibiting "flogging as a part of prison discipline," and later that year, North Carolina governor Cameron Morrison imposed strict limitations on whipping and offered a $400 reward "for evidence sufficient to convict" anyone not following the new guidelines.[12]

Even Colonel Sanders could not deny that in many respects, the South Carolina State Penitentiary was an antiquated facility. "I think we are about fifty years behind the times," the prison superintendent confessed. However, he argued that conditions had improved under his administration. Unlike before, inmates were now allowed to talk during their lunch break; after lunch they could sit in the prison yard and smoke; they were able to write home once a week instead of only once a month. Such minor improvements could not mask the institution's underlying brutality, and throughout the early 1920s, newspapers and political reformers regularly denounced conditions in the prison. In the words of an investigative committee, the penitentiary was "so obsolete, so inadequate, so unsafe and so unsightly that one cannot view it except as an expression of another age." As one South Carolina newspaper headline proclaimed, "State Penitentiary Is a Medieval Prison Out of Place in Present Day."[13]

In South Carolina, as in most Southern states, the penitentiary was one branch of a three-part penal system. In addition to the penitentiary and county-administered chain gangs, South Carolina incarcerated convicts on two prison farms that the state had purchased in the 1890s. Adjoining one another but operated as separate enterprises, the Reed and DeSaussure farms covered 4,200 acres in Kershaw and Sumter Counties, about forty miles east of Columbia. Colonel Sanders was in charge of the farms, but he delegated day-to-day supervision of them to resident managers and a handful of guards. Throughout the year, depending on the need for labor, inmates were transferred back and forth between the state penitentiary and the farms, where they tended livestock and raised cotton and other crops. On average, around 125 prisoners resided on the two farms. Nearly all of them were African American men, usually between twenty and forty-five years old, but a few white males and—especially in summer, when the workload was heavier—Black women were also sent there. To house the inmates, each farm had a three-story brick building; the first floor contained a dining room and kitchen, while the top two stories served as dormitories, with about fifty beds on each floor. Black male prisoners occupied the second floor, while the third floor held the occasional contingent of white male or Black female inmates.[14]

In 1922, the sociologist Frank Tannenbaum contrasted the typical penitentiary—"with its isolated cells, its narrow windows, its high walls, its constant dampness and semi-darkness"—with conditions on prison farms. Though "not ideal," the farms represented "an improvement on the old cell-block." Prisoners could work outdoors and generally had better quality food, prepared from crops and livestock that had been grown or raised on site. Nevertheless, the South Carolina prison farms remained a harsh environment. During an annual inspection, a state official noted that all toilets on one of the farms had been out of order for over a year; prisoners had to relieve themselves in the nearby fields and woods. Once a month, the prison chaplain came from Columbia to hold services; otherwise, the farm inmates spent the entire day on Sundays locked up in their dormitories. Some of the convicts wore shackles, and all were subject to whipping and other corporal punishments. The farm managers flogged inmates for infractions such as fighting and, in one farm manager's words, committing "buggery," which he defined as one man using "another man as a woman." Work conditions on the farms were similar to those under antebellum slavery, with prisoners toiling from sunup to sundown six days a week and—unlike the factory workers in the penitentiary—not receiving even a nominal wage for their labor.[15]

Although the prison farms resembled slave plantations, the profits derived from the convicts' labor were potentially greater than those enjoyed by slaveholders. Since the prisoners did not have to be purchased and arrived as full-grown adults, there was no initial investment cost for labor; as one critic observed, under such conditions, an enterprise was virtually guaranteed to turn a huge profit. However, the farms kept no financial records and paid no taxes. "These farms are conducted without a book being kept on either one," complained a member of the penitentiary's board of directors. "They ship out stuff, but where to, and how much the farms cost to run, we can't make out." When testifying before state lawmakers, Colonel Sanders claimed to have no idea if the prison farms were profitable, but on other occasions he boasted that they "were sources of great revenue." Though Sanders insisted he had not used his position to line his own pockets, the farms presented numerous possibilities for making money and bestowing financial favors, and he and other officials seem to have taken full advantage of such opportunities. The superintendent regularly sold cotton to preferred buyers at discounted prices, and on one occasion, Governor Wilson Harvey arranged for the state to pay a commission to a cotton broker for *buying* the state's cotton. In October 1922, officials claimed a suspicious fire had completely incinerated 174 bales of cotton stored in a farm warehouse; insurance paid for the vanished crop.[16]

Using the penal system as a money-making venture had a long history in South Carolina. In 1877, Wade Hampton—the state's first post-Reconstruction governor—announced that the prisons "should be made self-supporting as far as possible." However, Hampton's goal for the penal system extended beyond mere self-sufficiency. "With proper legislation," the governor noted, "the labor of the convicts in the penitentiary could be made profitable." A convict lease system, in which the state leased laborers to private companies outside the penitentiary, seemed the best way to realize Hampton's vision of profitability, so South Carolina immediately enacted legislation permitting convict lease. By the following year, prisoners were working for railroads, mining companies, and large plantation owners. The program became a major scandal after the press reported on the treatment of convicts leased by the Greenwood and Augusta Railroad. Confined to a disease-ridden stockade and overseen by brutal supervisors, dozens of the railroad workers died. In the wake of the incident, South Carolina largely abandoned the convict lease system, and by the early 1880s, the state had begun focusing on using convict labor within prison walls.[17]

The recently constructed penitentiary in Columbia provided the state with a suitable workplace. In 1883 the Columbia Hosiery company opened a mill within the penitentiary, using convict labor to produce stockings and knitted goods. For the state, the new arrangement proved more advantageous than convict lease. By bringing private companies to the penitentiary instead of sending prisoners to private companies, the state maintained absolute control of the convict workforce, could dictate workplace conditions, and increased its own share of the profits. By the 1890s the state had diversified its operations, purchasing the prison farms and sending contingents of prisoners from Columbia to labor on the farms. Thanks to the revenue generated by the hosiery mill and prison farms, the South Carolina penal system became entirely self-funding. Grateful for not having to appropriate any funds to the penal system, state lawmakers exerted no oversight over its finances, and though the farms and hosiery mill reaped huge profits, there was no public accounting of how much money was earned or how it was distributed.[18]

In the early 1910s, Governor Coleman Blease led a spirited fight to reduce the state's role in the penal system, arguing that all able-bodied prisoners should be placed under the control of local authorities and put to work on county chain gangs. "I have never believed . . . in keeping the Penitentiary for a money-making institution," the governor declared. Blease advocated abolishing the prison farms, and he displayed a particular animus for the hosiery mill, which he described as "a death trap" and "a tuberculosis incubator"—and whose convict labor force competed with the mill workers from whom he drew his political support. Under heavy pressure from the governor, state legislators and the penitentiary's board of directors abrogated the existing contract with the hosiery company. Blease heralded the closing of the mill as a wonderful accomplishment, asserting that "the most barbaric nation has never inflicted upon an innocent or a guilty man a meaner, nor more brutal punishment than South Carolina was giving to them in their hosiery mill." However, shutting down the mill did not end the penitentiary's joint ventures with private companies. Looking for a new industry with which to do business, prison officials soon signed a contract with the Fiber Craft Chair Company. In 1917, the company took over the abandoned mill, refurbished the building and installed new machinery, and converted the hosiery mill into a furniture factory. Fiber Craft supplied the equipment and materials, while the prison furnished the labor. The contract called for the prison and the company to divide all profits equally, but gave the penitentiary full indemnity from customers' bad debts. The prison's share of the net profits thus totaled more than one-half.[19]

In 1904—the same year Broadus Miller was born—W. E. B. Du Bois published a report on criminality among African Americans in the South. Du Bois argued that "the greatest single cause" for recidivism was the penal system's focus on making a financial profit instead of reforming and rehabilitating prisoners. Six years later, the scholar Albert Bushnell Hart observed that the penal system in Southern states "still retains the notion . . . that the prisoner is the slave of the state, existing only for the convenience and profit of those whom he serves." In his 1916 study of the South Carolina penitentiary, Albert Oliphant concluded that "the effort to derive a profit for the State from the labor of men sentenced by the courts to the penitentiary is the outstanding feature of the management of this institution." The desire to extract financial gain extended to every aspect of the facility. Some inmates suspected the penitentiary dining hall deliberately served inedible meals to force them to spend their factory wages at the commissary, which sold canned goods, fruit, candy, and tobacco. With the approval of prison officials, several years earlier an inmate had established the commissary, but after his sudden and suspicious death, Captain Roberts assumed control of it—and began pocketing its profits.[20]

The institutionalized brutality and dismal living conditions within the penitentiary fueled a simmering anger among the inmates, and on May 8, 1922—one year after Broadus Miller arrived—this anger reached a breaking point. During their lunch break, workers from the chair factory learned that guards had searched the cellblock and confiscated most of their personal belongings, including Bibles and letters from their families. After lunch, when Captain Roberts ordered the men to return to the factory, they stood in sullen silence and refused to leave the dining hall. One of the prisoners— known as "Jew" Frank—stepped forward and openly confronted the captain of the guards. "Captain, I don't believe it is right for you to be taking our Bibles and personal effects," he protested. Surprised by such audacity, Roberts backed down, assuring the men that the confiscated items would be returned. His reply mollified the prisoners, who finally obeyed the order to go back to work. But about twenty minutes later, Captain Roberts summoned two guards and told them to go to the chair factory, get "Jew" Frank, and bring him to the captain's office. When the guards arrived with the prisoner, Roberts announced that Frank would be whipped for his impudence and ordered him to be taken to the hospital basement.[21]

The sudden arrival of the guards in the chair factory and their departure with Frank had prompted a tumultuous reaction. Approximately two-thirds of the factory workers—some 150 men, most if not all of them white—abruptly declared a strike. Ignoring all commands to resume work, they clustered around the factory windows and door waiting to see what would happen to Frank, whose willingness to stand up to the captain had greatly impressed his fellow prisoners. As one inmate later noted, "If a man's a man at the penitentiary he is considered a leader." As they watched Frank being escorted from the main prison building in the direction of the hospital and the infamous "leather room," he suddenly broke away from the guards and ran toward the factory. Galvanized by his flight, many of the inmates seized makeshift weapons—shovels and hammers, bricks and rocking-chair arms—and rushed outside, milling about in the yard in front of the building. Those remaining inside the factory set fire to a trash can, while the two guards on duty in the building hurriedly took shelter on the second floor, holding off the inmates at gunpoint.[22]

From the administrative building, supervisors and guards watched in dismay as the prison yard erupted in chaos. Colonel Sanders began frantically calling up reinforcements from the Columbia police and fire departments and the Richland County sheriff's department. A session of criminal court was being held in downtown Columbia; when the judge heard of the situation at the penitentiary, he adjourned for the day so police at the courthouse could rush to the scene. Bolstered by reinforcements, Captain Roberts led a large detachment of guards and police officers into the prison yard. As they approached the factory, the captain drew his pistol and began firing into the crowd of inmates, and the men under his command followed his lead. All the prisoners quickly fell to the ground attempting to dodge the bullets. When the gunfire ended, one inmate had been fatally shot and a dozen others—including Frank—had been wounded. After marching the vanquished men back to the main cellblock and locking them in their cells, the guards and policemen stood in the well of the cellblock, drinking soda and smoking cigarettes. From a cell on the third tier an inmate angrily cursed down at the assembled officers. One of the policemen pointed up at the man and called, "Come out here you son-of-a-bitch, I want you." Two guards rushed to open the man's cell and dragged him down the stairs. With the entire cellblock watching, the policeman stepped up to the inmate and struck him savagely on the head with a heavy walking stick. A second blow sent him sprawling unconscious onto the concrete floor, and he was carried off to the prison hospital, blood streaming down his face.[23]

In the following days, prisoners who had participated in the riot were taken to the death house and flogged. A policeman who witnessed one of the men being whipped later described what he had seen. "He kinder twisted up when they put the lash to him," the officer recalled. The riot had attracted a great deal of press attention, prompting state legislators to organize an investigative committee. Having their actions called into question both angered and worried prison administrators. The prison doctor told inmates that "he would kill the first dam son of a bitch that testified against him," while Captain Roberts declared he would "make it very warm for anyone that testified." Despite such threats, a few prisoners spoke to the committee—and were promptly punished for doing so. One of the men who testified was subsequently taken to the death house, "stripped by two negroes," and held down on the table to be whipped by Captain Roberts. The captain then shackled the man's feet and chained him by the neck to the wall, where he remained for over a week "without having any other food except bread and water."[24]

The role of African American inmates in punishing white convicts undoubtedly exacerbated friction between white and Black prisoners, but like much of what happened within the penitentiary's walls, interactions among the imprisoned left no trace in the written record. Broadus Miller may have been present in the penitentiary during the riot and its aftermath, or he may have been laboring on one of the prison work farms. The recorded history of his incarceration can be summarized in a single sentence: Prisoner #20749 entered the South Carolina State Penitentiary on May 31, 1921, and was discharged on February 10, 1924. Sentenced to three years, he was released three-and-a-half months early for good behavior, which suggests he had been a cooperative prisoner, perhaps holding down other inmates as they were beaten by prison guards.[25]

CHAPTER EIGHT

The Chains of the Skyway

When Broadus Miller emerged from the South Carolina State Penitentiary in 1924, he re-entered a world that had dramatically changed while he had been away. Released from a strictly regimented environment, inmates such as Miller faced a bewildering future. "We furnish them clothes and give them railway tickets home," the penitentiary superintendent had explained the previous year, "but I imagine it is an incentive for them to commit other crimes when they get to a place broke and without any money." In Miller's case, he no longer had a place to call home, for while he was in prison, Tom and Alpha Walker and the rest of his family had departed Greenwood County.[1]

During the Great Migration of the 1910s and 1920s, hundreds of thousands of African Americans left the Deep South. Their reasons for moving varied from family to family, but for the vast majority of Black South Carolinians between 1921 and 1924, the primary cause for leaving the state was the devastation wrought by the boll weevil. Only a quarter of an inch long but with a seemingly limitless appetite for cotton, the insect ate away at the fragile social fabric binding tenant families to a particular community. The weevil ultimately had a limited effect on overall cotton production in the South, for as it laid waste to one locale, the price of the cotton harvested elsewhere increased. But for South Carolina during the early 1920s, with an agricultural economy already mired in deep depression, the weevil's arrival proved catastrophic. In 1920 the state's farmers produced over 1.6 million bales of cotton; the following year's harvest was cut by more than one-half, an estimated $100 million loss to the state economy. In 1922, fewer than 500,000 bales were harvested, with the weevil consuming about 40 percent of the cotton planted that spring. At the end of the decade, the African American scholar Asa Gordon looked back on the insect's impact on Black South Carolinians. "The effect of the cotton boll weevil on the average colored farmer can hardly be measured in dollars and cents," Gordon concluded. "Coming as it did and when it did, the average farmer could not adjust quickly enough to ward off disaster."[2]

Upstate South Carolina bore the brunt of the weevil's voracious fury, leaving bitter memories that lingered for years to come. "I almost went broke," a white farmer from Spartanburg County later recollected. "The boll weevil. We didn't know how to fight it . . . and it was heart-breaking to see a good crop go down. Some of my neighbors just gave up and moved away. You could get farm land for almost nothing." Many farmers attempted to counter the weevil by investing in more fertilizer. As one Black farmhand grimly remarked, the heavily fertilized fields produced only "a crop of boll weevils." Reacting to the weevil's arrival, state agricultural agents preached the virtues of crop diversification and the growing of foodstuffs, but the region's farmers continued planting cotton. As an agent in Greenwood County noted, it was "the one crop grown in this part of the country on which credit can be obtained." An Edgefield County farmer later described how he had "staked his all on cotton in the spring of 1922." That summer, weevils swarmed over his fields, destroying the crop and forcing him to mortgage the farm. The next year he planted cotton once again. The results were even worse. "The more it rained, the more the grass grew, and the more the weevil came," he recalled. By Christmas he had gone bankrupt and lost the farm to creditors.[3]

The boll weevil struck especially hard in Broadus Miller's native Greenwood County. In 1920, the county's cotton fields had produced 253 pounds per acre; the following year, the average yield per acre dropped to only 103 pounds. Between 1920 and 1925, cotton acreage in the county was cut in half. Over the course of the decade, local farmland lost two-thirds of its value, and one-quarter of the county's farms were abandoned. The cotton profits that flowed into town elites' coffers dried up quickly. In February 1922, Greenwood's United Methodist Church announced that "church finances were in bad shape and they were without funds to meet current expenses." But the people hit hardest were those least able to sustain the blow. Decades later, elderly African Americans in Greenwood County still vividly remembered the arrival of the weevil. They had desperately labored for weeks in the fields, attempting to protect the crop by coating each cotton boll with a homemade insecticide of sulfur mixed in molasses. Their efforts proved futile. With no cash crop to use for purchasing supplies, many families faced near starvation. "It was so bad we didn't have no food or nothing then," one man recalled. "The only crop we made that year was some peas," reminisced a woman. "We ate pea bread, pea soup, peas boiled up."[4]

Throughout the spring and early summer of 1922, the county's farmers hoped the previous year's weevil infestation had been a one-time occurrence, but late that summer the weather turned cool and rainy, with the damp nights and cloudy days in which the weevil flourished. Already beset by insatiable insects, farmers around Shoals Junction suffered a further calamity in August when a fierce hailstorm pummeled the region and destroyed most of the crops, including a 100-acre cotton field belonging to Tom and Alpha Walkers' sometime landlord, Harrison "Lat" Rasor. In the aftermath of the storm, wanting to retain agricultural laborers for future growing seasons, Rasor and other local landowners pleaded with the county to issue a roadwork contract to provide employment for their tenants and farmhands. A resident of Ninety Six wrote to the local newspaper offering to assist Shoals Junction's afflicted farmers. He had no work for agricultural laborers, for his own cotton crop had been wiped out by the weevil, but he wanted "the pleasure of helping such men as Rasor" by donating ten bushels of corn so they could feed their hogs.[5]

The invasion of the boll weevil seemed a plague of biblical proportions, and South Carolina public officials reacted accordingly. Governor Thomas McLeod proclaimed a statewide day of prayer, declaring that God had sent the weevil "as a judgment on our people not only for their sins, but as a means of bringing them back to Him." The governor requested state residents beg God "for deliverance from the ravages of the boll weevil, in such way or ways as may seem wise to Him, either by direct supernatural intervention or through the workings of natural causes which are under His control." Prayers for supernatural intervention went unanswered, but tenant farmers and field hands moved in less mysterious ways. In the months following the dismal harvest of 1922, around 50,000 Black South Carolinians departed the state, causing a momentous demographic shift: for the first time since the early colonial era, African Americans would no longer comprise a majority of South Carolina's population. The mass exodus included more than 2,400 Black residents of Greenwood County—over 12 percent of the local African American population. Among those leaving the county were Tom and Alpha Walker.[6]

For most African Americans emigrating from South Carolina in the early 1920s, dire necessity prompted their departure. As sharecroppers or renters, they owned no land, and their tenancy depended on coming to a mutual agreement with a farm owner. If their landlord lost the farm to the bank or sold out and moved, then sharecroppers or renters no longer had a home, and even if the farm owner managed to hold on to the land, when the weevil laid waste to the cotton fields, then the tenant family's source of income— and means of compensating the landlord—completely vanished. The relationship of landlords to tenants ran the gamut from outright brutality to paternalistic solicitude, but underlying all such relationships was cold hard economics. Landowning farmers such as the Rasors and Agnews had multigenerational feudal ties to specific Black families, and in many cases they wished for their tenants to remain in the area, but they could not or would not provide long-term support for unemployed farm workers.[7]

The boll weevil accelerated a demographic transition that had begun years earlier with the establishment of the cotton mills. By 1907, Greenwood County's mills already consumed 25 percent more raw cotton than the county's farmers produced. In the following years, as more mills opened and the existing mills increased production, industrial demand would far exceed local supply, while the major railway routes running through the county allowed raw cotton to be shipped in with ease from elsewhere. Because African Americans were barred from working in the mills, the transition from an agricultural to an industrial economy displaced many Black laborers. At the beginning of the twentieth century, Walnut Grove township had fewer than 1,400 residents, the majority of whom were African Americans. Following the completion of the Ware Shoals textile mill in 1906, the township's population rapidly grew; by the end of the 1920s, over 4,800 people lived in the township—and fewer than one-quarter of them were Black. Within a single generation, as Black tenant farmers played a progressively smaller role in the local economy, the township increasingly became the domain of white mill workers.[8]

The journey of most departing African Americans followed rigidly ironbound channels to a limited set of potential destinations. The growth of the Piedmont cotton mills had helped spur the rapid expansion of rail networks connecting the mills to national markets; displaced farmers and field hands would ride these same rails when exiting the region. From the town of Greenwood, both the Southern Railway and the Piedmont & Northern ran northward through Shoals Junction to Spartanburg, a major railway hub. At Spartanburg, the railways split into two main migratory channels. One set of railway lines led up through Charlotte and the North Carolina Piedmont to the urban centers of the Northeast. Most migrants followed networks of family and friends, moving to towns and cities where familiar faces could help ease the burden of being in unfamiliar places. For many African Americans from Abbeville and Greenwood Counties, the journey up the eastern corridor ended in Pittsburgh and Philadelphia, home to Black communities with extensive ties to these two counties.[9]

A second set of railway lines veered northwest from Spartanburg to the base of Saluda Mountain, where the highlands abruptly rose and formed a natural border between the two Carolinas. In the 1870s convict chain gangs had labored up Pacolet Creek and into North Carolina, laying tracks for the steepest stretch of standard-gauge mainline railroad in the nation. Work had slowed on entering the mountains, but in 1886 a rail link was finally completed to Asheville, the urban center of western North Carolina. Local boosters promoted Asheville and the surrounding region as the "Land of the Sky," a residential and vacation paradise with a steady need for domestic workers to cook the meals, clean the rooms, and chauffeur the cars of a wealthy white clientele. In the early 1920s, a speculative real estate boom caused a frenzy of new construction, leading to great demand for strong-backed manual laborers. With Asheville booming at the same time as the weevil ate its way through South Carolina, the city became a magnet for displaced tenants and farmhands, and South Carolina natives soon accounted for over one-quarter of the city's 16,000 Black residents.[10]

By the fall of 1923, Tom and Alpha Walker had relocated to Asheville, which was about 100 miles north of Shoals Junction. After arriving in the city, Tom Walker began working as a construction laborer, while his wife took a job as a maid. Over the next few years, the Walkers periodically moved from one tenement house to another on South Beaumont Street, which ran through a downtown African American neighborhood on the south side of Pack Square. Clustered around South Beaumont, Eagle, Valley, and South Market Streets, the neighborhood had developed during the late nineteenth century and would eventually come to be known as "the Block." At its heart stood a multipurpose community center called the Young Men's Institute (YMI), which included a kindergarten, drugstore, and library. On the streets around the YMI were several Black-owned businesses, including barbershops, doctors' offices, restaurants, and funeral homes. In the early 1920s, as Black South Carolinians arrived in large numbers, hastily constructed tenement houses sprang up throughout the neighborhood.[11]

After his release from prison in February 1924, Broadus Miller traveled north and rejoined the Walkers in Asheville. At some point, either on his journey or soon after arriving in the city, he met a young Black woman named Mamie Wadlington. Like Miller, the eighteen-year-old Wadlington was a native of South Carolina, having grown up just north of Columbia in Fairfield County, where her parents still lived. On a warm, sunny Monday in early summer—June 30, 1924—Miller and Wadlington walked into the Buncombe County courthouse and visited the Register of Deeds office to obtain a marriage license. In an awkward scrawl, the groom-to-be signed his name as "Broads Miller" (see figure 8.1). The license listed him as the son of Robert and Alice Miller, both deceased—the only recorded mention of Miller's birth parents. Later that afternoon, a justice of the peace married the young couple,

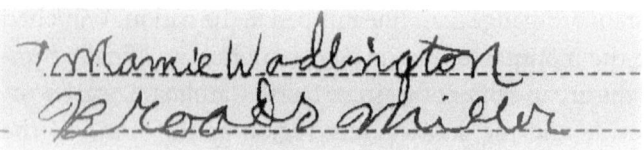

FIGURE 8.1 Signatures of Broadus Miller and his bride on their 1924 marriage license. (Buncombe County Register of Deeds, Asheville, NC. Photograph by author.)

who took up residence in a tenement house at 63 Valley Street, just a few hundred feet from the Walkers.[12]

The writer Thomas Wolfe had grown up on the opposite side of Pack Square from where Miller and his family settled. As a newspaper delivery boy, Wolfe had regularly made the rounds of South Beaumont and Valley Streets, and he would later use this experience as a source of artistic inspiration. The year before Tom and Alpha Walker's arrival, Wolfe wrote a play titled *Welcome to Our City* about downtown Asheville's Black neighborhood. The play's stage directions gave a white outsider's perspective on a place where "white-washed shacks and cheap one- and two-story buildings of brick" were interspersed with empty lots "littered with rubbish, bottles, horseshoes, wagon wheels, and junk of every description." A few years later, in his autobiographical novel *Look Homeward, Angel*, the writer again portrayed the African American neighborhood and its "celled hive" of tenement houses. In Wolfe's words, most residents of the neighborhood were "decent and laborious darkies." However, the ones who fascinated him were those whom he knew as "floaters," the "young men and women of precarious means, variable lives, who slid mysteriously from cell to cell, who peopled the night with their flitting stealth"—individuals like Broadus Miller.[13]

CHAPTER NINE
Law and Order in a White Supremacist State

Unlike Broadus Miller's native South Carolina, the Tar Heel State never had a majority Black population. But in the 1890s, beset by economic hardship, many white North Carolinians turned to the recently formed Populist Party and gained power by allying with the state's Republicans, most of whom were African Americans. During the election of 1898, the Democratic Party responded by launching a massive white supremacist campaign designed to shatter the fragile multiracial coalition of its political opponents. One of the architects of this campaign was Josephus Daniels, the owner of Raleigh's *News and Observer*, which poured forth an unrelenting barrage of rabidly racist editorials and cartoons. At the same time, armed white men organized into groups known as Red Shirts and paraded throughout the state, threatening African Americans and keeping them away from the polls. What could not be gained by threats would be taken by brute force. North Carolina's largest city, Wilmington, had a majority Black population and an integrated government. During election week that November, white mobs and a local militia seized power in Wilmington, killing scores of African Americans and causing hundreds more to flee the city. Two years later, an amendment to the state constitution set forth literacy and poll tax requirements for voting, and the disfranchisement achieved at gunpoint was sublimated into law.[1]

After African Americans had been politically disempowered, the leaders of the white supremacist campaign shifted their focus to strengthening the authority of the state government that they now controlled. In the years after inciting the violence of 1898, Daniels's *News and Observer* took a strong editorial stance against lynching. Charles Aycock had spearheaded the successful fight to disfranchise Blacks; after becoming governor in 1900, Aycock regularly used the National Guard to quell potential lynch mobs, setting a precedent that subsequent governors would follow. By the 1920s, North Carolina had attained a higher stage of white supremacy, one in which mobs had been superseded by state authority and formal law. In 1920, Cameron Morrison was elected governor. As a young man, Morrison had played a leading role in organizing the Red Shirts, but as governor, he did not hesitate to deploy the National Guard against potential mob violence, even in the face of opposition from local authorities. When Nash County officials criticized the National Guard's deployment to their county in 1923, Governor Morrison summarily dismissed their complaints. "I am determined to use every particle of power given to me by the Constitution of the State to prevent lynching while I am governor," Morrison asserted, "and I am going to do it by sending troops to any community as soon as I learn there is need for them to prevent violence."[2]

The governor served as the commander in chief of the National Guard, but a career military officer—an adjutant general—directed its daily operations. In 1920, John Van Bokkelen Metts was appointed adjutant general, an office he would hold for over three decades. While governors came and went, Adjutant General Metts remained in place, a powerful figure behind the throne. The son of a Confederate officer, Metts was a native of Wilmington. As a twenty-one-year-old sergeant in the Wilmington militia, he had participated in the bloody massacre of African Americans in November 1898. Two days after the massacre, he penned a letter describing the militia's actions. "We killed a 'few negroes,'" Metts reported, but "we have not killed enough negroes—two or three white men were wounded and we have not gotten enough to make up for it." After becoming adjutant general, Metts would work to suppress lynching and other forms of mob violence with the same zeal with which he had participated in such violence in 1898.[3]

A primary goal of the state government was to protect and promote the interests of the economic elite. During the early 1920s, African American laborers in North Carolina annually created an estimated $500 million in wealth, and the farm owners and businessmen who profited from their labor had a vested interest in ensuring their security. In the autumn of 1923, events in Mitchell County—a rural mountain county northeast of Asheville—demonstrated the threat that mob violence posed to business interests. Mitchell's resident population was overwhelmingly white, but a few companies had hired African Americans to come to the county and work in mining, road construction, and the installation of water and sewer lines. At the same time, a chain gang that included Black convicts from eastern North Carolina was also laboring in the county. After one of the convicts escaped and allegedly assaulted an elderly white woman, an angry mob turned on the recently arrived African American workers in the county—about 200 people—and marched them at gunpoint to the Spruce Pine train station, where they were forced onto boxcars and deported. Without these Black laborers, road construction came to a halt and a mining corporation had to suspend operations. Business leaders complained to Governor Morrison, who quickly sent Adjutant General Metts and two National Guard units to

Spruce Pine. Protected by armed troops, about fifty African Americans returned and resumed work on the roads and in the mines.[4]

The recorded number of lynchings in the South vary, depending on the criteria used to define "lynching." But on one point these various compilations all agree: during the first three decades of the twentieth century, North Carolina had the fewest lynchings of any Southern state. In 1924, William Richardson—Governor Morrison's former personal secretary—penned a laudatory article about the governor with the headline "No More Lynchings! How North Carolina Has Solved the Problem." In the previous year alone, Morrison had deployed the National Guard five times to prevent a potential lynching. "North Carolina has learned that threatened violence must be met by stern force," Richardson concluded. When mobs of private citizens confronted well-trained and heavily armed agents of the state, the state's superior strength proved invincible. In most cases, the simple display of overwhelming force was sufficient to cow any would-be lynch mob. Writing for the *American Mercury*, W. J. Cash acerbically noted that Governor Morrison's "really grand feat in arms was the putting down of lynching," with the awe-inspiring parade of military strength providing at least some compensation to spectators deprived of witnessing more explicit violence.[5]

In the early 1920s, at the same time that North Carolina officials were striving to eradicate mob violence, the newly formed incarnation of the Ku Klux Klan soared to national prominence. The new Klan's reactionary populism attracted a broad audience of white Protestants, ranging from devout churchgoers and mainstream businessmen to opportunistic grifters and thugs. The organization attained a national membership numbering in the millions, but its message and tactics varied from state to state. In North Carolina, whereas the Reconstruction-era Klan had waged a campaign of terror against the state government and politically active African Americans, the Klan of the 1920s had no reason to engage in such activities: at the turn of the twentieth century, avowed white supremacists had regained complete political control of the state government and most African Americans had been disfranchised. Though some Klan chapters occasionally flogged bootleggers and committed other acts of violence, leaders of the North Carolina Klan envisioned the organization as a means for civilians to support state-sanctioned law enforcement.[6]

One of the first manifestations of the new Klan in North Carolina appeared on December 30, 1920, when an organizational meeting was held in Durham and dozens of the city's "leading citizens" signed the charter. In the following weeks, Klan chapters began organizing in Raleigh and elsewhere. As

Josephus Daniels later recalled, the organization initially attracted some of Raleigh's "best people," for they believed "that a few masked parades would frighten the criminals and build respect for law and order." Among those joining the Raleigh Klan was Frederick Chaillé Handy—the head of the North Carolina office of the US Department of Justice. Handy's position within the Justice Department made him a valued asset for the Klan, and he was appointed to a national leadership role—Imperial Night Hawk, in charge of investigating the organization's enemies and raking up dirt to be used against them. However, in the summer of 1922, J. Edgar Hoover—the assistant director of the Bureau of Investigation, as the FBI was then known—became alarmed at Klan violence in Louisiana and began a major purge of federally employed Klan members. Less than a month later, Frederick Handy abruptly resigned from the US Department of Justice and was replaced by an agent from New York.[7]

The 1920s Klan was embraced by many prominent North Carolinians, including the Durham industrialist and civic leader Julian Carr. As head of the North Carolina division of the United Confederate Veterans (UCV), Carr traveled throughout the state to give dedication speeches at the unveiling of Confederate monuments, and in 1921 he was appointed the national commander in chief of the United Confederate Veterans of America. In April 1923, the UCV held its annual convention in New Orleans. On the last day of the convention, Carr addressed the assembled veterans and openly proclaimed himself to be a "Ku Kluxer." Though motivated in part by nostalgia for the Reconstruction-era organization, Carr's support of the reborn Klan was largely a reaction to contemporary issues. During the 1920s, US congressmen Leonidas Dyer and George Tinkham lobbied for federal anti-lynching legislation and voting rights for African Americans, while industrialists and labor unions waged an ideological battle over the workplace. In a speech given the same year as the reunion in New Orleans, Carr warned the rest of the nation to "muzzle your Dyers and your Tinkhams," and using the new Klan's favorite catchphrase, he declared that "real one hundred per cent Americanism" could count on "reinforcement from the South whenever revolution comes."[8]

The Klan reached its peak in North Carolina under the leadership of Henry Alexander Grady, who became Grand Dragon—the state-level Klan head—in September 1922. Grady came from a prominent Duplin County family; his father had been a US congressman in the 1890s. Three years before becoming Grand Dragon, Grady had been elected Grand Master of Masons in North Carolina, and within weeks of being chosen to lead the Klan, he was elected to the bench as a North Carolina Superior Court judge. His judicial position conferred an aura of respectability and legally sanctioned authority, thus making him a highly regarded figure in the Klan's national organization. In the spring of 1923, he was appointed to the fifteen-member Imperial Kloncilium, the Klan's national leadership council; his fellow council members included such luminaries as Gutzon Borglum, who would later sculpt Mount Rushmore.[9]

In January 1924, Judge Grady issued a lengthy public statement defending his role as Grand Dragon. The judge proudly noted that Klansmen took an oath to protect "the sacred constitutional rights and privileges of free public schools, free speech, free press, separation of church and state, liberty, white supremacy, just laws, and the pursuit of happiness." The inclusion of "white supremacy" in such a list might seem incongruous, but white supremacy was a basic tenet of North Carolina's established political and legal systems. In April 1924, Grady published an editorial in *The Searchlight*, the Klan's national newsletter. "White Supremacy was engrafted into the platform of the Democratic party in North Carolina in 1898," he declared. "If the Democratic party was right in 1898, the Ku Klux Klan is right now." By the 1920s, even the Democratic Party's white opponents had long since accepted African American disfranchisement as a fundamental principle of North Carolina politics. "The negro as a class does not desire to enter politics," Republican gubernatorial candidate Judge John Parker asserted in 1920, and "the Republican Party of North Carolina does not desire him to do so." That same year, the state's Republican Executive Committee sent out an open letter endorsing the idea of "a strictly white government" and promising that "the Republican Party's policy will be to let the Negro stay out of politics."[10]

Grand Dragon Judge Henry Grady wore two robes—the white robe of the Klan and the black robe of state-sanctioned judicial authority—and he viewed these two robes as complementary, not clashing. From local segregation ordinances to the state's anti-miscegenation statute, white supremacy was an integral part of North Carolina law, and Judge Grady believed in both white supremacy and the primacy of the law. The grandson of a large slaveholder, the judge saw himself as a paternalistic guardian of African Americans—if they remained in their designated place. If they transgressed the boundaries of that place, then they would be punished, but Grady insisted that such punishment be sanctioned and administered by the state. From the judge's perspective, the North Carolina Klan was an anti-lynching organization, dedicated to defending the rule of law in a white supremacist state. Addressing the Klan's annual statewide rally in 1926, Judge Grady boasted that

Law and Order in a White Supremacist State

"there had not been a lynching in North Carolina since the Klan was organized in the state." At the time of his speech, North Carolina officials, the national press, and independent observers such as the Tuskegee Institute all agreed with his assessment; according to Tuskegee's annual reports, there had not been a lynching in North Carolina since January 1921.[11]

WHEN BROADUS MILLER and his relatives arrived in Asheville, a local chapter of the Ku Klux Klan was already well established and very active in the city. The Asheville Klan had been organized in the summer of 1921 by thirty-four-year-old Lawrence Laban Froneberger. Born in Gaston County, Froneberger had previously worked as a pharmacist in Florida before becoming an avid crusader for the enforcement of narcotic laws. In 1915, the self-titled "Doctor" Froneberger showed up in Atlanta, where he passed himself off as a federal agent and participated in police raids on opium dens. After a stint as a traveling salesman for a Florida pharmaceutical company, he returned to his native North Carolina and began selling automobiles in Charlotte. When the new incarnation of the Klan emerged in the state, Froneberger—with his vigilante zeal and flair for salesmanship—joined and moved to Asheville to start marketing the organization.[12]

Froneberger's recruitment efforts gained momentum in September 1921, when a lecturer came from national headquarters in Atlanta and spoke at the Asheville City Auditorium, attracting an audience of some 800 people. In the following weeks, around 450 men joined the local Klan chapter, which found an enthusiastic supporter in Reverend Arthur T. Abernethy, a former college professor who would later be appointed North Carolina's first poet laureate. Reverend Abernethy's First Christian Church of Asheville became a hotbed of Klan activity, and when local Klansmen needed money for expenses, they turned to a member of Abernethy's congregation, the wealthy businessman Nathaniel Augustus "Gus" Reynolds. One of the city's most prominent residents, Reynolds had served as chairman of the Buncombe County Board of Commissioners and then established Reynolds Funeral Home. He had married his brother's widow—and thus became the stepfather of his own nephew, the future US senator Robert "Buncombe Bob" Reynolds. Headed by Froneberger, with Reverend Abernethy as a public spokesman and Gus Reynolds bankrolling its operations, the Klan launched a widely publicized campaign for "law and order" in the city.[13]

On November 1, 1921, Buncombe County sheriff deputies raided a house in Asheville's downtown African American neighborhood and arrested two white women whom they found "in company with negro men." Charged with violating the state's anti-miscegenation statute and released on $400 bond, the women immediately left town. Froneberger and a handful of Klansmen set out in pursuit. They seized the two women in Saluda and brought them back to Asheville, where they successfully demanded that officials increase the bond and levy harsh punishments. Bond was raised to $1,000 each; one of the women would be sentenced to thirty days on a chain gang, while the other served time in jail. The two Black men in whose company the women had been found had also been arrested. One of them received a two-year sentence on the chain gang. "Maybe when you serve that sentence and get off, you will stay in your place," the judge told him. The second man—Louis Sisney—was a veteran of the World War and had fought in France. After posting the initial bond, Sisney received death threats and fled the state, fearing "he would get a rope around his neck if he remained."[14]

Though Froneberger had been deputized as a special officer of the Asheville police department, he had no warrant to seize the women in Saluda and would be indicted on federal charges of kidnapping and conspiracy. Gus Reynolds provided bond for the Klan leader, and the charges were dropped after defense attorneys got the case transferred to Judge Thomas A. Shaw—who, as Froneberger approvingly noted in a letter to Klan headquarters in Atlanta, was a "fair one hundred percent American Judge." Reverend Abernethy applauded the Klan's relentless pursuit of anyone accused of miscegenation. "It might as well be understood once [and] for all that we men of Asheville who value the sanctity of our homes and the superiority of our Caucasian blood do not intend to permit such social and sexual equality," the minister declared. "If the law will assert itself to repress these crimes we will approve and sustain the law. If the law will not, then . . . there are enough red-blooded men among us in Asheville to see that the higher law of civilization and God is executed."[15]

Two weeks after illegally seizing the women in Saluda, Froneberger arranged for a search warrant to be sworn out against George Masa, a Japanese immigrant who operated a photography studio in downtown Asheville. An acclaimed landscape photographer whose work would later play an instrumental role in establishing Great Smoky Mountains National Park, Masa was accused by Froneberger of taking nude photographs of high school girls. The Klan leader accompanied several policemen on a nighttime raid of Masa's studio, where they arrested the photographer and confiscated his negatives. The local solicitor proclaimed that dozens of girls had posed nude for Masa—and was then forced to retract his claims when the photographs turned out to be formal portraits with the girls modestly clad. The girls

FIGURE 9.1 Asheville Klansmen participating in the city's annual Armistice Day parade, November 1924. (Buncombe County Special Collections, Pack Memorial Public Library, Asheville, NC.)

were students at Asheville High School, the city's leading secondary school, and the accusations against them outraged their parents. In the wake of the incident, the Asheville city council passed an ordinance against slandering public school students, punishable by a fifty dollar fine.[16]

In the spring of 1922, Lawrence Froneberger stepped down as leader of the local Klan. He had profited handsomely from his few months as a Klan recruiter, earning several thousand dollars for organizing chapters in Asheville and other western North Carolina towns, and he used this money to open a real estate office on Pack Square. Following Froneberger's departure, the Klan remained a potent force in the city, playing a prominent role in civic affairs and maintaining close ties to law enforcement (see figure 9.1). In 1923, the same year Tom and Alpha Walker arrived in Asheville, the city hosted the first annual meeting of the Klan's Grand Dragons, attended by Judge Henry Grady and other Klan leaders from across the United States. Among the speakers at the meeting was the Grand Dragon of South Carolina, who demanded that immigration be stringently regulated "to prevent America from becoming the melting pot or dumping ground of the world."[17]

The influx of Black South Carolinians to Asheville caused many white residents to fear the city was becoming a "dumping ground," and they had no desire for this "dumping ground" to turn into a "melting pot." In July 1924 — just three weeks after Broadus Miller's marriage in the Buncombe County courthouse — county commissioners ordered the racial segregation of water fountains on Pack Square. Considered a "progressive" measure and already well established in the large urban centers of the South, such formal segregation had been slow to come to "primitive" mountain regions. After the commissioners' action, signs were installed on Pack Square designating separate facilities for whites and Blacks, but these signs were inconspicuous and African American residents had long been accustomed to drinking from whichever fountain they wished. The *Asheville Times* reported that local "negro haters" delighted in guarding the fountains reserved for whites and harassing any unsuspecting Black who tried to drink. The newspaper deplored such actions, worrying that tourists might "carry erroneous impressions back home of this city's methods of enforcing race segregation."[18]

CHAPTER TEN

Asheville's "Sordid Saturnalia"

During the late summer and fall of 1925, the backlash against Black South Carolinians arriving in Asheville reached its peak with a series of rape accusations that shook the city to its core. Described by the press as "a sordid saturnalia of bestial ravishment," the alleged assaults began in August, when a white woman claimed she had been attacked on Sunset Mountain by a Black man. Police arrested some twenty-five suspects, but she did not identify any of them as her assailant. Five weeks later, on the morning of September 19, a second woman alleged she had been assaulted at the same location. Doctors and police who examined the woman found her story highly implausible; she seemed to be mentally unstable, but her vehement insistence that she had been attacked led to a manhunt that lasted several hours and resulted in numerous arrests. She described her assailant as a large, light-skinned African American in his thirties. Late that afternoon, police arrested Alvin Mansel—a diminutive and dark-complexioned boy, weighing less than 125 pounds and only seventeen years old (see figure 10.1). Nevertheless, when the police took him to the woman, she identified him as her assailant.[1]

Like Broadus Miller and hundreds of other African Americans, Alvin Mansel had moved to Asheville from upstate South Carolina. He had grown up in Pickens County, the son of a shoe repairman. His mother died when he was a child, and after completing a fifth-grade education he held various menial jobs such as picking cotton, cleaning the streets, and waiting tables at a roadside inn. Prominent white residents of Pickens would later testify that Mansel was "trustworthy" and had a "good character," and they had frequently employed him as a caretaker for their children. In the summer of 1925 he visited his sister in Asheville and ended up taking a job in the kitchen of the local tuberculosis sanatorium. Within weeks of starting work, and based solely on the alleged victim's dubious accusation, Mansel was charged with rape and taken to the Buncombe County jail, located directly behind the county courthouse.[2]

On the evening of Mansel's arrest, angry whites began gathering into a would-be lynch mob on the streets of downtown Asheville. Local Klan leaders warned Sheriff E. M. Mitchell about "the formation of the mob and offered their services if needed"; if the sheriff wished, Klansmen would assist

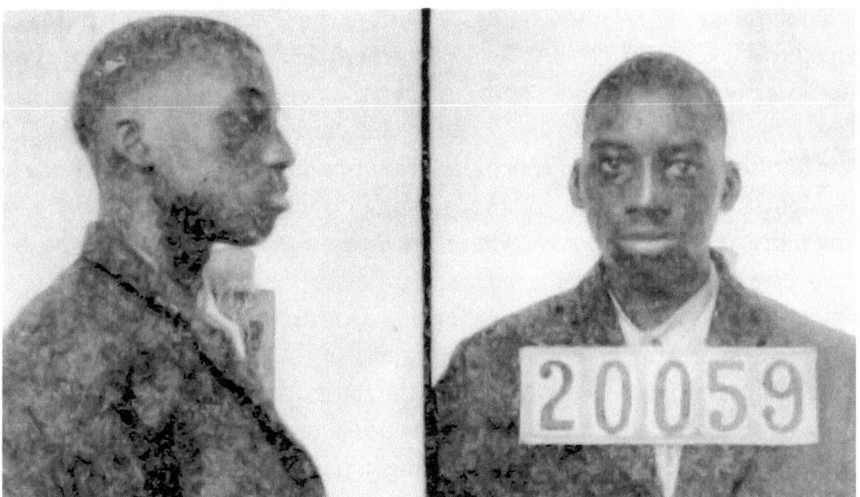

FIGURE 10.1 Alvin Mansel. In 1925, a false rape accusation against Mansel inflamed racial tensions in Asheville to the boiling point. (North Carolina State Board of Public Welfare, *Capital Punishment in North Carolina* [Raleigh: North Carolina State Board of Charities and Public Welfare, 1929], 96.)

him in guarding the Black prisoner and defending the state-sanctioned judicial system. Declining the Klan's offer to put "as large a force of men as he desired" at his disposal, the sheriff quietly rushed Mansel to Charlotte. Authorities then invited the mob to select a committee to tour the jail and verify that the prisoner was no longer there, but as the inspection was in progress, several hundred men stampeded the jail's entrance, broke down its iron gate, and stormed inside. After ransacking the entire building searching for the accused rapist, the mob finally dispersed.[3]

One month later, another alleged assault—this time, in West Asheville—led to a manhunt lasting several days. On October 26, police arrested an African American named Preston Neely after the purported victim "recognized him in a local store and followed him down the street until she could summon an officer to make the capture." Neely had arrived in Asheville the previous year from Lancaster, South Carolina, and was employed as a dishwasher in a café. Following his arrest, a large mob once again congregated outside the county jail, prompting Sheriff Mitchell to transfer the prisoner to Greensboro. That evening the entire city was on edge, and when pedestrians on a downtown street accused a Black man of "annoying a white woman," police detained him; the next morning a special police court ordered the man to be "sent to the chain gang for two years."[4]

Asheville's "Sordid Saturnalia" 87

In the wake of the latest assault accusation, the *Asheville Citizen* published an editorial addressed "To Asheville Negroes" that castigated the city's entire Black population for not doing enough to prevent these alleged attacks. Declaring that "its women are dearer to the white race than everything life has to offer," the editorial concluded with an ominous ultimatum to Black residents: "There must be no other assault on a white woman by a Negro—one more and peril will stare you in the face—a fearful peril. It will be no respecter of persons—the powers and influences which have restrained it will no longer avail." Leaders of Asheville's African American community responded by organizing a mass meeting at the Young Men's Institute on a Sunday afternoon; speakers at the meeting roundly condemned the *Asheville Citizen* for giving "encouragement to the possible shedding of blood should some irresponsible negro commit a crime in the future."[5]

Motivated in part by a sense of self-preservation, longtime Black residents of the city spoke to a reporter and drew a sharp distinction between themselves and the recently arrived immigrants from South Carolina:

> These newcomers, in large measure, are of the so-called "boll weevil" type. They were brought to Asheville by construction workers to aid in the gigantic developments that have called for hordes of robust day laborers. The creation of the white man's residential paradise, the miracle of forming new business districts . . . , the erection of factories and the placing of machinery in an industrial revival have required men of muscle. They have arrived in multitudes. . . .
>
> Many of these strange negroes have been picking cotton and hoeing corn in the flat lands with a month's earning absorbed by a month's appetite, with overseers ruthless and unscrupulous. Suddenly transplanted to a tolerent [sic] city like Asheville, they have shown a tendency to run riot and have exercised a bad influence on their fellows. With pockets bulging with money, they have made possible such dives and rendezvous as exert a wicked sway. The Asheville negro can not disclaim a certain racial responsibility for them but neither can he assume a personal guarantee of their good behavior, especially since he had nothing to do with bringing them here.

Though members of Asheville's established Black community may have felt some resentment toward the workers pouring in from South Carolina, the charges against Alvin Mansel and Preston Neely upset all African Americans, natives and newcomers alike. Based entirely on unsubstantiated allegations, two Black men had been charged with rape, a capital crime, which served as a stark reminder of how precarious the place of any African American was within the state's judicial system.[6]

The cases against Mansel and Neely would be energetically pursued, especially after the local press publicized off-the-cuff comments made by the prosecutor, Ed Swain. When chatting with a reporter, Swain blamed the alleged victims for wearing provocative clothing. "Women do not seem to realize that suggestive wearing apparel has a demoralizing effect upon ignorant negro men and boys," the prosecutor opined, and he then added that "negroes, lacking the culture and understanding of white men, cannot reconcile these things with modern fashion and their primitive feelings are liable to get away from them." After his criticism of the alleged victims appeared in print, the prosecutor quickly issued a statement trying to limit the political damage. "I wish to say that I am a Southern white man," Swain declared, "who holds the protection of our woman [sic] above anything on earth, and consideration of any shadow of excuse for outrages which make my blood boil is totally beyond my conception." A headline in the *Asheville Citizen* proclaimed, "Solicitor Will Wage Relentless Fight against Negroes," and Swain assured the public that the "prosecution in court of those charged with such abominations shall be driven aggressively and zealously with every energy I can command."[7]

As trial preparations began, Adjutant General Metts visited Asheville to assess the situation. Alarmed at conditions in the city, Metts ordered a detachment of thirty National Guard troops from Morganton—including Lieutenant Sam Ervin Jr., the future US senator—to come reinforce the local guard unit. On the morning of Monday, November 2, the Buncombe County sheriff brought Alvin Mansel and Preston Neely back to Asheville. Two carloads of National Guardsmen met the sheriff outside the city and escorted him and his prisoners to the downtown courthouse. The impending trials had attracted a huge crowd of spectators, and as the defendants were arraigned, troops stood guard "with their Springfield rifles at a business-like angle, attracting much attention and sending a chill over the throng." Following the arraignment, police took Mansel and Neely to the county jail, where over fifty National Guardsmen were billeted. The state's show of superior force deterred any would-be lynch mob; a journalist noted that "there has been not the slightest indication of mob action against the negroes."[8]

The next morning, Alvin Mansel's trial began. Mansel testified he had been at work during the time of the alleged rape, but the prosecution argued there had been a half-hour interval in which he could have left the sanatorium, walked over a mile to the scene of the purported crime, waylaid and raped the woman, and then returned and resumed work. On Thursday, November 5, a jury swiftly convicted the hapless Mansel and the judge sentenced him to death. It was then Preston Neely's turn. For two days the judicial proceedings played out the same way as they had before, and the verdict seemed a foregone conclusion. As a journalist covering the trials for the Associated Negro Press noted, when Black men were accused of assaulting white women, Southern courts seemed to issue convictions automatically, one after another. "They turn these things out like sausages," the journalist bitterly complained. In Neely's case, jurors deliberated nearly four hours — and then acquitted the defendant. The unexpected verdict stunned the courtroom audience. The prosecution and defense began offering a series of competing motions, a prearranged tactic designed to keep the audience in their seats while National Guardsmen with fixed bayonets rushed Neely out of the courthouse and to a waiting convoy of police cars. The convoy sped south to an undisclosed location in South Carolina, where Neely was released. Though acquitted of rape, he had been both literally and figuratively driven out of Asheville and back to his native state.[9]

As Alvin Mansel awaited execution, further details about his case began to emerge. His accuser's testimony had blatantly contradicted her previous statements to the police, and several white witnesses provided signed affidavits that Mansel had indeed been at work when the alleged assault occurred. This exculpatory evidence had not been presented to the jury; a defense attorney had been appointed to represent Mansel only a few hours before the trial began, and the court had rejected the attorney's request for more time to investigate the case and interview witnesses. After learning of these new revelations, many of the jurors who had convicted him changed their minds and expressed serious doubts about his guilt. Doctors who had examined the purported victim, bystanders who had heard her original account of the alleged rape, and even the assistant prosecutor in the case joined some 4,000 other residents of Buncombe County—including attorneys, judges, and religious leaders—in signing a petition urging executive clemency for the wrongly convicted Mansel.[10]

The petition went to the desk of Angus McLean, a former banker who had succeeded Cameron Morrison as governor. Derided by critics as being a mere figurehead for the state's "conservative plutocracy," McLean had been elected in 1924 with the support of the Klan, but the election was largely a formality: three years earlier, North Carolina's political bosses had publicly decreed he would be the next governor. On assuming office, he continued Morrison's policy of using the National Guard to suppress lynching and other forms of mob violence. As McLean explained in one of his speeches, "The Negro is a most valuable element in our population because he controls our labor supply," and the governor would not let the actions of illicit mobs drive away an important segment of the state's workforce. In July 1926, Governor McLean responded to the Buncombe County petitioners. Despite overwhelming evidence of Mansel's innocence, the governor declined to issue a pardon, but he commuted the sentence to life imprisonment. Alvin Mansel would end up spending five years in the state penitentiary before McLean's successor Max Gardner pardoned him for the alleged crime he did not commit.[11]

But though Governor McLean did not pardon Mansel, he also refused to pardon members of the mob that had invaded and ransacked the Buncombe County jail. In the aftermath of the attack on the jailhouse, fifteen men had been tried, convicted, and sentenced to various terms in prison or on the chain gang. More than 6,000 persons, including numerous law enforcement officials, petitioned the governor on their behalf. "No man can calculate the damage that may be done to the good name and fame of North Carolina by even one lynching," McLean responded, "and the only way to suppress lynching is to let those who engage in it understand that they will be punished and punished severely." The governor aimed to maintain public order, not to administer idealized notions of justice. Lynch mobs that challenged the supreme authority of the state's judicial system, and African Americans wrongfully convicted by that system, would both be punished by the state.[12]

THE RAPE ACCUSATIONS that rocked Asheville in 1925 were almost certainly complete fabrications. But though Alvin Mansel's innocence became increasingly clear, many white North Carolinians stubbornly persisted in believing that *someone* must be guilty of the purported crimes. Two years later, after Broadus Miller gained sudden notoriety, the press would speculate that perhaps he had attacked the women in Asheville. However, it is not clear if Miller was present in the city when the alleged assaults occurred. At the end of 1924, as the city directory was compiled for the coming year, Miller and his wife resided on Valley Street, only a few minutes' walk from the Buncombe County courthouse and jail, but when 1925 came to an end, the couple were no longer listed as living in the city. Precisely when Miller left Asheville is uncertain, but like many African Americans from the Deep South, he had apparently maintained ties with the region from whence he came, for at some point in 1925 or early 1926 he returned to his native Greenwood County.[13]

For much of Broadus Miller's life, the only evidence of his travels comes from the criminal record he left behind. On March 2, 1926, he was arraigned in the Greenwood County courthouse on charges of housebreaking and larceny. He had allegedly attempted to burglarize a local clothing store owned by a Russian-born Jewish immigrant named Louis Mark. According to a press account, Miller confessed to breaking into Mark's store, but he denied stealing anything. "They caught me before I got any goods," he reportedly told the prosecutor. It would be the only known recorded statement Broadus Miller ever made. Having already served time in the South Carolina penitentiary, and having likely spent some part of that sentence on a prison farm, he would now become intimately familiar with the third branch of the state's penal system. After pleading guilty to breaking and entering, he was sentenced to one year of hard labor on a county chain gang.[14]

By the 1920s, because of the ever-growing number of automobiles and the resulting need for expanded and improved public roads, chain gangs had become the primary form of incarceration throughout the South. In most Southern states, including South Carolina, counties operated their own chain gangs with near complete autonomy. A state inspector visited once a year, but local supervisors organized the gangs, and armed guards had day-to-day authority over the prisoners. Whenever a county needed more workers, then county officials showed greater zeal for catching and punishing lawbreakers. In 1927, the sociologists Jesse Steiner and Roy Brown published a groundbreaking study of the chain gang system. "Without doubt the motive underlying the establishment and the continuance of the county chain gang is primarily economic," Steiner and Brown concluded. "The average county official in charge of such prisoners thinks far more of exploiting their labor in the interest of good roads, than of any corrective or reformatory value in such methods of penal treatment."[15]

Greenwood County operated two chain gangs, each having a dozen or so prisoners whose sentences ranged from a couple of weeks to several years. Accompanied by a mule-driven wagon that carried their tools, tents, and supplies, the men toiled throughout the county, repairing wooden bridges and using pickaxes to widen and level the roads (see figure 10.2). Except for the "trusty"—a loosely supervised prisoner who performed mundane tasks such as fetching water—all the convicts were continuously shackled. Each man had his ankles cuffed together with a heavy iron chain a few feet in length. While he worked, the chain could be hitched to his belt so it would not drag on the ground; at other times, a much longer chain was threaded through each of the individual ones, joining all the men in a coffle. Though the gangs served as a source of cheap labor, they were the most expensive item in the county's budget. Greenwood County annually spent over $20,000 to pay

FIGURE 10.2 Chain gang at work in upstate South Carolina, 1917. Photograph taken at Camp Wadsworth, Spartanburg County. (National Archives Record Group RG:165, Training Camps and Schools—Camp Wadsworth, NARA165-WW-530B-011.)

the superintendent and guards, feed and clothe the prisoners, supply the tools for roadwork and lumber for bridge construction, and furnish the mules and wagons. One of the gangs consisted entirely of African Americans. Though known as "the white gang," the second group included both whites and Blacks, who slept in segregated tents and were "given separate work to do on the roads." For most of the year, the two chain gangs worked on opposite ends of the county, periodically moving and pitching camp at various places in the countryside, then wintering for a few weeks on a work farm outside the town of Greenwood.[16]

Conditions on the chain gangs were wretched. In 1919, a state inspector visited one of the Greenwood County camps and was appalled by what he saw: "The beds provided for the men are totally unfit for human beings. They are nothing more than poor straw ticks and old mattresses laid flat on the ground [and] full of grit and other dirt." Two years later, an inspector described the county's camps as dismally unsanitary. "The most outstanding fault of both camps is the failure to properly dispose of the sewage," he noted. For toilets, the prisoners used buckets that were then dumped on the open ground with the sewage left uncovered, which resulted in "the breeding of flies and the spreading of disease." The same week Broadus Miller was sentenced to the chain gang, the press reported on a Black convict in Greenville County who had been forced to labor barefoot through the previous winter, leading to severe frostbite and the amputation of both his feet. Chain gang guards had virtually no oversight and their treatment of prisoners was often brutal. In his 1924 book *Darker Phases of the South*, the sociologist Frank Tannenbaum cited reports from South Carolina that whenever a new convict arrived at a road camp, he would be summarily flogged in order "to impress him with due reverence for his superiors."[17]

For nine months, Broadus Miller labored on a Greenwood County chain gang. After his early release in December 1926 for good behavior, he once again headed to Asheville and resumed living with his wife in a tenement house on South Beaumont Street. The following spring, a stonemason named Dante Martin hired Miller as a manual laborer. A native of Italy, Martin had emigrated to the United States in 1913, then worked on various construction sites in West Virginia and Kentucky. The early 1920s real estate boom in Asheville brought Martin to the city, but as the frenzied wave of new construction subsided, he had to search further afield for building projects. In the spring of 1927, he contracted to build a house about sixty miles east of Asheville, so at the beginning of June, the Italian-born stonemason and his crew of African American workers embarked on a fateful journey to Morganton.[18]

CHAPTER ELEVEN

Morganton—Natives and Outsiders

On May 5, 1927, a front-page headline in the Morganton *News-Herald* announced "Mr. and Mrs. Frank Tate to Build Stone House." Franklin Pierce Tate was one of Morganton's most prominent residents. Bank director, president of an insurance agency, primary investor in several textile mills, appointee to various state committees—the middle-aged Tate held multiple positions of power. Five years earlier, the longtime bachelor had married a younger woman, Martha "Pattie" Thomason, a South Carolina native who had moved to Morganton to become principal of the North Carolina School for the Deaf. Following their marriage, Mrs. Tate resigned from the school and the couple settled in an exclusive neighborhood on West Union Street. After the birth of a son, the Tates wanted a grand house befitting their social status, so in the spring of 1927 they hired a New York architect to design an elegant colonial revival mansion, made of granite, that would stand on a lot directly across the street from where they were presently living. At the beginning of June the stonemason Dante Martin and his crew of construction workers—including Broadus Miller—arrived in town to build the Tates' new home.[1]

Frank Tate's father Samuel McDowell Tate had been a near-legendary figure in Burke County. A Confederate officer and forever thereafter referred to as Colonel Tate, he was one of the postwar leaders of North Carolina's Democratic Party. He served several terms in the state legislature, then became state treasurer, and because of his political influence, Morganton was chosen as the site for two large public institutions—the State Hospital for the Insane and the North Carolina School for the Deaf. The colonel's premier accomplishment was his role in creating the Western North Carolina Railroad. On the eve of the Civil War, contractors had used slave labor to begin building a railway from the Piedmont to the western end of the state. After the war ended and construction resumed, the railroad's board of directors appointed Colonel Tate to head the company. Political infighting and financial malfeasance led to Tate's removal, but in 1875, now a legislator in Raleigh, the colonel arranged for the state to acquire the railroad and reassumed personal control of the project.[2]

More than any other state, North Carolina in the late nineteenth century relied on convict labor for railroad construction, and convicts would take the place of slaves in completing the Western North Carolina Railroad. In March 1873, the state legislature approved the leasing of convicts to the railroad company, which paid the state forty cents a day per prisoner. Two years later, when the state acquired the company, Colonel Tate ensured the authorizing legislation mandated the use of convict labor. Over the course of nearly two decades, 3,600 prisoners—almost one-half of all men sentenced to the state penitentiary—were shipped in boxcars to western North Carolina to labor on the railroad. Nearly all these prisoners were African Americans. Housed in outdoor stockades and fed seven cents' worth of food daily, they did extremely hazardous work, and collapsing tunnels and other accidents claimed over 400 lives. When the railroad finally reached Asheville in 1880, Black men had left a trail of blood laying the tracks through the mountains.[3]

The convict laborers were forcibly transported to work on the railroad. Nominally free people faced a more subtle compulsion, but dire necessity drove indigent workers forward as implacably as a whip. On the eve of the Civil War, enslaved African Americans had comprised one-quarter of Burke County's population. During the half century following emancipation, the number of Blacks in the county remained roughly constant—around 2,500 people—but the lack of any natural increase indicated a steady stream of African American out-migration. In this same period, the white population more than doubled, and by 1920, Blacks comprised fewer than 12 percent of the county's inhabitants. Most local white workers were happy to see African Americans leave. In 1879, a Morganton editorialist declared that "only the large landed proprietor" was "at all troubled about" the exodus of Blacks, whose departure made "room here in this favored country for thousands of industrious white laborers." Even the landed proprietors agreed that some newcomers were more welcome than others. "Burke is a good and pleasant county for *white folk* to move to, but carpet-baggers and dead-beats 'need not apply,'" proclaimed Colonel Tate in 1884. However, unlike working-class whites, families such as the Tates profited from African Americans' labor. In the colonel's words, Burke County elites "would prefer to do 'head work' and let the negro do the digging."[4]

When Broadus Miller came to Morganton from Asheville, he almost certainly rolled in on the railroad with which Colonel Tate had connected the

FIGURE 11.1 Franklin Pierce Tate House, West Union Street, Morganton, NC. The construction of the Tate House brought the itinerant laborer Broadus Miller to Morganton. (Courtesy of the North Carolina State Historic Preservation Office.)

two towns. He arrived to dig the foundations and carry the heavy granite blocks for the house being built for Colonel Tate's son (see figure 11.1).

BY THE 1920S, Morganton's population had grown to some 6,000 people, many of them employed in local furniture factories and textile mills. Residents took pride in their handsome downtown, its newly paved streets lit by electric lights and lined by two- and three-story brick office buildings and stores. "Morganton is a pleasant town," noted one visitor. He was especially impressed by the nearly century-old Burke County courthouse standing at the town's center (see figure 11.2). "It is almost covered with ivy and has a look of having always been there. All about the building are magnificent shade trees, and a lovely lawn adds much to the charm of this Hall of Justice." At the northwest corner of the courthouse lawn stood a Confederate monument, its large granite base topped by a nine-foot-tall bronze statue of an armed soldier defiantly facing north. Dedicated in 1918, the monument served as the focal point for the town's annual observance of Confederate Memorial Day in early May.[5]

FIGURE 11.2 A 1928 photograph of the Burke County courthouse and Confederate monument, Morganton, NC. (History Museum of Burke County, Eugene Willard Collection, submitted to Picture Burke, a digital photograph collection of the Burke County Public Library, Morganton, NC.)

The World War had helped reignite a martial spirit in Morganton, and in November 1922, recruiters began organizing a local military company that would be incorporated into the North Carolina National Guard as Company B of the 105th Engineers. Men between the ages of eighteen and thirty-five signed up to hold drills once a week and attend fifteen-day summer encampments. Exempted "from county and town poll taxes and jury duty," these volunteers were furnished with uniforms and equipment and paid $1.25 for every training session. "The weekly drills of the boys in full uniform are attracting much local interest," the *News-Herald* noted in the spring of 1923. That October, Governor Morrison deployed the company to Mitchell County, where for ten days they protected African American laborers who had returned to the town of Spruce Pine after being driven out by a mob; two years later, a detachment from the company would be sent to Asheville to stand guard over the trials of Alvin Mansel and Preston Neely.[6]

National Guardsmen were not the only civilians volunteering to defend law and order. In May 1922, a local chapter of the Ku Klux Klan made its first public appearance, with robed and hooded men appearing at the burial service of a Morganton storekeeper and placing a wreath in the shape of a burning cross on their fellow Klansman's grave. Two weeks later, in one of his last engagements as a Klan leader, Lawrence Froneberger came from Asheville and lectured on the principles of "true Americanism" to an audience of nearly 400 people at the high school auditorium. The town's Baptist and Methodist churches provided a bedrock of support for the Klan. In the summer of 1922, Morganton's East Baptist Church sponsored a three-week tent revival in a vacant downtown lot by the evangelist Oney Williams Triplett, who attracted an audience of some 1,200 people every evening during the week and double that number on weekends. "He is a civic-minded preacher, siding always with law enforcement and good government," the *News-Herald* reported. On the Fourth of July, Reverend Triplett delivered a sermon titled "The U.S.A. and the K.K.K.," in which he "commended the Ku Klux Klan" for fighting against "some of the imminent perils" threatening "our government." The following week, two Klansmen in robes and hoods appeared at the revival and presented Triplett with thirty dollars and a note thanking him for having "so admirably expounded the doctrine of the true, Christian religion as it should be followed by all 100 per cent Americans." Two months later, when the evangelist George Eastes held a revival at the First Methodist Church, a pair of Klansmen once again showed up, giving Eastes fifty dollars and a note of appreciation. "We believe in one hundred per cent Americanism, the obedience of our laws and Christian living," the note explained.[7]

Other than their visits to revivals and appearances at graveside services, the Morganton Klan's activities received little coverage in the press. In November 1922, "reliable sources" reported to the *News-Herald* that Klansmen were planning to take "drastic measures" against Burke County bootleggers. Klan leaders quickly responded with a letter to the newspaper disavowing any such plans. "We investigate such cases that are brought to our notice and if our investigations justify we report to our local town and county officers, they being the proper persons to enforce the law," the writers claimed, and they went on to defend the Invisible Empire's "great principles," which included "white supremacy," "Protestant Christian religion," "prevention of mob violence and lynching," "upholding of the Constitution of the United States," and "100 per cent Americanism." The Klan had little reason *not* to work with local law enforcement officials, many of whom were themselves Klansmen. When fighting against miscegenation in Asheville or campaigning against bootleggers in Burke County, the Klan was demanding stringent enforcement of state-sanctioned laws, and the coercive authority of a lawman's badge went hand in hand with the power of a hood and sheet.[8]

The Klan of the 1920s captured the public imagination, but as the contemporary sociologist Guy B. Johnson observed, there was "nothing new" about its ideology. "It is part of the social heritage of a great many Americans," Johnson explained, "and therein lies the strength of the Klan, not in a mere organization of a million members, but in the kindred and sympathetic attitudes of many millions of Americans—the real Invisible Empire." In North Carolina, the Klan had many partners. The largest fraternal organization for native white male Protestants was the Junior Order of United American Mechanics. Formed in mid-nineteenth-century Philadelphia following violent clashes between Protestants and Irish Catholic immigrants, the Junior Order had begun expanding into the South in the early 1890s. North Carolina proved fertile recruiting ground for the Junior Order; by the 1920s, membership in the state numbered some 50,000 men, far more than anywhere else in the South. As the organization expanded, it outgrew its working-class roots and included many of North Carolina's leading businessmen and politicians. The Junior Order provided various social services for native white Protestants and proclaimed "the promotion of education" as one of its primary goals. However, this "promotion of education" consisted of nothing more than distributing Bibles and flags, with the organization handing out these twin symbols of Protestant patriotism at presentation ceremonies in public schools throughout the state. Its activities may have seemed benign, but the Junior Order shared the same constituency as the Klan, and during the 1920s the two organizations maintained close ties, had an often-overlapping membership, collaborated on a national newsletter, and sometimes conducted joint meetings.[9]

Unlike the new incarnation of the Klan, which had risen to prominence seemingly overnight, the Junior Order's roots in Morganton dated back to the 1890s. In the early twentieth century, the local newspaper editor T. G. Cobb served a term as the organization's state leader. After Cobb's death in 1916, his daughter Beatrice took over the Morganton *News-Herald* and became the town's leading spokesperson (see figure 11.3). In 1921, *Editor and Publisher*—the national trade journal of newspapers and periodicals—ran a feature article on Beatrice Cobb. "Miss Cobb comes pretty near running the town of Morganton," the article concluded. As publisher of the only newspaper in Burke County, she served as an "advisor and mentor" to county residents, and when she editorialized on an issue, voters were "sure to back up her judgment." The following year, twenty-five-year-old Sam Ervin Jr. ran

FIGURE 11.3 Beatrice Cobb (1888–1959), the influential editor of the Morganton *News-Herald*. (Photograph attributed to Greene Studio, submitted by Susan Fitz McAninch to Picture Burke, a digital photograph collection of the Burke County Public Library, Morganton, NC.)

for the state legislature. Cobb energetically promoted his candidacy, praising him as possessing "all the vigor and enthusiasm of young manhood." "Sam Ervin would be a credit to the county," she proclaimed. "Let's send him to Raleigh!" That November, Burke County's voters heeded the editor's impassioned plea and launched the young Ervin on his political career.[10]

In the words of the renowned Raleigh *News and Observer* columnist Nell Battle Lewis, Beatrice Cobb's editorship was "one of the unquestionable triumphs of feminism in Tarheelia." In a male-dominated profession, the Morganton editor stood out as a remarkable figure. For many years she was the only female member of the North Carolina Press Association; in 1922, she was elected secretary of the association, an office she would hold until her death three decades later. Though she served as a Democratic precinct chairwoman in Burke County and as a delegate to several Democratic National Conventions, she insisted the *News-Herald* was nonpartisan. However, the paper did more than simply report the news; it carefully cultivated an image of an idyllic town—one that would attract investors. In a 1923 editorial titled "It Pays to Boost," Cobb pointed to the example of Buncombe County, where property values had increased by 25 percent over a three-year period. "The tax books of Buncombe present a mighty strong argument in favor of boosting your community," she asserted. The following spring, Cobb issued a special "Prosperity and Publicity" edition of the *News-Herald*. Lavishly illustrated with state-of-the-art photography, it was praised and emulated by other newspapers throughout the state. "Miss Cobb believes in progress and practices it," enthused the *News and Observer*. A front-page headline in the special issue promoted one of Burke County's most marketable assets: "Pure Anglo-Saxon Blood."[11]

When writing about local African Americans, Cobb mixed patronizing affection with nostalgia for the starkly defined racial hierarchy of the past. After an elderly Black man died in 1922, the editor eulogized him as someone who "held the respect of both the white and colored people," for he had been "one of the few remaining old darkies of antebellum days." In 1923, the Southern Railway's newsletter included a brief tribute to Jones Erwin, a station hand at the Morganton train station; Cobb reprinted it in the *News-Herald* and declared that his "friends here, both white and colored, are delighted at the recognition thus given the faithfulness of 'Uncle Jones.'" The following year, Erwin's wife passed away. "Good Colored Woman Dies," announced a front-page headline in the *News-Herald*. The accompanying obituary described the woman's husband as "one of the best known darkies in the community." Cobb believed African Americans had a role to play in Morganton, but her conception of "Southern people" simply did not include Blacks. In a 1926 editorial, she claimed "the average Southern negro, who lives and works for Southern people," thought "that in almost every situation his best friends are the white people." Such "friendship" was what scholar John Dollard later termed a "feudal protectoral relationship": these "friends" had status in a white supremacist state and could provide protection and support. In 1927, the *News-Herald* told of a local Black man who had been arrested for gambling. "Whenever he comes in conflict with the law, negro-like, he thinks first of his 'whitefolks' and tries to figure who of them will have the softest heart and help him out," the paper reported.[12]

In her role as editor, Beatrice Cobb frequently served as a feudal protector of the town's African American residents, defending them when she believed they had been unfairly attacked. But though Cobb embraced many forms of social and economic progress, she held the same deeply conservative views on race as her fellow white townspeople. A staunch prohibitionist and member of the First Methodist Church, the politically active Morganton editor resembled Rebecca Latimer Felton, the Georgia suffragist and first woman to serve in the US Senate. Like Felton, she had a horrified fixation on the idea of Black men raping white women. At the turn of the century, Felton had demanded that African Americans accused of such crimes be lynched. Though not as outspoken as the fiery Georgian, Cobb reacted to alleged assaults on white women by Black men with a far greater fury than she displayed toward any other topic. In 1919, an African American named Tom Gwynn was charged with raping a sixteen-year-old white girl in neighboring Catawba County. After a mob attempted to storm the jail and lynch Gwynn, police rushed him to Morganton, where Burke County officers guarded him until he was transported to the state penitentiary to await trial. Beatrice Cobb gave a lurid account of Gwynn's alleged crime—"The black beast overtook his intended victim and caught her arms," she breathlessly reported—and though she editorially praised the officers who had helped prevent a lynching, she empathized with the mob. "It is but natural," she contended, "that red-blooded white men would want to see a brute have immediate punishment."[13]

In the spring of 1925, just two years before Broadus Miller arrived in Morganton, racial tensions in the town came to a head when a young Black man named Arthur Montague was accused of raping a white girl. Born about 1903—only a few months before Miller—Montague had grown up in Pierce County in southeast Georgia, where his family rented a home in the town of Blackshear. His mother had given birth to two sons as a teenager, then married an illiterate day laborer and had an additional two children, the youngest of whom was Arthur. Both of his parents had moved to Pierce County in the late 1800s, for the swampy pine woods of southeastern Georgia offered various job opportunities for Blacks. Women worked as laundresses and cooks, while men labored in sawmills, lumber camps, and the turpentine industry. In addition, a large factory in Blackshear employed African Americans to shovel and mix guano and other ingredients for the commercial fertilizers used on cotton farms throughout the South.[14]

In the 1910s Arthur Montague's parents died, leaving him and his siblings to fend for themselves. Cast adrift in an adult world, the young Montague lived a hand-to-mouth existence. When he was about twenty-one years old, he arrived in Morganton, perhaps as part of a large crew of African American laborers brought in from Savannah to help construct new buildings at the State Hospital. On January 31, 1925, Montague married a local girl named Louise Avery. His teenage bride belonged to Burke County's largest extended Black family, the descendants of slaves once held by the plantation owner Isaac T. Avery. She had grown up in a fatherless household, supported by a mother who worked as a laundress, and she lived with her mother and her mother's elderly aunt in a two-room rented cabin on Concord Street at the edge of downtown. An unpaved street of small homes fronted by grassless dirt yards, Concord ran parallel to West Union Street with its residential mansions, and many of the women on Concord were employed as domestic servants by West Union's white elites.[15]

In April 1925, Montague found work as a substitute cook at the North Carolina School for the Deaf, the large public institution Colonel Tate had secured for the town. The school's 200-acre campus sat atop a scenic hill on the outskirts of Morganton, with a view stretching across open fields to the South Mountains on the horizon. A largely self-sufficient community, the School for the Deaf was home to around 300 boarding students from across the state, ranging in age from six-year-olds to adults in their early twenties. With a curriculum emphasizing both academic and vocational training, the school had its own farm and dairy, and the resident staff included everyone from administrators and teachers to farmhands and laundry workers. Among the staff were a handful of African Americans, most of whom worked as cooks in the dining hall, and though Montague was married, he took up residence alone in the servant quarters on campus.[16]

On the evening of April 23, only a few days after he started working at the school, Montague accompanied two Black teenage boys to a party in the nearby countryside. His companions supplied him with alcohol that Montague would later claim had been spiked with some type of drug. Late that night, senselessly drunk, he staggered back to the School for the Deaf, where at three o'clock in the morning a supervisor discovered him wandering the first floor of a girls' residence hall. After ordering him to leave, she reported the incident to a security guard. A few minutes later, the supervisor heard a scream coming from the third floor. Rushing upstairs, she found a frightened young woman who had been woken by Montague coming into her room and approaching her bed. When the young woman turned on a light and began screaming, he had turned and fled. The nighttime disturbance created havoc on the normally tranquil campus. Police were quickly summoned and together with the school's staff, they began a campus-wide search for the intruder. At dawn they found him. After fleeing the residence hall, Montague had gone to a dormitory for younger students and entered a second-floor infirmary where three girls were sleeping. He had crawled into the bed of one of the girls—a fourteen-year-old student—and was passed out drunk beside her. Doctors examined the girl and declared she had been raped. To prevent a potential lynching, officials immediately rushed the accused rapist to the state prison in Raleigh.[17]

Three weeks later, Arthur Montague was brought back to Morganton to stand trial, with the local National Guard company deployed to provide security for the courthouse and jail. The trial would expose the uneasy relationship between the town's Black community and African Americans who arrived from elsewhere. Morganton's Black residents strove to distance themselves from Montague and his actions. "He just drifted in and didn't belong here," local African Americans told Beatrice Cobb. The two teenage boys who had accompanied Montague to the party and supplied him with alcohol were natives of the town. They testified against him, stating that after he became drunk, he had boasted about planning to assault some student. Montague argued the two witnesses were former boyfriends of his wife and thus motivated by jealousy. Describing the accused rapist on the witness stand, the *News-Herald* acknowledged "he was by no means lacking in wit and sense, answering the questions with more intelligence than might have been expected." But Montague's wit and sense could not save him, and after deliberating for seven minutes, the jury convicted him of rape and the judge sentenced him to death.[18]

The accusations against Arthur Montague infuriated Morganton's white residents. "To say that the entire community was shocked and mortified by the horror of the crime . . . is putting it mildly," Beatrice Cobb observed. In her words, "the helpless little deaf girl was outraged in an unspeakably terrible manner by a negro brute—a crime that would be calculated more than anything else to raise to fever heat the Anglo-Saxon blood of every decent-minded white man in the State." When a judicial appeal temporarily postponed Montague's execution, an irate Cobb hinted that a lynching would have been preferable to such delay. The apparent victim had been a boarding student from eastern North Carolina. "If she had been the daughter of a local citizen," fumed the editor, "the situation would have never been allowed to reach its present state." Cobb's desire for vengeance would ultimately be sated, for in January 1926, eight months after his conviction, Montague was at last strapped into the electric chair, his final words "frantic appeals to Jesus to 'save my soul.'"[19]

Two weeks after Montague's trial, an annual outdoor drama took place on the grounds of the School for the Deaf, attracting an audience of some 2,000 spectators. Composed by a local high school teacher and starring an amateur cast of many Morganton residents, *The Birthright* presented the story of Burke County's history in several acts. The drama opened with a prologue recounting how Native Americans had been driven out of the region and "Burke became the home of the white people." Subsequent acts included a portrayal of "the merry-making in the negro quarters during the slave period." After a mournful requiem for the Lost Cause, the drama reached its climax—a vivid rendition of Reconstruction, replete with mounted and costumed Klansmen who rode to the rescue "bearing the fiery cross." The actors were depicting the events of half a century earlier, but their appearance immediately evoked the newly reborn Invisible Empire. "The horsemen in their Ku Klux Klan robes brought a storm of applause," noted a visiting journalist, "and this was taken to indicate that there are numerous Klansmen in Burke county." Staged on the same school grounds where Montague's actions had taken place, and occurring only a fortnight after he was sentenced to death, the performance helped celebrate the restoration of the established order the Black outsider had so profoundly upset.[20]

CHAPTER TWELVE

The Convergence of the Twain

Despite Beatrice Cobb's highly inflammatory rhetoric, she consistently drew a distinction between Morganton's native African American residents and itinerant laborers who arrived in town from elsewhere. When indicting Arthur Montague for rape, a grand jury had issued a public statement to the *News-Herald* recommending "that the two State institutions located in Burke county, that is the State Hospital and the School for the Deaf, not employ in or around the buildings of said institutions any colored help." Though Cobb printed the jury's recommendation, she editorialized against it and defended "our negroes," who were "above the average." Local Blacks had been "almost as much aroused by Montague's crime as the white people," Cobb argued, and his actions "should not be laid at their doorsteps." The following week, the *News-Herald* published an editorial by schoolteacher Daisy Moore Avery, who wrote on behalf of Morganton's African American community to thank the editor "for so kindly defending us." Black residents had been "deeply humiliated" by the grand jury's proposal. "There are pitifully few jobs open to us here," Avery noted, and if the jury's recommendation were followed, then "several men and women who have given years of faithful service at the State institutions will have to leave home to find employment."[1]

In the early twentieth century, African Americans in Morganton had very limited job opportunities. The average Black woman could look forward to nothing more than a lifetime of cooking the meals, cleaning the houses, and caring for the children of the town's well-to-do white residents, but she had better prospects of finding work as a domestic servant than a Black man had of obtaining any type of steady job. As the sociologist Arthur Raper noted, "Her employment is regular, and her services are sought, while his work is casual and seasonal." In 1922, Morganton's First Baptist Church spent over $10,000 to build a parsonage; a local Black man was paid fifteen cents an hour to carry the bricks and mortar the white masons used. Burke Tannery employed African Americans for the malodorous task of skinning animal hides and tanning leather, but Blacks were barred from most industrial jobs. In North Carolina, state law never formally mandated the exclusion of African Americans from the textile mills, but the mills themselves adopted this policy because of their mostly female workforce. In 1906, the scholar Holland Thompson noted that "the working of negroes, particularly negro men, beside white women within walls would not be tolerated," so "the only negroes employed directly in the Southern textile industry are a few outside the mill proper."[2]

Among the various types of textile mills were those producing hosiery, which typically offered better pay and less hazardous conditions than other types of mill work, without the swirling clouds of cotton dust that turned mill hands into "lint heads." Decades later, looking back on the development of the hosiery industry in North Carolina, a business analyst concluded, "The year 1898 appears to have been a turning point." That year, Julian Carr formed Durham Hosiery Mill Company, which quickly grew into the largest hosiery manufacturer in the world. Over the next three decades, as hosiery mills sprang up throughout the Piedmont, North Carolina would become home to about one-fifth of all such mills in the nation. In the early years, Carr and other owners experimented with using African American labor, but they abandoned this idea in the face of adamant opposition from working-class whites.[3]

By the beginning of the 1920s, Burke County had nine hosiery mills. Three of these mills were owned by an Italian immigrant named Francis Garrou. He and other members of a Protestant sect called the Waldensians had moved to Burke County in the early 1890s and formed the community of Valdese, about eight miles east of Morganton. At the beginning of the twentieth century, Garrou partnered with investors and opened a mill in Valdese, and in the following years, as he accumulated considerable wealth, he expanded operations. On East Union Street in downtown Morganton stood an abandoned furniture factory. In 1917, Garrou took over the abandoned factory, refurbished the building and installed new machinery, and converted the furniture factory into a hosiery mill (see figure 12.1). With $150,000 in capital investment, Garrou Knitting Mill became the most valuable hosiery mill in Burke County. One of its primary investors, Franklin Pierce Tate, sat on the board of directors and served as the mill's vice president.[4]

At the beginning of June 1927, around the same time Broadus Miller arrived in Morganton to work as a construction laborer on Frank Tate's new house, fifteen-year-old Gladys Kincaid began toiling in Garrou Knitting Mill. She belonged to a family that had lived in Burke and adjacent counties for several generations. The Kincaids had settled in the western Piedmont during the 1760s and over the next century and a half had multiplied exponentially. Some branches of the family had prospered, owning land and slaves

FIGURE 12.1 A 1920 photograph of Garrou Knitting Mill and some of its workers. (Morganton *News-Herald*, May 13, 1920.)

and accumulating wealth that they passed down to their descendants, but others had become dirt poor. Gladys Kincaid was the child of landless tenant farmers. She had grown up in the community of Chesterfield, about five miles north of Morganton, and like many mill workers, she had been forced to leave a rural farm because of family tragedy. Her father James Kincaid died of influenza in January 1923 at the age of forty-seven, leaving a widowed wife and eight children.[5]

After her husband's death, Mary Jane Kincaid found it increasingly difficult to make ends meet on her own, so she and her children eventually moved in with her brother, a sharecropper who lived in a two-story farmhouse by the Catawba River, about a mile and a half from downtown Morganton. In the spring of 1927, because of the family's poverty, Gladys Kincaid had to quit school and find employment. Some of her friends and former schoolmates worked at Garrou Knitting Mill and they helped her obtain a job there. A week after her fifteenth birthday, she began working ten-hour days from Monday through Friday and half a day on Saturday. New employees started at $5.50 a week, but after finishing training and beginning work on a production basis, they could look forward to receiving a weekly paycheck of around eight dollars. With this hard-earned money, Gladys Kincaid would help support her widowed mother and younger siblings.[6]

On her daily walk along Bouchelle Street to and from the mill, Kincaid regularly passed Will Berry's house where Broadus Miller boarded. In the late afternoons Miller and the other lodgers would sit and socialize on the front porch facing the street along which Kincaid walked. After the girl's death, witnesses stated that her accused killer had "watched her for several days" as she walked down the street and had sometimes "followed her for a short distance down the road." According to a salacious account in the *Charlotte Observer*, "Miller had for several days followed the girl's movements . . . with bestial lust in his eyes. On two occasions at least he had skulked behind her as she, a wistful looking girl of appealing beauty, had wandered her way home." No one witnessed the fatal encounter between Kincaid and her assailant, but Beatrice Cobb portrayed a "blood-curdling" scene in which "a pretty, innocent young girl, just blossoming into her teens," had become "the victim of a savage-minded, unspeakably brutal black beast." The *Hickory Daily Record* described the murdered girl as the "attractive little victim of a mad negro's lust," but doctors who performed an autopsy concluded she had not been raped. In the words of the *News-Herald*, Kincaid had been attacked by a "would-be rapist" who "fatally wounded the girl before he was able to accomplish his fiendish purpose." The Winston-Salem *Twin City Sentinel* suggested it was fortunate the blow had been "harder than her assailant intended," for "this very violence saved her from the ravages of the brute."[7]

The scene of the fatal assault quickly became a sort of shrine, attracting carloads of "spectators and curiosity seekers" from across the state. During her lifetime the young mill worker had not been well known in Morganton, but after she died, newspapers clamored to obtain her photograph and press accounts emphasized her physical beauty. In the words of one reporter, her "timid charm and happy disposition had made her a popular favorite of all who knew her." Supervisors at the knitting mill described her as "a slender, timid brunette of unusual popularity with her fellow employees," while neighbors spoke of "a girl of good character, quiet and unassuming in demeanor." Years later, one of her former teachers could still recall the girl's "dark blue eyes peering at me in the classroom from out of a wan white face." The teacher remembered her clearly: "A fair student, Gladys was quiet, but courteous, kind and friendly. She seemed to be something of a dreamer, gazing often with unseeing eyes beyond persons and objects within her immediate presence." One of her childhood friends later reminisced about Kincaid, who had been "the quiet type" and "lady-like" but loved playing baseball with her schoolmates. "She was a beautiful girl," her friend recalled. "Her mother made all her clothes, and she always looked so pretty" (see figure 12.2).[8]

On the Wednesday afternoon following her death, Gladys Kincaid's body was prepared for burial. The deeply rutted dirt road leading to her family's farm had turned to mud from the previous night's downpour, so Kincaid lay in state at the home of a cousin in Morganton. Throughout the day a steady

FIGURE 12.2 The only known photograph of Gladys Kincaid, this family portrait from c. 1919 shows the young Kincaid (standing at center) with her parents and siblings. (Photograph provided by Armantia.)

stream of visitors came to pay their respects. On Wednesday night, Mae Fleming—who was a cousin, former schoolmate, and coworker of the dead girl—stayed to help care for Kincaid's mother, who had been briefly hospitalized for shock and then released. Fleming spent the night sleeping in the same room with Mary Jane Kincaid. They were woken the next morning by the sound of the hosiery mill whistle announcing the start of another work day. Seventy years later, Fleming still vividly remembered the bereaved mother's reaction: "And we were laying there in the bed, and when that whistle went off, she said, 'Oh Lord, I'm thinking about Gladys, it's time for her to go to work.' And she cried, she cried. She was so pitiful."[9]

On the morning of Thursday, June 23, exactly one month after her fifteenth birthday, Kincaid's funeral took place at Catawba Valley Baptist Church. The wooden church stood on a high bluff about two miles upriver from the Kincaids' farm, halfway between Morganton and Chesterfield. Her family had attended Catawba Valley when they lived in Chesterfield, and the young girl had continued going there after they moved. About two years earlier, she had been entered on the church roll as an official member, a momentous event in the lives of rural Southerners. Her family had never owned their own home, moving from one tenant farm to another, but the church provided continuity in a changing world. The funeral drew a large crowd, including several of Kincaid's former schoolmates and teachers and many of her colleagues from the mill. Reverend Rufus Bradshaw of Morganton's First Baptist Church was known as an eloquent speaker and had been asked to deliver the eulogy. With a "voice choking with emotion," the minister "spoke the few words of condolence to the bereaved ones, while a crowd that overflowed the church fought hard to control its feelings and keep back the tears from its eyes." Following the service, a soft rain fell from a darkened sky as Kincaid was lowered into the ground in the adjacent church cemetery. In the words of a reporter, it seemed "as if the pathos of Burke's greatest tragedy had stirred the depths of nature's own heart."[10]

Because of her family's poverty, donations paid for Gladys Kincaid's funeral and for the marble tombstone subsequently placed atop her grave. "She was the flower of our home," read an inscription on the stone, which was crowned with the sculpted form of a young lamb—a common design for children's graves in the 1920s, but in Kincaid's case, the stone served as a visual representation of her portrayal in the press. She had been an innocent lamb; her accused killer would be demonized and hunted down as a beast.[11]

CHAPTER THIRTEEN

Outlawed

On Wednesday, June 22—the morning after Gladys Kincaid was fatally attacked—Sheriff Jules Hallyburton swore out an affidavit stating that Broadus Miller was wanted "for the crime and felony of murder and rape," but that he had fled and evaded "the usual process of law." According to all contemporary press accounts, Kincaid had not been raped. But she had been killed, and the fate of her accused murderer would be decided by proclamation. The sheriff's affidavit initiated the process by which Burke County authorities could utilize a provision of North Carolina's legal code and proclaim Miller an outlaw. Immediately after the sheriff signed the affidavit, two justices of the peace—George Battle and William Hallyburton, a cousin of the sheriff—issued a joint proclamation: "It is . . . ordered that any citizen of the County of Burke may arrest, capture and bring said Broadus Miller to Justice, and in case of flight or resistance by the said Broadus Miller, after being called on and warned to surrender, may slay him without accusation or impeachment for crime."[1]

When outlawing the fugitive, county officials scrupulously followed the steps set forth by state law; they were undoubtedly advised in this process by Sam Ervin Jr., who had been appointed county attorney the previous December. The sheriff's affidavit and the justices' proclamation closely copied the wording of the state's outlawry statute, with one notable exception: the law permitted all North Carolina citizens, regardless of their county of residence, to act on a proclamation. In the coming days, Governor Angus McLean would frequently and wrongly be credited with designating Miller an outlaw. The statute did not grant the governor this power; the only persons authorized to issue outlawry proclamations were "any two justices of the peace, or any judge of the supreme, superior, or criminal courts." The governor merely voiced his approval of an action that had been taken at the local level.[2]

Following the proclamation, Burke County commissioners approved a $250 reward for Miller, dead or alive, which the state of North Carolina promptly matched with an additional $250 reward. In addition, a much larger private reward fund was organized by Morganton resident Sam Taylor, who distributed a sign-up sheet among local businesses and private individuals. At the top of the sheet was a simple statement: "We the undersigned promise to pay the sum opposite our names for the brute who murdered Gladys Kincaid, and as the Governor [sic] has outlawed him we agree to pay the party or parties for his person dead or alive." Over the course of one week, some 800 signatories would pledge a total of nearly $1,500; among the main contributors were three local furniture factories. Because of the proclamation and the offered rewards, every North Carolina citizen had both a legal right and a financial incentive to kill Broadus Miller.[3]

BEING DECLARED AN OUTLAW meant that an individual was "outside the law"—that is, had been stripped of the legal protections enjoyed by members of a civil society. The practice of outlawing individuals had distant origins in English common law. In the eighteenth century, colonial officials in North Carolina had sometimes enacted legislation to outlaw "evil Disposed Persons in the Frontier Parts" and individuals who engaged in "riotous assemblies." However, the provision of state law used to outlaw Miller was not modeled on these occasional legislative acts. Instead, in both its wording and the procedures it set forth, the state's 1866 outlawry statute had been closely copied from a previous North Carolina law concerning fugitive slaves.[4]

Implemented in 1715, North Carolina's first slave code authorized private citizens to "kill any Runaway Slave" who had been a fugitive for more than two months, stipulating that the killer would not be held legally accountable "if he give Oath that he could not apprehend such slave but was constrained to kill him." In 1741 the General Assembly expanded this legislation into a comprehensive legal code, with one section detailing the process to be used against runaway slaves who "lie out hid and lurking in the Swamps, Woods and other Obscure Places." When two justices of the peace were jointly notified that a runaway was "killing cattle and hogs" or committing any other unspecified "injuries," the justices were required to issue an outlawry proclamation that would be posted at the door of the local courthouse. Such proclamations stated that if the fugitive did not "immediately return home," then it was "lawful for any Person or Persons whatsoever to kill and destroy such Slave or Slaves, by such ways and means as he shall think fit, without Accusation or Impeachment of any Crime."[5]

After the American Revolution, the slave code of colonial North Carolina—including the guidelines for outlawing runaway slaves—remained in effect and continued to be used. In 1821, New Hanover County slaveholder Robert Brown advertised a reward for an outlawed runaway's capture "or for his HEAD." Northern newspapers widely reprinted Brown's reward notice as evidence of the evils of slavery. The abolitionist Harriet Beecher Stowe was horrified by the outlawry provision of the North Carolina slave code and the "awful possibilities" implicit in allowing anyone to kill a fugitive "by such ways and means as he shall think fit." In 1841, the British and Foreign Anti-Slavery Society published a report detailing the ways and means used against runaway slaves in North Carolina: "A slave who runs away, lurks in swamps, &c., and kills a hog or any other domestic animal to keep himself from starving, is subject to a proclamation of outlawry, and then whoever finds him may shoot him, tear him in pieces with dogs, burn him to death over a slow fire, or kill him by any other tortures."[6]

As the abolitionist William Ingersoll Bowditch noted, nearly all slaves were illiterate and could not read any outlawry proclamation issued against them. "This is truly a Christian law!" Bowditch bitterly declared. "A written proclamation to men, not one in ten thousand can read a letter of it!" But though outlawry proclamations were ostensibly addressed to fugitive slaves, ordering them to return to their masters, the true audience for such decrees was bounty hunters. A proclamation of outlawry legally authorized the killing of a runaway, and such proclamations could always be obtained by any slave owner who wished a runaway dead. In November 1836, William Cobb of Jones County secured a proclamation against two fugitive male slaves; he then offered a $200 reward for the men "or for the killing of them, so that I can see them." Throughout the late 1840s and the 1850s, outlawry proclamations regularly appeared in the newspapers of Wilmington, a busy seaport and the largest city in the state. In August 1849, a Wilmington resident named Miles Costin—a wealthy merchant, real estate speculator, and sometime slave trader—obtained a proclamation against a runaway. Published in the *Wilmington Journal*, the proclamation was accompanied by a reward notice from Costin offering fifty dollars for the man's capture—"or One Hundred Dollars for his head."[7]

The Civil War rendered the entire North Carolina slave code—including the outlawry provision—null and void. In the war's aftermath, state legislatures throughout the South rushed to implement legislation known as Black Codes that restricted the movement and labor of newly freed African Americans. In January 1866, North Carolina legislators convened for a two-month special session and spent much of that time drafting a Black Code. Produced in the same legislative session that created the state's Black Code, the outlawry statute took most of its wording directly from the slave code's provision for outlawing fugitive slaves. However, the new statute could be used against any individual, regardless of race, who had been charged with any type of felony. As before, two justices of the peace (also known as magistrates) could jointly issue a proclamation, but the statute authorized any superior or supreme court judge to do so as well. Most importantly, whereas outlawed slaves could be killed without any restrictions, the new law specified that fugitives must first be "called on and warned to surrender." Outlawed fugitives could be killed even if they were unarmed, but only "in cases of flight or resistance."[8]

During Reconstruction, Henry Berry Lowry and the so-called Lowry Gang of Robeson County became the most famous outlaws in North Carolina. The Lowries belonged to a people who would come to be known as the Lumbee. The mixed-race descendants of Native Americans, African Americans, and whites, the Lumbee had been designated in antebellum records as "free persons of color," and during the Civil War, they were persecuted by the Confederate Home Guard and forcibly impressed into service as manual laborers. In the closing months of the war, Lowry and his companions waged a bloody tit for tat against state and county authorities, a fight that continued long after the war officially ended. African Americans and Lumbee—who together comprised nearly one-half of Robeson County's population—viewed the Lowries as heroes. However, in the eyes of most local white residents, the "Lowry Gang" were nothing but bandits, which led to outlawry proclamations being issued against them.[9]

In February 1872, the state legislature authorized unprecedented rewards of $10,000 for Henry Berry Lowry and $5,000 apiece for five of his companions, including Andrew Strong and Lowry's brothers Stephen and Tom. Henry Berry Lowry disappeared around the time of the large reward offer, reportedly dying from an accidental gunshot wound. In July 1872, bounty hunters hid next to a road and ambushed the unsuspecting Tom Lowry, waiting until he was only a few feet away to unleash a volley of gunfire. After loading his body in a wagon, the killers drove to the county seat of Lumberton, where curious spectators swarmed to get a glimpse of the corpse, and there they posed for a studio photograph with their prey, kneeling with rifles in hand and Lowry's body sprawled on the ground in front of them. On Christmas Day 1872, as Andrew Strong stood on the porch of a country store, a clerk eager to claim the reward quietly walked up behind Strong and shot him in the back of the head. The following year, bounty hunters shot and killed Stephen Lowry as he sat playing a banjo, then transported his body back to town. "Lumberton is in a high state of excitement caused by the bringing in of the dead body of this notorious outlaw," a journalist reported. "The streets are crowded with anxious citizens, who are feverish to learn the particulars of his death and to gaze upon the visage of one so famous."[10]

Though the outlawry statute explicitly stated that individuals had to be "called upon and warned to surrender" and could be killed only "in cases of flight or resistance," Tom Lowry, Andrew Strong, and Stephen Lowry were all gunned down in cold blood—and the state then rewarded their killers for what they had done. As the sociologist Max Weber later noted, "The state is considered the sole source of the 'right' to use violence." Ultimately, however, state-sanctioned violence was not constrained by strict adherence to the constructs of written law.[11]

FOLLOWING RECONSTRUCTION, North Carolina officials regularly used the outlawry statute as a law enforcement tool against fugitives charged with various felonies, ranging from murder to burglary. During the late nineteenth century, African Americans comprised approximately 70 percent of outlawed fugitives in the state. Press coverage of these Black outlaws frequently depicted them as hunted animals. In 1878, magistrates in Wilmington outlawed an escaped Black convict named Tom Johnston and county officials offered a reward for him dead or alive. "When the darkeys go out bird-hunting now, they keep one barrel of their guns loaded with buck-shot, and only shoot out the other," the *Wilmington Sun* claimed. "They all want to be prepared for Johnston. His hide will command a premium in the market at any time." In the fall of 1892, an alleged wave of burglaries in Durham led to the outlawing of a young Black man named Henry Rogers. "Load your gun for bear, and go after him," the *Durham Daily Globe* urged its readers, advocating that Rogers be killed so "the law may be saved trouble and expense." After the 1895 killing of an African American storekeeper in Wilmington, the culprit Magnus Slade was outlawed and pursued into a nearby swamp, leading the *Wilmington Morning Star* to facetiously suggest that the posse erect "a barbed-wire fence . . . around the swamp" and "set bear traps for the outlaw." In 1896, Wake County magistrates outlawed Jim Booker, an African American who had killed his estranged girlfriend. "No Crime to Kill Him," the Raleigh *News and Observer* announced about Booker. "Any man may shoot him like a dog and the law will hold it no murder."[12]

In the early twentieth century, a Black man named Will Harris gained fame as an outlaw. After escaping from a Mecklenburg County chain gang in 1901, Harris reportedly committed a series of barn burnings, burglaries, and assaults. Arrested and sentenced to the state penitentiary, he escaped and returned to Mecklenburg. In August 1903, two justices of the peace outlawed Harris, but though he would be blamed for various crimes over the next few months, he remained elusive. In 1906, a stranger arrived in

Asheville claiming to be the notorious Will Harris. On the evening of November 13, the man got drunk in a home on Valley Street, the same street where Broadus Miller would reside less than two decades later. He emerged from the house with a high-powered rifle and walked up the street, firing with cool deliberation and uncanny accuracy. In his wake he left five men dead—two white police officers and three local Black residents. The following morning a superior court judge issued an outlawry proclamation against "a certain person, a colored man, calling himself, and supposed to be, Will Harris." County and state authorities quickly posted rewards for the fugitive. Hundreds of armed men with bloodhounds pursued him for the next day and a half, and when they finally overtook him about a dozen miles south of the city, he exchanged gunfire with them and was cut down in a hail of bullets. His body was then brought back to Asheville and publicly displayed in a South Main Street undertaker's parlor, where it was viewed by an estimated 2,000 people.[13]

The writer Thomas Wolfe was six years old when the purported Will Harris went on his shooting rampage. Years later, Wolfe would give a fictionalized retelling of the incident in his short story "The Child by Tiger." Valley Street was only a few hundred yards from Wolfe's home, and he likely drew from childhood memory when describing the sound of the bloodhounds as they were taken to the crime scene and set on the killer's trail. "The baying of the hounds," wrote Wolfe, was "one of the most savagely mournful and terrifying sounds that night can know." The writer seemed haunted by the subsequent public display of the outlaw's corpse, marveling at how his fellow townspeople had taken "that ghastly mutilated thing and hung it in the window of the undertaker's place, for every woman, man, and child in town to see." Yet Wolfe well understood the morbid attraction of such spectacles. "I think it has always been the same with people," the narrator of his story concluded. "They protest. They shudder. And they say they will not go. But in the end they always have their look."[14]

A decade after the events in Asheville, the outlawing of a fugitive in eastern North Carolina concluded in a similar fashion. In 1916, an African American named Dave Evans was serving time on a Pitt County chain gang. When a guard threatened to flog him, he responded that "he would never be whipped again" and killed the guard with a pickaxe. He and a few other convicts then fled, stopping at a nearby farmhouse to remove their chains. Pitt County officials immediately launched a massive manhunt. Because Evans had killed the guard, he alone would be outlawed. Most of the escapees were quickly recaptured, but Evans managed to stay a step ahead of the bloodhounds on his trail. Before fleeing, he had taken the slain guard's pistol, and two weeks after his escape, he shot and killed the county's chain gang supervisor, who was at the forefront of a pursuing posse. The following morning the posse finally caught up with Evans and gunned him down. They first took his body to the nearby town of Ayden, where it was viewed by hundreds of people, then drove on to Greenville and displayed the corpse in front of the Pitt County courthouse. In the words of a local journalist, the manhunt's conclusion provided "a most satisfactory ending to one of the most exciting incidents in the history of Pitt county."[15]

From the beginning of the twentieth century through the spring of 1927, the cases of Dave Evans and the presumptive Will Harris are the only known instances in which outlawed African Americans in North Carolina died at the hands of a posse; in both cases, the outlawed men carried guns and fired on their pursuers. Though an outlawry proclamation provided the legal authority to kill a fleeing fugitive, most outlaws—both Black and white—were either taken alive or successfully eluded capture. If apprehended, African Americans outlawed for interracial homicide were quickly convicted and put to death, but there are no known cases of an outlawed white man being captured and then executed, no matter how heinous his crime. In 1916, eleven years before Broadus Miller was outlawed, Burke County officials issued an outlawry proclamation against a white bootlegger named Charles Mace. Mace lived in the South Mountains, an outcropping of rugged hills a few miles south of Morganton. In a fit of drunken rage, he savagely beat his wife and then shot her in the head. After her body was discovered, a sheriff's posse pursued the homicidal husband through the South Mountains, opening fire when they glimpsed him scaling down a cliff, but he escaped and made his way to South Carolina, where police captured him a month later. Brought back to Morganton to stand trial, Mace was convicted and sentenced to thirty years in the state penitentiary.[16]

Unlike Charles Mace, Broadus Miller was a Black man accused of killing a white girl, and if apprehended alive and put on trial, he would undoubtedly end up sitting in the electric chair. As the North Carolina press emphasized, his death was "just as certain at the hands of the State as at the hands of a mob." But few observers thought Miller would be taken alive. According to the *Hickory Daily Record*, the odds were "more than ten to one" that he would be "shot down in flight or fight." The outlawry proclamation gave every citizen of the state the legal right to shoot and kill the fleeing fugitive, and Morganton's white residents devoutly wished for such an outcome. If Broadus Miller were quickly killed, the threat of a lynch mob would be averted and the town spared a tumultuous trial. "Many law-abiding citizens," observed the editor Beatrice Cobb, "have expressed the hope that the negro outlaw would be killed in resisting arrest."[17]

CHAPTER FOURTEEN
Mountain Manhunt

During the first thirty-six hours of the manhunt for Broadus Miller, newspapers throughout North Carolina reported that a lynching was imminent in Burke County. Members of Morganton's National Guard company had been voluntarily assisting with the manhunt, but Governor Angus McLean waited in vain for county officials to request that National Guard troops be officially deployed to prevent potential mob violence. Local authorities in the South were generally reluctant to make such requests, for they viewed any deployment of troops as "outside interference." Finally, on the morning of Thursday, June 23—the day after Burke County justices of the peace outlawed Miller—Governor McLean took the initiative and telephoned Sheriff Hallyburton. The sheriff admitted that the accused killer would likely be lynched if he were caught, so the governor called up the Morganton National Guard and ordered them "to guard the life of Miller in the eventuality of his capture." According to the *Washington Post*, the troop deployment had also been prompted by fear "that the mob . . . may seek vengeance upon some of the negroes who have been arrested on suspicion." Police took Miller's wife from Morganton and held her in another county, and they transferred Will Berry—in whose house Miller had boarded—to the jailhouse in Lenoir. Authorities continued to worry about potential mob violence against Berry, who was rumored to have helped the fugitive escape, so they later removed him from Lenoir and held him in an undisclosed location.[1]

On Thursday evening, after receiving reports about the "menacing disposition" of the men hunting Miller, Adjutant General Metts dispatched an additional National Guard company from Hickory. Their sudden departure sparked a rumor "that Miller had been captured and was being lynched," causing hundreds of Hickory residents to jump in their automobiles and speed toward Morganton, eager to see the rumored lynching. Bounty hunters and vigilantes from a wide area were also converging on the town. As a journalist for the *Winston-Salem Journal* reported, "Four Mitchell County citizens, armed to the hilt, who said they hailed from the Big Rock Creek section, where a negro is not allowed to alight or stay after sundown, drove over to Morganton . . . to help Burke County citizens run down the murderer of the Kincaid girl. They were itching for a chance to try their marksmanship." Overwhelmed by a situation beyond his control, the Burke County sheriff spoke with reporters. "If Broadus Miller falls into the hands of some of the citizens," an exasperated Sheriff Hallyburton declared, "they would lynch him even if the Governor himself were on hand." Thursday ended with another "night of wild chases and false rumors," but with National Guardsmen officially on duty and patrolling the town, the sheriff finally got some sleep. He had been up for over forty-eight hours, ever since pandemonium had erupted in the wake of Kincaid's murder.[2]

The following day, newspapers noted that civic leaders in Morganton had "expressed resentment over reports tending to indicate that mobs, bent on lynching, had held sway since Tuesday." The *Charlotte Observer* quoted Beatrice Cobb, who indignantly denied the existence of any would-be lynch mob in the town. "There is no danger of a lynching here," Cobb insisted. "The searchers are orderly and calm. Except for a few younger boys with hot heads, there has been no talk of lynching." In her own newspaper, Cobb was a bit more candid, noting that if Miller were captured alive, "the common sense of the officers in charge is sufficient assurance that they would not aggravate the situation here by attempting to bring him to Morganton." The editor strove to maintain an idealized representation of her hometown, both to outsiders and to the local audience, and she minimized or ignored any news that challenged such a portrait; the *News-Herald* never once mentioned the presence of National Guard troops on the town's streets.[3]

The National Guard's deployment lasted two days, Thursday and Friday, June 23 and 24. By Friday evening, law enforcement officials were convinced that Miller had escaped from the vicinity of the town and Governor McLean demobilized the men. Their deployment had irritated local officials and white civic leaders. But for Morganton's African American residents, the troops' presence had provided a reassuring sense of security. As angry mobs hunted Broadus Miller, Black domestic servants stopped going to work, afraid to venture into white neighborhoods, and some families barricaded themselves inside their homes, sending anyone who could pass as white to buy groceries and supplies. On the Sunday afternoon following Kincaid's murder, leaders of the Black community held a meeting at Gaston Chapel African Methodist Episcopal Church. A committee of spokespeople—including pastors, schoolteachers, and a local businessman—drafted a series of resolutions to be published in the *News-Herald*. In these resolutions, the committee denounced the killing of Kincaid and thanked a number of people—including Governor McLean and Captain Owen Connelly of the Morganton National Guard—"for the protection they have given us."[4]

Notably, Beatrice Cobb was one of the persons thanked by the committee. In the immediate aftermath of Kincaid's death, Cobb had published an editorial titled "The Outsider" emphasizing that Broadus Miller was not a native of Morganton, and she drew a distinction between the town's Black residents and African Americans who came from elsewhere. "It is to the credit of the local negroes that this crime is not to be charged against them," the editor asserted. "As a whole the Morganton negroes are fairly law-abiding and live in peace and amity with the white citizens of the community. In practically every instance of startling and outstanding crime during recent years some negro from a distance has been the principal." She deplored "that the local negroes" had to suffer "the discredit and reflected disgrace of the disreputable acts of these drifters." As rumors circulated that Will Berry had helped Broadus Miller escape, Cobb spoke up in his defense, arguing that Berry knew "nothing of the crime, or of Miller, merely becoming scared so that he got tangled up in answering questions."[5]

But though Beatrice Cobb defended local African Americans, she tacitly endorsed the lynching of Gladys Kincaid's accused killer. "How would you feel," she demanded of her readers, "if this girl, the helpless, innocent victim of a devil in human guise, were your sister or your daughter?" In Cobb's words, death was "too lenient a punishment" for Broadus Miller. During the manhunt for Miller, newspapers throughout North Carolina urged that the outlawed fugitive be tried and punished by the state, but no such message appeared in the *News-Herald*. Almost forty years earlier, in September 1889, a local newspaper called the *Morganton Star* had angrily denounced the state judicial system for being too slow and lenient. "The murders in the county . . . cannot be counted on your fingers," the *Star* declared, "and not a man has suffered the penalty under the gallows." Less than a week later, a mob dragged two accused killers—one white, the other Black—from the Morganton jail and hanged them from a railroad bridge. The *Star* then published a second editorial, ostensibly deploring mob violence but mainly objecting to criticism of the lynching from newspapers in other counties. No one outside Burke County, the paper argued, had any right to pass judgment on local matters.[6]

The *Star*'s editor was T. G. Cobb—Beatrice Cobb's father. When advocating swift vengeance and asserting county sovereignty, Cobb followed in her father's footsteps.

IN THE DAYS FOLLOWING GLADYS KINCAID'S MURDER, the manhunt for Broadus Miller "spread over three states, with authorities and posses in

North Carolina, South Carolina and Virginia engaged in the search." Across a wide area—from Raleigh to Lynchburg, Virginia, to Gaffney, South Carolina—railroad detectives and police detained scores of young Black men. The *Hickory Daily Record* reported that Morganton deputies were "speeding back and forth over the foothill section of North Carolina in an effort to quickly identify the many captures that have been made.... Asheville, Marion, Lenoir, Hickory and other sections of this country have captured and held tall ginger-cake negroes until the Burke officers could identify them." Two men traveling together were detained six different times and taken to the Morganton jail to be identified; they finally managed to continue on their way after officials gave them a signed affidavit certifying that neither of them was Broadus Miller. At Spencer, a small community near Salisbury, railroad workers spotted and chased a Black man, and after he eluded them, they summoned the Rowan County sheriff to continue the pursuit. When farmers outside Charlotte "reported that a strange negro was wandering around the fields," a police officer arrested the man after a daylong search and "put the negro through a severe cross-examination." Not all the targeted suspects were African Americans. A "dark complexioned" man from India "was frightened mightily when a mountain posse dragged him from a bus" and interrogated him about Kincaid's murder.[7]

A physical description of Broadus Miller appeared in newspapers throughout the state: "About 5 feet 10 inches, light brown color, slender, weight about 150 pounds, clean shaved, hair shaved from eyebrows, thin brown eyes, scar on left forearm, wears band ring on finger of left hand." In addition, police obtained and distributed a photograph of the wanted man (see figure 14.1). The grainy and blurred image was in great demand, and the press reported that a Morganton studio "has capitalized upon the situation by turning out hundreds of postcard pictures of the alleged negro culprit which are sold at 15 cents apiece." The photograph strikingly resembled a man named Eugene Martin, who had once worked for several months as a construction laborer in Hickory. Arrested in eastern North Carolina and taken back to Catawba County and jailed, Martin confessed to being an escaped convict from an Asheville chain gang. Sheriff Hallyburton publicly confirmed that the prisoner was not Broadus Miller, but after a Morganton resident visited the jail and wrongly identified him as the outlaw, an angry mob gathered outside on the street. Local police rushed Martin to Gastonia, where he was held for several days before being returned to the chain gang; officials were so concerned by the possibility of a lynch mob pursuing Martin that they refused to disclose where he had been taken.[8]

FIGURE 14.1 Reward notice and photograph of Broadus Miller. (*Winston-Salem Journal*, June 25, 1927.)

Among the many alleged sightings of Broadus Miller, the most credible reports indicated he had fled north from Morganton on foot and passed through Chesterfield, the rural community where Gladys Kincaid had been born and spent her childhood. In the countryside around Chesterfield lived a number of African American families, some of whom fed the fleeing fugitive. Their motives for assisting him varied, but when confronted with a Black man being chased by angry white mobs, many African Americans assumed the man was innocent, and even if they believed him guilty, they did not want to see him lynched. However, no one would give Miller shelter, which would have put a family in grave danger as accomplices, and when some persons in the community reported to the police that they had seen him, law officers brought bloodhounds to the scene. Bloodhounds had not been able to pick up the trail of Kincaid's accused killer anywhere in Morganton, neither at the scene of the attack nor at Will Berry's home. Only after police took them to Chesterfield did they finally strike a trail, which officers followed "in an almost direct route" up the Johns River valley and into the Blue Ridge Mountains of western Caldwell County (see map 14.1).[9]

Over the following week, manhunters combed some fifty square miles along the heavily wooded eastern slopes of Grandfather Mountain. Concentrated around Wilson Creek, the hunt began on Friday, June 24, when a man resembling Miller was spotted near Adako, a small community close to the Burke-Caldwell county line. In the words of the *News-Herald*, "some negro, who for some reason is dodging, has been giving the inhabitants of that section occasional glimpses of his dusky form and has been leaving traces of his flight." In 1920s North Carolina, both law officers and private citizens could claim the rewards offered for fugitives, and though he had no jurisdiction in either Caldwell or Burke Counties, Hickory police chief Eugene Lentz went to Adako on Friday to check out the reported sightings. Lentz soon concluded that Miller had indeed been seen in the area. An elderly Black man described giving food to a stranger who claimed to be on the run for accidently killing a man in Asheville; the stranger had requested shelter, but the old man had refused and sent him away. A group of African American children near Brown Mountain said the suspect had stopped at their family's cabin around one o'clock in the afternoon, "then left hurriedly going in the direction of the mountains." That afternoon Lentz tracked the fugitive for several miles before losing his trail. In the evening a posse of 300 men cordoned off Adam's Knob, a few miles north of Adako, but did not find anyone.[10]

The following morning someone allegedly glimpsed the suspect in the woods near Adako, and another reported sighting in the nearby community of Collettsville caused several carloads of sheriff's deputies to race to the scene. As the day progressed, the hunt centered on a heavily wooded area between Johns River and Mulberry Creek. In the words of the *Charlotte Observer*, "All day the pursuit was hot, with a bloodhound leading the pursuers almost to within sight of the fugitive." Hunters chased the suspect "until his shoes were worn off and his feet were bleeding," and bloody footprints indicated "the killing speed which the fugitive has been forced to keep up to stay ahead of the pursuers, both man and dog." The footprints showed the

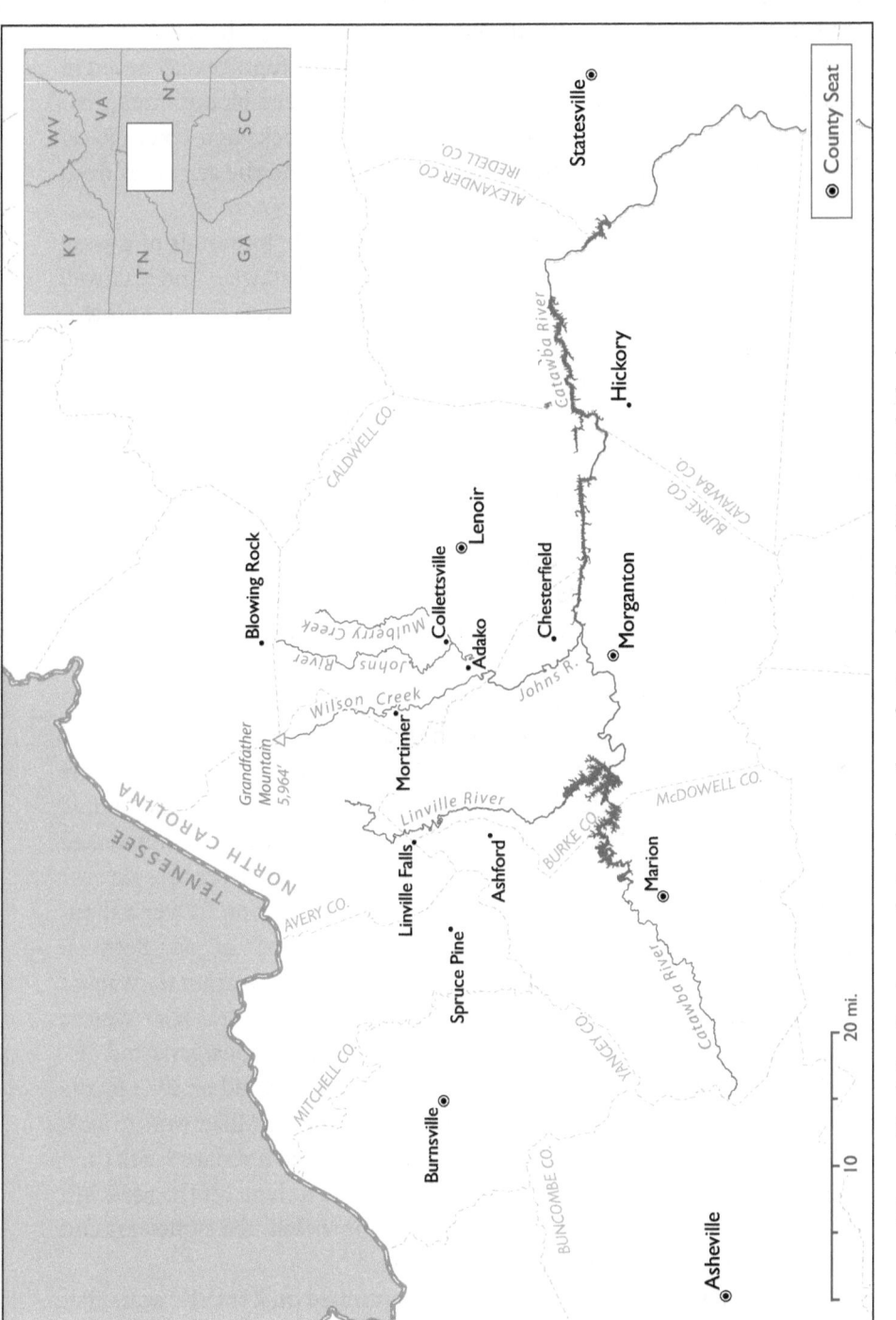

MAP 14.1 Western North Carolina in 1927 during the manhunt for Broadus Miller. (Map by Josh Platt.)

pursued man was removing his cap and using it to cover his raw and bleeding feet. Late Saturday evening the bloodhound's handlers believed the dog was within a few hundred feet of their prey, but the fugitive succeeded in doubling back on his trail and losing his pursuers. The bloodhound, "exhausted by long hours of trailing, dropped in his tracks and could go no farther," so the posse stopped to wait for morning and the arrival of fresh hounds from Salisbury and Asheville.[11]

On Sunday the hunt resumed. From dawn to dusk, hundreds of private citizens and law enforcement officials from Burke, Catawba, and Caldwell Counties swept the mountains north of Collettsville. Among the hunters that day was Sam Ervin Jr., who came from Morganton to participate personally, while a Catawba County police chief, wearing overalls and "with a pistol strapped under his left arm," directed one of the hunting parties. One member of the posse—described in press reports as a "hearty young hillsman from near Morganton"—claimed to have "jumped the negro from his night's bed and stayed close on his heels until early afternoon before he lost the trail," but none of the other hunters could find any clear sign of their prey. Nor could the bloodhounds pick up the fugitive's scent, which had been erased by the hordes of men tramping through the woods over the previous two days.[12]

The Sunday manhunt attracted a "typical holiday crowd," with people swarming to the mountains to witness the latest developments in the case—and to be present if Miller were captured and lynched. "Hundreds of cars went from Morganton, Hickory and Lenoir to Adako and Collettsville," noted the *Charlotte Observer*. Throughout the day, a long line of traffic slowly snaked its way along the narrow mountain backroads, traveling "from one place to another" as "various reports and rumors gained circulation." Over a thousand people parked their cars and walked along a stretch of road between Collettsville and Olivette, but they did not enter the woods to hunt the wanted man. Instead, in the scornful words of one reporter, the horde of spectators only "paraded the broad highway and displayed their vicious guns and pistols"; they "walked up and down in places where they could be seen by the most persons and threatened extreme violence if Broadus Miller were to walk out in that big and thickly populated highway," but did not dare "stick their toes under a patch of shrubbery, unless a car pushed them off the road." In the late afternoon as the sun sank and the air grew chill, the sightseers and highway strollers began heading back to town.[13]

Over the next couple of days, the hunt continued on a smaller scale. Police and bounty hunters combed the woods near Collettsville, while a posse of twenty men from Blowing Rock spent Monday searching a nearby rocky crag. The fugitive's trail had grown cold, however, and law enforcement officials began "talking among themselves to the effect that the negro has made good his escape." Hoping to pick up the trail again, police brought in fresh bloodhounds from eastern North Carolina. One of the hounds was accompanied by six puppies, for its handlers wanted the young dogs to learn "their first lesson in man hunting under the most adverse circumstances it is possible to imagine." As the Raleigh *News and Observer* explained to its readers, the area of the manhunt was "the rugged land at the very foothills of the uncharted Blue Ridge and Grandfather ranges." Though the terrain was daunting, the mountain woods contained "plenty of water and fine huckleberries." Journalists and police speculated that Miller might also be receiving food from some mountain residents. About four miles north of Collettsville lived a number of rural African American families, descendants of slaves from the Johns River valley. As the *Charlotte Observer* reported, "Officials have searched every negro house in this community and are keeping a close watch on them."[14]

Eighty years later, several elderly Caldwell County residents still remembered the 1927 manhunt. Many oral histories emphasized the theft of food from isolated cabins and springhouses. When one family discovered that some of their milk had been stolen, they threw away the remaining milk and butter because "Broadus had been in the springbox." From another family's house, Miller stole a bowl of food and some rags to wrap around his raw and bleeding feet, discarding the empty bowl a few hundred feet from the home. Late in the afternoon on Tuesday, June 28, the fugitive entered the home of Charlie Ingram, who lived on Cold Water Creek near Mortimer. Ingram's wife was outside with other local women, hoeing a nearby cornfield, when the intruder stole milk and cornbread from the family's kitchen. The Ingrams' daughter saw him and screamed, causing Miller to jump out the open kitchen window and flee. Posse members with bloodhounds soon arrived. Seeing movement in the bushes near the Ingrams' home, the posse opened fire, killing two chickens. After the hounds caught scent of the man's trail, the chase began anew. Late that night, the family of a woman giving birth to a child heard the baying of the hounds and looked out their kitchen window. They glimpsed the fleeing fugitive and, minutes later, the posse and dogs, hot on his trail.[15]

On the morning of Wednesday, June 29, as news spread of the previous day's sightings, hundreds of men again headed into the mountains. In the words of one reporter, "Cars began passing Collettsville at an early hour this morning and the search began to resemble one of its earlier days." Unlike the weekend sightseers, these midweek arrivals "went into the thickets of the mountains," determined to claim the large rewards offered for the outlaw. Late Wednesday afternoon, a woman near Mortimer saw him breaking into her family's springhouse. Hunters quickly arrived with hounds and began a relentless pursuit lasting late into the night. After sunset, members of the posse spotted and fired at the fugitive as he crossed a railroad trestle over Wilson Creek. From there his trail "led the men and dogs on into the untracked region west of Mortimer." That night, a journalist on a nearby ridgeline reported hearing "a continuous but faint roar of the barking dogs as they stick to the course over the rugged cliffs."[16]

Far from the mountains, the *Charlotte Observer* provided a vivid summary of unfolding events:

> With the bass voices of half a dozen bloodhounds echoing through the stillness of the night in these Caldwell county mountains, the man-hunt . . . was believed by officers in charge of the search to gradually be coming to a close. Reports coming out of the dense mountains are that the negro . . . is just a few paces ahead of the pursuing posse. From Collettsville to Adako, and then from Adako to Globe, the chase for the outlawed man has been resolutely pushed, and tonight the pack of bloodhounds, increased from all parts of the state, has battled its way through the thicket of mountain growth on toward Mortimer, near the line of Avery county.

But predictions of an end to the manhunt proved premature. West of Mortimer, the fugitive entered one of the most rugged areas in the Appalachians, with twelve-mile-long Linville Gorge at its center. On each side of the gorge, steep wooded cliffs plunged down some 1,400 feet to the Linville River. Entering this wilderness after a week of desperate running, Broadus Miller managed to vanish. As a press report noted, "The sole hope now, officers declare, is to wait until he comes out of the thicket again."[17]

CHAPTER FIFTEEN

A Killing and a Celebration

On Saturday, July 2, an envoy from Governor McLean arrived in Morganton. The North Carolina National Guard—including the Morganton company—planned to depart early the following morning for their annual summer encampment in South Carolina and would thus be unavailable to guard Broadus Miller if he were taken alive, so Pardon Commissioner Edwin Bridges had been sent to confer with local officials about preventing a possible lynching in the troops' absence. An attorney from Charlotte, the thirty-three-year-old Bridges was a trusted assistant to the governor, and though his official duties as pardon commissioner were limited to examining potential pardons and summarizing these cases for the governor's review, McLean regularly dispatched him to places threatened by potential mob violence. On arriving in Morganton, he met with Sheriff Hallyburton and county attorney Sam Ervin Jr. The pardon commissioner and Ervin were longtime friends and political allies; three years earlier, Bridges had been an invited guest at Ervin's wedding, and when Ervin sought to become a district attorney in 1926, Bridges had penned a flattering campaign biography on his behalf. In their meeting, the officials discussed stationing "one or two high powered cars" in the area of the manhunt in order to "rush the negro to some unknown location for safe keeping" if he were captured. But as they all undoubtedly realized, the most effective way to preempt a lynch mob was for the outlawed fugitive to be shot and killed on sight.[1]

Numerous Morganton residents had spent the past week in the mountains hunting Broadus Miller. That weekend, with the outlaw's trail growing cold, they began making their way back to town. Among the returning hunters was the improbably named Commodore Vanderbilt Burleson. Born in 1885, Burleson had grown up in Linville Falls, a small community at the upper end of Linville Gorge. The son of a renowned mountain guide and bear hunter, he had become a skilled tracker and hunter in his own right. In the early twentieth century, the photographer Frank W. Bicknell extensively documented life in Linville Falls. Several of Bicknell's photographs featured Burleson and his kinsmen, guns in hand, proudly standing over the bodies of black bear they had killed (see figure 15.1). After marrying a Morganton native, Burleson moved to her hometown, where he worked as a town policeman and then

FIGURE 15.1 Bear hunters in Linville Falls pose with their trophy, c. 1900–1905. Standing, third from left in the middle row, is Commodore Burleson, who holds a long-barreled pistol. Kneeling at the far left is Burleson's father, Mitch Burleson. (Courtesy of Pat Burleson Howell.)

a carpenter. In the 1920s he joined the Ku Klux Klan, and at some point he became head of the local klavern. The Klan's militant Protestantism and its war against bootleggers resonated with Burleson, who belonged to Morganton's First Methodist Church and was a teetotaling former alcoholic. But one aspect of the Klan's message especially appealed to him: its emphasis on white supremacy. No African Americans lived in Burleson's native Linville Falls, and after moving to Morganton, he was outspoken in his dislike of Black people. In 1925, during the Arthur Montague case, he had been one of the grand jurors who recommended that Burke County's public institutions quit employing African Americans.[2]

At noon on Saturday, around the same time that Pardon Commissioner Bridges was conferring with Burke County officials, deputies in Yancey County detained an African American who resembled the physical description of Broadus Miller. The man stated that he was from Buncombe County and had spent the past week and a half "in a Virginia mining town," and though he produced receipts corroborating his alibi, Yancey County sheriff

Hugh Banks locked him in the Burnsville jail pending positive identification. On hearing of the arrest, a group of Morganton residents led by the town's police chief traveled to Burnsville and "demanded that the man be turned over to them." The sheriff refused; he did not trust their intentions, and the large rewards offered for Miller provided a strong incentive to retain full custody of the prisoner until his identity was conclusively established.[3]

That evening in Morganton, Commodore Burleson met with Harrison Pritchard, a tenant farmer who, like Burleson, had spent the previous week in the mountains searching for Broadus Miller. At a local general store, the two men discussed the ongoing manhunt with Fons Duckworth, a former town alderman and leader in the Junior Order. Duckworth told Burleson and Pritchard that he planned to drive to Burnsville the next day and check out the suspect who had been arrested. He would be accompanied by John C. Burnett, a white resident of Morganton who knew Miller by sight and could identify him, and he invited Burleson and Pritchard to come along. Early the following morning, Sunday, July 3, the four men set out in Duckworth's Model T Ford. They were not acting in any official capacity, and if the prisoner did turn out to be Miller, they had no legal authority to take him. But when they left that morning, all of them were armed. Along the way, they stopped in the town of Marion. There they learned that the Yancey County sheriff, fearing that "news of the negro's arrest might spread" and attract a lynch mob, had taken the man to Asheville and secured him in the Buncombe County jail. They also learned that during the night there had been a burglary in Linville Falls that had likely been committed by the long-sought outlaw. The men from Morganton immediately turned and sped north, following the fugitive's trail to Burleson's own birthplace.[4]

THE LINVILLE FALLS community sits along a mountain ridge at the intersection of Burke, Avery, and McDowell Counties, about ten miles west of Mortimer, where the fugitive had last been sighted. Commodore Burleson's uncle John Wiseman owned and operated a general store in Linville Falls. Early that Sunday morning, Wiseman noticed that a café across the road from his store had been broken into during the night. Candy bar wrappers marked the intruder's trail going down into the North Cove valley and toward the small rural community of Ashford. Suspecting the culprit might be Broadus Miller, the storekeeper telephoned the Morganton police. That same morning, a farmer in Ashford discovered that someone had stolen a jar of milk from his springhouse; the farmer's daughter claimed to have glimpsed a Black man with a gun crossing the road at the nearby Concord United Methodist Church.[5]

At the turn of the twentieth century, a writer had described the six miles between Linville Falls and Ashford as "some of the wildest scenery of the South," in which "vast chasms, ghastly rents, massive towering rocks, seared and seamed, are on every hand." It was through this terrain that the fugitive's trail led. By the time Burleson and his companions arrived in Ashford, several cars were parked beside the road near the Methodist church and a few dozen hunters had converged on the scene. The McDowell County sheriff had brought bloodhounds, and starting at the farmer's springhouse, members of the loosely organized posse traced the fugitive's trail to an empty milk jar a hundred yards away. From there, footprints led up the wooded mountainside behind the church. Burleson and Pritchard recognized the tracks as the same they had followed in Caldwell County a few days before, for one of the man's feet was "covered with rags with two toes [sticking] through." The group of hunters split up and went in separate directions, agreeing that whoever came upon any sign of their prey would give a bobwhite whistle to alert the others. As Pritchard and Duckworth circled the top of the mountain, they came upon a fresh trail through the brush and whistled. Hearing the signal, Commodore Burleson worked his way up through the dense undergrowth with a .45 caliber pistol in hand—and suddenly encountered Broadus Miller.[6]

As the crow flies, Ashford is only some twenty miles from Morganton, but during twelve days on the run the outlawed fugitive had covered a much greater distance—up the Johns River valley, back and forth across the rugged foothills below Grandfather Mountain, and over the steep rock faces and thick scrub brush between Mortimer and Linville Falls. In a mad zigzag course, going in circles and doubling back on his own trail, he had frantically tried to shake off the incessant hounds and hunters on his heels. He had worn out his shoes in the first few days of running, and from then on he had been barefoot, his bleeding feet wrapped in rags, as he pushed blindly forward through dense laurel thickets and snake-infested creek bottoms. Living on wild berries and occasional food and milk pilfered from homes and springhouses, he had lost thirty pounds while on the run. When he emerged in Linville Falls, hungry and tired, he had broken into a café desperately seeking food. Apparently no longer making much effort to cover his tracks, he had littered the ground with candy bar wrappers as he stumbled with exhaustion down the mountainside toward Ashford. There he drank milk from a farmer's springhouse, tossed aside the emptied jar, and wandered back into the woods.[7]

Commodore Burleson shot and killed Broadus Miller on the thickly wooded mountainside behind Concord United Methodist Church. The details of the killing are shrouded in controversy. Burleson claimed the fugitive was armed and had fired at him with a 12-gauge shotgun stolen from some isolated mountain cabin. His companions from Morganton supported his story. Duckworth asserted that when he arrived on the scene "less than a minute" after the shooting, a shotgun was "lying at the negro's side," and when the gun was broken open, "it was still smoking" from having been fired. The press had previously reported vague rumors that Miller might be armed, and as one journalist noted, posse members were "prepared to shoot without a great deal of provocation." In the coming days, newspapers throughout the United States would give a melodramatic account of the encounter between the hunter and the outlaw, portraying the shooting as an epic gunfight in which Burleson had heroically triumphed. However, other witnesses would soon challenge the official account of Miller's death.[8]

The sound of gunshots quickly brought the rest of the posse to the scene. Broadus Miller lay on the ground, shot in the chest and mortally wounded; he "never spoke and in a moment or two closed his eyes and was dead." Burleson and his companions then tied a rope around Miller's legs and dragged him like a dead animal out of the woods and to the road, where they threw his body into the back of the Model T. With Duckworth at the wheel, they set off for Morganton, eager to show off their trophy and claim the large rewards. Although Burleson was a deadly hunter, he had never learned to drive, and he sat nervously in the cramped and crowded car as Duckworth raced at breakneck speed down the curving mountain road, passing Sheriff Hallyburton, who—accompanied by Pardon Commissioner Bridges and Sam Ervin Jr.—was driving in the opposite direction, to the scene of the manhunt in Ashford. Once out of the mountains, the road straightened and flattened and ran directly toward Morganton, where around noon the manhunters arrived with their prey.[9]

The journalist Ben Dixon MacNeill of the Raleigh *News and Observer* happened to be in Morganton that Sunday. Known as "the most colorful newspaperman in North Carolina," and seeming to have a "mysterious gift for being where things happened," MacNeill had stopped in the town on his way to a Fourth of July celebration scheduled for the following day in the community of Little Switzerland. The timing of his visit proved serendipitous, for he witnessed the triumphant return of the bounty hunters and provided a graphic account of their arrival:

> An automobile swept into [town] with its siren shrieking. Four men rode in the car, and over the right rear door projected the feet of a figure

thrown carelessly on the floor. The feet were wrapped in rags. The left foot was partially bare and very black. It hung loosely over the side of the car. The streets were filled with people going home from their places of worship.

One of the men sat still and tired in the seat but the other three leaned far out of the car to yell jubilantly to the crowds going home from church "Here's your Nigger—come and look at him." People stopped to stare as the car swept along and then they turned toward the court house in the center of the town. . . .

Shooting half across the sidewalk before it was brought to a stand still, the car drew up before the courthouse. The rear door was opened, and two men grabbed the feet that projected. The body was dragged to the pavement, its head hitting sharply as it fell. For a moment it lay there, with its red, gaping wounds in the naked breast and stomach still dripping. The clothing had almost all been torn off in his wandering through mountain forests. . . .

Again grasping the figure by the feet, two men dragged it across the sidewalk, across the courthouse lawn, pausing a moment before the door and then going in. A vast throng collected with miraculous speed. They yelled in exultation. Women embraced one another and men shook one another by the hand and slapped one another on the back. Before the doors of the courthouse they all clamored for a sight of the dead, naked fugitive.

Commodore Burleson's twelve-year-old daughter Margaret and his son Gillam, who was eleven, were walking home together from Sunday school at the First Methodist Church when their father and his companions arrived. Standing on the sidewalk across from the courthouse, the two children saw the men open the back door of the car and drag out the body, and they ran across the street to look at the dead man. They then rushed home to tell their mother, who made them stay at home for the rest of the day and not return to the courthouse square.[10]

After Broadus Miller's body was dragged inside the courthouse, it "lay in a huddled heap" on the floor for half an hour while people crowded into the building to look at it. As Sunday services at the local churches ended, the crowd around the courthouse swelled. In the words of the *Charlotte Observer*, "Thousands of people, in varying moods and temperaments, began to pour into town and fill the streets about the courthouse." The rapidly growing crowd all wanted to see the body, so some men dragged the corpse out of the

FIGURE 15.2 The Morganton courthouse square on the Sunday afternoon of July 3, 1927. A crowd gathers around the Confederate monument, with Broadus Miller's body (not visible in the photograph) on display at the monument's base. (*Raleigh Times*, July 6, 1927.)

courthouse and to the north side of the lawn, where they placed it on the ground beside the large Confederate monument. Dressed in their Sunday best, the crowd—mostly comprised of men, but with a few women and children as well—clustered around Miller's body, with several men standing on the base of the monument to look down at the dead Black man on the ground below (see figure 15.2). Two months earlier, a procession of schoolchildren had celebrated Confederate Memorial Day by gathering at the monument to hear Reverend Rufus Bradshaw—the same pastor who would preside over Gladys Kincaid's funeral—deliver a prayer for the Confederate dead.[11]

Broadus Miller's body lay at the base of the Confederate monument for about an hour. During that time, the crowd grew restless, with individuals pushing forward to get a glimpse of the body—and threatening to do more than just look at it. In MacNeill's words, "Some proposed to hang him up in sight of everybody and others demanded that he be dragged through the streets behind an automobile." Because of the large rewards offered for the outlaw, Commodore Burleson and his companions had a vested interest in protecting the corpse until it had been conclusively identified, and though decades later, some people would claim that Miller's body had been dragged by car on the streets around the courthouse, there is no evidence that this occurred. Instead, alarmed at a situation that threatened to spiral out of control, law officers seized the body and dragged it by hand across the lawn to the jailhouse, a small two-story building on the opposite side of the courthouse square. There they removed it from public view and locked it in a cell. While the body lay inside the jail, authorities brought in Broadus Miller's wife—who had been held in an undisclosed location—and a dozen of his coworkers to confirm the identity of the emaciated corpse. "That's Broadus," his wife said. Two policemen then escorted Mrs. Miller back to her home in Asheville by train.[12]

The large crowd on the courthouse lawn attracted the attention of motorists on a nearby highway, who stopped to see the cause of the excitement. Traffic on the highway came to a standstill, and as news spread by telephone and telegraph throughout Burke and adjacent counties, carloads of more spectators rushed to the scene, clamoring to see the dead outlaw. After the crowd grew to a few thousand people, they began threatening to storm the jailhouse. Sheriff Hallyburton's "own inclination was to send the body immediately to an undertaking establishment," but "after a conference with other officials" he acquiesced to the crowd's demand. However, the authorities took steps to maintain a more orderly exhibition than before. While some fifty town and county officers stood guard, police took the body back outside and laid it "on a board at the foot of the steps of the north portico of the jail." Officers roped off a narrow aisle leading to the steps and allowed the crowd to pass by in single file in front of the body. Not everyone on the crowded courthouse lawn stood in line to see Miller's corpse. Beatrice Cobb later declared that though she "felt no uneasiness or hesitancy in mingling with the crowd," she had "no desire to gaze upon a dead negro and did not look at the body."[13]

As the organized public exhibition of Miller's body began, Commodore Burleson sat in the law office of Sam Ervin Jr. across the street from the courthouse, giving a formal statement to Pardon Commissioner Edwin Bridges. Burleson claimed the outlaw had been armed with a shotgun and had fired at him, the load of shot going over his head. Ervin spoke up and said three witnesses had told him the shotgun blast hit a tree stump directly in front of Burleson. "Is that right?" the outlaw's killer responded. "I thought he shot over my head." The pardon commissioner would subsequently report to the governor that "the slaying of Broadus Miller was necessary and justifiable," and he praised local officials, especially his friend Ervin, for having "worked diligently and wisely in taking precautionary measures for the purpose of preserving law and order." The meeting with the governor's envoy abruptly ended when a police officer stepped into the office and announced that the huge crowd outside was demanding to see the man who had killed Broadus Miller. When Burleson emerged from the law office, the crowd cheered wildly. Police officers escorted him across the courthouse lawn and to the jailhouse porch. Eerily reprising the trophy photographs from his bear-hunting days, Burleson stood "above the body of the dead negro" throughout the afternoon, occasionally waving in response to the people shouting his praises.[14]

That afternoon, a local photographer named Walter Greene took pictures of Burleson standing on the courthouse lawn with his .45 caliber pistol tucked in his belt (see figure 15.3), and of Broadus Miller's body on display outside the jailhouse. Greene worked for a downtown studio owned by Lloyd Webb, and hordes of people stampeded the studio demanding copies of the photographs. "We had to sell the pictures while they were still wet," Webb recounted a few days later. "If we had waited until they were dry that crowd would have torn the building down." In the photographs of the dead outlaw, the shotgun Miller had allegedly carried is prominently displayed on top of his body. The shirtless dead man wears a pair of knee-length shorts, while a knotted sheet has been looped around his shoulders, presumably to use in carrying or dragging the body by hand. The photographs clearly demonstrate that the body had not been dragged by car, for the corpse shows no evidence of the great physical trauma such an action would have caused.[15]

When Pardon Commissioner Bridges learned Miller's body was on public display, he protested and urged "that an end be put to the morbid spectacle," but Sheriff Hallyburton replied that he feared "what the crowd would do if denied an opportunity to look at the man." Throughout the afternoon a constant stream of spectators moved through the roped aisle at the jailhouse. A journalist counted more than 5,000 people passing in front of the body, but some persons went through the line more than once. Spectators who waited in line "came out expressing profound satisfaction" at having had "a glimpse of the huddled ragged figure." Many of these spectators spat on the corpse, but police protected it from greater desecration. When one man "paused at the side of the dead negro and then kicked it mightily," deputies intervened and detained him. Another person "showed an open knife up his sleeve and the officers pushed him on down the line hurriedly." As people passed through the line, two men solicited donations for Gladys Kincaid's

A Killing and a Celebration 139

FIGURE 15.3 Commodore Burleson standing on the Morganton courthouse lawn. The pistol that he used to kill Broadus Miller is tucked into Burleson's belt. Sunday afternoon, July 3, 1927. (Photograph by Walter Greene.)

family, collecting more than $300. Kincaid's mother was brought to see the body of her daughter's accused killer, but she did not allow her young children to accompany her.[16]

By late afternoon the scene on the courthouse lawn was becoming chaotic. On their way back from Asheville, a Winston-Salem family stopped in Morganton to see the cause of the large commotion; they described witnessing a "wild" celebration involving thousands of people in which "joy reigned unconfined." Several people in the crowd were drinking, and county officials feared that they might attempt to seize the corpse in order to desecrate it. Although hundreds of spectators were still waiting in line to see Miller's body, police took the corpse back inside the jail, placed it in a coffin, and prepared to ship it by train for burial in an undisclosed location. At six-thirty that evening, "thousands were lined up at the railway station as officers placed the body in an express car." A funeral home employee and sheriff's deputies accompanied the coffin. According to one account, the men planned to disembark in nearby Hickory and bury the body there, but some members of the crowd, intent on desecrating the corpse, had sped to Hickory and were waiting when the train arrived, so the body's handlers decided to continue further east. Late that evening the train stopped in Statesville, about fifty miles east of Morganton, where the men unloaded the coffin and turned it over to a funeral home. The following morning, Broadus Miller would be buried in an unmarked grave at the edge of a local African American cemetery.[17]

With the outlaw dead and his body removed, the danger of mob violence in Morganton was over. On Sunday evening Pardon Commissioner Bridges headed home; after arriving at the Charlotte train station, he entertained waiting reporters with stories of what he had seen and heard in Burke County. Back in Morganton, the large crowd slowly began to melt away. However, some people lingered on the courthouse square late into the evening, wanting Commodore Burleson to recount "over and over the same story." His listeners "wanted details about such particulars as the bread and candy found in the negro's pockets, the one shell in his gun, the kind of gun—a 12 gauge breech-loader—how he looked when surprised, etc., etc." Burleson would not get home until ten thirty that night. The *News-Herald*'s account of the day's events ended on an idyllic note. "By sundown," Beatrice Cobb wrote, "the crowd had dispersed and nightfall saw Morganton again quiet and peaceful."[18]

CHAPTER SIXTEEN

Reverberations and Patterns

On the day after the exhibition on the Morganton courthouse lawn, many people tried calling Commodore Burleson on the telephone or stopping by his house to congratulate him. But Burleson wasn't home. He had left early that morning for Statesville, where Broadus Miller's burial took place on the same day that the city would celebrate the Fourth of July by hosting the long-planned annual state rally of the Ku Klux Klan.[1]

By the time of the Statesville rally, Judge Henry Grady no longer headed the North Carolina Klan. In January 1927, the judge had fallen out with Hiram Evans, the Klan's national leader. Evans had launched a campaign demanding states enact various anti-Catholic legislation, including a law prohibiting recognition of Catholic marriage ceremonies. Catholic weddings endangered "the sanctity of marriage," Evans declared, and attempting "to change the established American customs concerning marriage would produce social confusion, discord, and finally civil war." Judge Grady denounced the proposed laws as "silly, unseemly, and unconstitutional," and he stepped down as Grand Dragon and resigned from the Klan. Evans replaced Grady with thirty-five-year-old Morgan Belser, an Alabama native who had been serving in the Klan's Washington, D.C., office and had no close ties to the state. On taking charge in North Carolina, Belser relocated the Invisible Empire's state headquarters from Raleigh to Charlotte. There he spoke to reporters on July 4 and denounced the "American Association for the Advancement of Atheism," which he claimed was preparing to invade the South. He then got in a car and headed to Statesville to join his fellow Klansmen.[2]

In the wake of Judge Grady's resignation, several Klan chapters in North Carolina had dissolved and membership had declined, but though its heyday had passed, the Invisible Empire still maintained significant support. By noon on the Fourth of July an estimated 2,000 Klansmen had gathered in Statesville, with hundreds more arriving throughout the day. They came "from all parts of North Carolina," as well as from South Carolina, Tennessee, and Virginia. The Klan rally was held in conjunction with an afternoon horse show featuring an honored guest: Commodore Vanderbilt Burleson, killer of Broadus Miller and member of the Morganton Klan. With Burleson mounted behind him, a former local sheriff "rode in front of the grandstand and around the grounds, announcing, 'Here's the man who killed the negro.' Cheers came from all sides of the grounds, many enthusiasts yelling out, 'Bring him around and let me see him.'"[3]

In the evening, a large parade wound its way through the crowded streets of downtown Statesville. Two policemen on horseback "accompanied by two mounted Klansmen, with both riders and horses in white robes, led the procession," followed by city officials and hundreds of robed Klansmen waving American flags. After circling the downtown streets, the procession stopped in front of the Iredell County courthouse. The featured speaker for the celebration was Dr. William Hamlett, a Texas minister who had resigned from Austin's First Baptist Church in order to become a full-time spokesman for the Klan. From a podium on the courthouse lawn, Hamlett proclaimed "the importance of keeping the human race pure, illustrated by the clear, pure mountain stream, as contrasted with the sluggish, stagnant streams of the lowlands." Following the speech, a crowd of thousands watched a large fireworks display, capped off by "the burning of the fiery cross."[4]

AS KLANSMEN GATHERED in Statesville to celebrate the Fourth of July, Ben Dixon MacNeill's account of the previous day's events in Morganton appeared on the front page of the Raleigh *News and Observer*. His graphic description of the way Broadus Miller's body had been treated prompted a storm of editorial condemnation from many of the state's leading newspapers. "Morganton Church-Goers Applaud a Gory Matinee," proclaimed a headline in the *Raleigh Times*. "When the automobile brought the dead body through the streets, the people were just emerging from church, meditating sermons," the *Times* lamented. "The siren announcing the kill changed them instantly from a collection of pious sheep and demure doves into a pack of wolves ravening after the event." Other papers joined the chorus of criticism. The *News and Observer* editorialized that the exhibition had been "a carnival of community hate" and "a gruesome spectacle to satisfy the fierce exultation and the morbid blood lust of a group of white men," while the *Greensboro Daily News* castigated "a community where so many persons have happily utilized a Sunday afternoon to drench themselves in savagery."[5]

The criticism infuriated Morganton's white residents. In the words of Beatrice Cobb, the townspeople were "spitting fire." Newspapers throughout western North Carolina rallied to the town's defense. "What other conduct could have been expected of an outraged people?" the *Charlotte Observer* demanded. "Why should they not have manifested a desire to view the body of the outlaw whose acts had brought so much distress upon that community?" The *Cleveland Star* argued that the desire "to see the body of a slain man" was "a curiosity that has evidenced itself enough to be termed natural." Whether "natural" or not, such manifestations of morbid curiosity regularly occurred and were not limited to the dead bodies of Black men. The previous year, on a Sunday afternoon in August 1926, six white teenage girls in an automobile had been killed at a railroad crossing on the outskirts of Gastonia. "The bodies, taken to local undertaking establishments, were viewed by an endless chain of curious men, women and children up until a late hour Sunday night and also Monday morning," the press reported. "Force had to be used to keep back the crowd Monday morning."[6]

The crowd on the courthouse lawn had celebrated Miller's death, but vengeful celebrations were by no means unique to the South. The first executions in the United States in the year 1927 had taken place in Boston, where on an evening in early January a crowd numbering in the thousands gathered outside Charlestown State Prison. Fifteen months earlier, three young white men had robbed a railway storage yard; during the robbery one of them had killed a night watchman, a crime for which he and his two companions were all sentenced to die. At midnight, as the condemned men were led one by one to their deaths in the electric chair, the huge crowd outside celebrated raucously, with triumphant shouts and blaring car horns. In a scene lit by the incessant flashing of reporters' camera bulbs, they surged forward, pressing squads of deployed policemen up against the prison's outer walls. The following week, the nationally syndicated columnist Arthur Brisbane reflected on the spectacle that had occurred in Boston. "Crowds that howled around the French guillotine," concluded Brisbane, "were not entirely different from human beings of today."[7]

Yet, clearly the spectacle in Morganton was more than morbid curiosity or vengeful celebration. Unlike the girls in Gastonia and the young men in Boston, Broadus Miller was an African American, and his dead body had been dragged across the courthouse lawn and displayed at the foot of a Confederate monument by an angry crowd of white men. The *Hickory Daily Record* quoted an unnamed "prominent Morganton citizen" who defended the treatment of the body, declaring that "the negro was in advanced stages of a dangerous disease when he was killed and . . . nobody wanted to fondle him around." In response to the widespread editorial condemnation, Beatrice Cobb admitted that "at first the corpse was not handled as carefully as it might have been," but she rationalized what had occurred: "No man likes to touch the body of a mad dog; by his act Broadus Miller had practically lowered himself to that classification." Local law enforcement officials had prevented the crowd from dragging the body behind an automobile, and when Miller's body was later brought back out of the jailhouse and placed on public display, officers had guarded it. But the spectators who stood in line did more than just look at the corpse. As a man later recalled, he had gone through the line twice in order "to spit on Broadus."[8]

What took place on the Morganton courthouse lawn highlights the difficulty in precisely defining the term "lynching." An extrajudicial killing? Burke County officials had carefully followed state law in issuing the outlawry proclamation, and the proclamation gave every citizen of North Carolina the legal right to shoot the fleeing fugitive. The death of an individual at the hands of a mob? Commodore Burleson acted alone in pulling the trigger. Could a dead man be posthumously lynched? Anti-lynching activists in the 1920s argued against expanding the definition in such a way. But placing a dead Black man on public display—first at the base of a Confederate monument, then on the steps of the jailhouse—sent a clear and stark message to all African Americans. Decades later, an elderly white resident of Morganton would candidly remark that Broadus Miller's dead body had been exhibited in order to "put the fear of the Lord into Negroes."[9]

Neither the NAACP nor the Tuskegee Institute—two national organizations that kept track of lynching deaths—classified the killing of Miller as a "lynching," but the NAACP thus categorized a North Carolina case that occurred a few weeks later. On the evening of July 30, 1927, an African American named Tom Bradshaw allegedly assaulted a white girl in Nash County. After being arrested later that night, he escaped under highly suspicious circumstances. A police officer transporting the handcuffed prisoner to jail stopped and let him out of the car, supposedly because Bradshaw wanted to kneel beside the road and pray, then shot and wounded him as he fled. Still wearing handcuffs, and suffering from a gunshot wound, Bradshaw was chased by a large posse for three days, then shot and killed on the afternoon of August 2. For the rest of the afternoon his body lay in the field where he fell, while large crowds of people flocked to the scene to look at his corpse. Many of the spectators had cameras and took photographs. "Some drove up within a few feet of the Negro's body in their Fords," a reporter noted. "Others parked a mile away and walked." A local minister brought a group of children to see the dead body, then led them away after "they had one good, awed look."[10]

As an editorial in the *Greensboro Daily News* later noted, the cases of Tom Bradshaw and Broadus Miller were "in many respects similar." The newspaper asserted that it had "no disposition to argue the question" of whether the killing of Bradshaw constituted a lynching. "Obviously the pursuers were more interested in killing him than capturing him," the paper observed. "Morally it was so close to a lynching, as that term is generally used, that the difference is inconsequential." The *Daily News* concluded there were "many acts" in North Carolina that could be classified as lynchings but would never be catalogued as such.[11]

But though the cases of Miller and Bradshaw had similarities, there were also significant differences between the two. Most importantly, whereas Miller had been outlawed, no proclamation had been issued against Bradshaw. The fleeing Bradshaw was still wearing handcuffs when he was killed and was universally acknowledged to have been unarmed; even his pursuers seemed embarrassed by the circumstances of his death, and no member of the posse would admit having fired the shot that killed him. Miller, in contrast, had allegedly carried and fired a gun. In the eyes of the law, his alleged possession of a shotgun was irrelevant—fleeing outlaws could be legally shot regardless of whether they were armed. But the gun made a profound difference in how the killing would be perceived by the public, providing an aura of respectability to what Commodore Burleson had done.[12]

Among the hunters pursuing Broadus Miller had been a group of men from Caldwell County who tracked him for several days through the mountains, staying continuously on his trail and arriving on the scene in Ashford around the time Burleson killed him. The following week, two of these men—H. W. Gragg and Clyde Dula—spoke to reporters and insisted Miller had been unarmed, for his trail had led through nearly impenetrable laurel thickets, places where a person "had to crawl considerable distances on hands and knees," and "it would have been almost impossible" to traverse the thickets while toting a shotgun. There had never been "any sign of any gun on this trail," the men declared. "Burleson showed us a shot gun, which he said the negro had fired at him," Dula told reporters. "That gun had not been fired. Of that I am positive." According to Gragg and Dula, they had heard Burleson's pistol shots, but no corresponding blast from a shotgun, and the position of the entrance and exit wounds on the outlaw's body demonstrated that the unarmed Miller had been killed while either asleep or attempting to surrender.[13]

Gragg and Dula's account made a mockery of the heroic "gun duel" narrative that had been publicized by newspapers nationwide, and Beatrice Cobb angrily editorialized that it was "very unfortunate" the men's statements "ever got into print." However, as the *Charlotte Observer* noted, "the desirability for North Carolina to preserve her record of fair play for accused men" required that the accusation be answered. Commodore Burleson hired Sam Ervin Jr. to represent him and sued the two men for slander. H. W. Gragg then publicly apologized for having doubted "the manner in which Mr. Burleson killed the negro outlaw." "It made no difference to me how he was killed, just so he was dead," Gragg hastened to assure the press. Clyde Dula never retracted his claim, but he acknowledged it could not be definitively proved and agreed to pay Burleson a symbolic one cent in damages.[14]

North Carolina would maintain "her record of fair play for accused men," but there was rarely any doubt of that play's outcome. In December 1927 in Wayne County, an African American in his early twenties named Larry Newsome killed a fifteen-year-old white girl, the daughter of a bootlegger for whom Newsome worked. The girl's body was found about 150 feet from her home, with her throat cut and her body badly slashed. When police apprehended Newsome his clothes were bloody and he had a bloodstained knife, and he confessed to having killed the girl while drunk. The crime had been brutal; so was the killer's background. He had grown up in a family of sharecroppers who drifted from one farm to another in eastern North Carolina. One of ten children, he had only a few weeks of formal education. His grandfather and at least one other relative had been declared insane. As a child, Newsome had suffered from spasms, and he contracted syphilis when he was nineteen. Two years later, he married. At the time of the murder, he, his wife, and child were living with his parents and three other people in a two-bedroom shack. On examining Newsome, doctors concluded he was "subnormal in general intelligence and decidedly psychopathic."[15]

On Sunday, December 11, less than three days after the murder, a hastily scheduled special court session convened in Goldsboro to try Newsome. Presiding over the trial was Judge Henry Grady, who had resigned from the Klan earlier that year but still wore his judicial robes. As the trial commenced, the victim's relatives attempted to seize Newsome and drag him outside, where a crowd of 10,000 people had gathered to lynch him. Chaos erupted in the courtroom and the sheriff physically intervened, drawing his pistol and firing it twice into the ceiling, then handing the gun to the judge and rushing the prisoner into the safety of the jury deliberation room. Judge Grady covered the crowd with the pistol and announced, "Gentlemen, I would not willingly harm a man among you, but the next man who undertakes to lay hands upon this prisoner I will shoot dead. There is not going to be a lynching here."[16]

Once again demonstrating his uncanny ability to be on the scene of dramatic events, the journalist Ben Dixon MacNeill was present in the

Goldsboro courtroom. MacNeill described the expression on the face of the pistol-wielding former Klan leader as "the look of a man who would not hesitate on the trigger for an instant if the occasion arose for pressing it." Half an hour later, after National Guard troops had been deployed inside the courtroom, the trial resumed. When the jury retired for deliberations, Judge Grady lectured the victim's family. He could empathize with their anger, the judge announced, and he would not penalize them for disrupting the trial, but state law must be followed in punishing offenders. "I am morally certain," Judge Grady told the packed courtroom, "that the verdict will be guilty and that I shall presently sentence this prisoner to death. That ought to be sufficient for you." Newsome was indeed quickly found guilty, and Grady then imposed the death sentence he had predicted.[17]

The week after Judge Grady defended at gunpoint the rule of law, Beatrice Cobb reflected on what had happened in Wayne County. The crime, which she predictably described as the act of "a negro brute," had been very similar to "the atrocious murder of Gladys Kincaid" six months before. But there was one important difference between the two cases: "We did not have to go through the ordeal of a trial. For weeks all of us lived in dread of what might happen should it be necessary to have a trial for Broadus Miller. We hoped and tried to believe that the law would be allowed to take its course. However, somebody might have tried to 'start something' and in that event there was no telling what might have happened." In Cobb's opinion, shared by many in Burke County and elsewhere, Commodore Burleson's actions had provided an ideal ending to the case. The outlawed fugitive had been quickly killed and Morganton had been spared both a trial and potential mob violence.[18]

If Broadus Miller had been taken alive, and if he had been successfully guarded from any would-be lynch mob, then there can be little doubt he would have been convicted and sentenced to death. From the spring of 1924, when Miller first arrived in North Carolina, until the summer of 1927, when he was outlawed and killed, the state executed twenty men. Only two of these men—father and son C. W. and Elmer Stewart—were white; convicted of killing two law officers who raided their moonshine still, the Stewarts had been sentenced to death by Judge Henry Grady. Of the eighteen African Americans put to death by the state, two of the men came from unknown backgrounds. From the sixteen African Americans whose origins can be determined, only six were North Carolina natives. The remaining ten men—including Arthur Montague—had moved to North Carolina from out of state, had been tried and convicted of rape or murder, and had died in the electric chair. Nine of the ten men had come from South Carolina and Georgia.[19]

In the early 1920s, the boll weevil played a major role in driving tens of thousands of farmworkers out of South Carolina and Georgia, many of whom arrived in North Carolina homeless and indigent. On the same day Arthur Montague allegedly assaulted a girl in Morganton, police in Forsyth County arrested two African Americans and charged them with murdering a local merchant; both men were South Carolina natives who had taken up residence in the tenement houses of Winston-Salem. Sometimes such newcomers became the target of false accusations, as happened with South Carolinians Alvin Mansel and Preston Neely in Asheville. In other cases, the new arrivals almost certainly committed the deeds for which they were convicted. In January 1925, the state executed Kenneth Hale and John Leak for robbing a Lexington taxi driver and beating him to death with an iron bar and a rock. The teenage Hale was the son of a Kentucky father and a mother from West Virginia. His companion John Leak had only recently arrived in North Carolina. Before coming to the Tar Heel State, Leak had been a farm laborer in Laurens County, South Carolina—adjacent to Broadus Miller's native Greenwood.[20]

In 1908, the journalist Ray Stannard Baker had identified "a growing class" of African Americans: men "who float from town to town, doing rough work, having no permanent place of abode, not known to the white population generally." This same class of people later fascinated Thomas Wolfe, but neither Baker nor Wolfe addressed the question of why the "floater" drifted. Children of landless menial laborers, frequently orphaned, sometimes mentally ill, uprooted and cast out into a large and hostile world without money or formal education, neither belonging to any community nor having any feudal protector, condemned on sight wherever they might go—such men had been effectively outlawed without any proclamation.[21]

Broadus Miller's background helps explain what happened in Morganton, but reducing an event to discernable causes never fully answers the question of why it occurred. On the first day of summer in 1927, innumerable threads converged. If any of those threads had been woven differently, the outcome would have changed. What would have happened if an Anderson jury had not deadlocked in 1921, leading to a mistrial and a three-year sentence for Miller? When Frank Tate and his wife decided to build a new house, could anyone have imagined the chain of events that had been set in motion? If the stonemason Dante Martin had never departed Italy, would Miller have ever ended up on a work crew coming to Morganton? If Gladys Kincaid's father had not fallen ill and died, would her family have still moved to town?

Such hypothetical questions are unanswerable. History unfolds along a linear course, seemingly implacable but with a destination known only in hindsight. When the railroad connected Shoals Junction to Anderson, and South Carolina to Asheville, and when another railway linked Asheville with Morganton and Statesville, then the tracks were laid that Broadus Miller would follow from his birthplace to his grave. Gladys Kincaid would be eulogized as a lamb and Miller demonized as a beast, but indigence and need drove a fifteen-year-old girl into a hosiery mill and those same forces brought an itinerant laborer to Morganton. Growing up on rural farms, then cast into a swirling world, two fatherless travelers whose paths crossed on a lonely road.

Epilogue

The week after the exhibition of Broadus Miller's body on the courthouse lawn, stung by the wave of criticism from North Carolina's leading newspapers, Beatrice Cobb announced in the *News-Herald* that she "had decided to try to help Morganton get over the effects" of the Miller case by refraining from any further commentary "on any of the circumstances connected with the affair." In the same issue of the paper, she made an exception to her new policy in order to defend Will Berry, in whose home Miller had boarded. Berry had been released from jail but continued to face hostility from local whites, and the editor asserted that he was "a quiet, orderly type of negro" who should be allowed to "live and work here unmolested."[1]

In the wake of Gladys Kincaid's murder and the manhunt for Miller, racial tensions simmered in an atmosphere of mutual fear and suspicion. One month after Kincaid's death, a white girl in neighboring Catawba County claimed two African American boys had jumped "at her from behind a clump of grape vines" as she walked along a road. Learning of the alleged incident, a local resident drove to the scene and found the two boys standing by the roadside hitchhiking. He invited them to get in his car — and then took them to the Hickory police chief. Though the boys "bitterly denied" the girl's accusations, they were jailed. As news of the arrests spread, Sheriff Hallyburton and his deputy Roscoe Cuthbertson drove from Morganton to Hickory and persuaded the police chief "to send the negroes to some other place for keeping." Later that fall, under unclear circumstances, Deputy Cuthbertson shot and killed an African American circus worker at the Morganton train station.[2]

The events of 1927 would live on in the collective memory of Burke County residents for decades to come, with a broadside poem and three ballads serving as a primary means of recollecting these events. The weekend following Broadus Miller's death, an amateur poet named Henry D. Holsclaw and his acquaintance Harry Lee Pennell penned a long narrative poem called "The Murder of Gladys Kincaid." In racially explicit language, the poem told how the Black man "was waiting to slay the poor child," and in a chilling image that evoked the frequent immolation of lynching victims, Holsclaw and Pennell declared that Miller "ought to have been burned the day he was born."

The poem concluded with a warning to African Americans "to stay in their place" and for "little white girls [to] be careful where you go." The authors sold numerous copies of their work as a printed broadside for twenty-five cents apiece. Some years later, Beatrice Cobb published it in the News-Herald, and many people clipped the poem from the paper and preserved it.[3]

The murder of the young mill worker also inspired three folk ballads—"The Tragedy of Gladys Kincaid," "Gladys Kincaid," and "The Dreadful Fate of Gladys Kincaid." The first two were the work of unknown lyricists who set their words to traditional melodies, while the third was composed in the fall of 1927 by the Morganton musicians Tim and Britt Poteat. These ballads were sung for many years in Burke County and the surrounding region. All of them used racially explicit language to describe Kincaid's death and the subsequent pursuit and killing of Broadus Miller. The folk song collector Mellinger Henry included "Gladys Kincaid" in his 1934 work *Songs Sung in the Southern Appalachians*. Two years earlier, Henry's informant had recorded an Avery County woman singing the ballad, with its concluding verse a stark summation of the way many local whites remembered Kincaid's death: "Oh, this beats all I ever heard / In all this wide, wide world / The idea of a Negro beast / Killing a poor white girl."[4]

The ballads portrayed the hunt for Broadus Miller as a heroic quest to bring a murderer to justice. As "The Tragedy of Gladys Kincaid" proclaimed, "Go tell it to the country / To both the black and white / That old Burke County / Shall e'er defend the right." However, a subsequent dispute cast an embarrassing light on one of the manhunters' main motivations. Three separate rewards had been offered for Miller dead or alive: $250 by Burke County, $250 by the state of North Carolina, and a total of about $1,500 by a group of private subscribers. Though Commodore Burleson single-handedly shot and killed Miller, he had been assisted in the manhunt by Fons Duckworth and two other companions. Two months after the killing, they sued Burleson and demanded a share of the rewards. The lawsuit dragged on for two years, with at least one mistrial and several continuances, and would not be settled until July 1929. Existent court records pertain only to the county reward, with the three plaintiffs dividing $150 and Burleson receiving $100. It is unclear what share—if any—the plaintiffs eventually received of the state and private rewards. The Morganton attorney John Mull represented the plaintiffs in their lawsuit. Mull also taught the adult Sunday school class at the First Methodist Church, where the Burlesons were members; following the lawsuit, Commodore Burleson never attended Sunday school again.[5]

Beatrice Cobb apparently viewed the lawsuit as an embarrassing coda to the Broadus Miller saga, and the *News-Herald* provided virtually no coverage of the prolonged court battle over the reward money. The Statesville *Landmark*, however, delighted in Burke County's embarrassment. In a caustic article titled "Man-Hunters Hunt Gold," the newspaper noted that after killing the outlaw, "the Commodore" had been acclaimed as "the fair-haired boy of the countryside," but this "rare and radiant character" had then been forced to wage "a stubborn defense of his right to hold as much as he wants to of the reward." The *Landmark* proposed a simple solution to the financial dispute: "The contestants are claiming distinction in a man-hunt. Let some worthy judge scatter the gold, for which they now war, over the countryside, set the man-hunters on a mark and bid them go, with a fair start and no favors. Then Burke will learn who best can scour the hills."[6]

In May 1929, the town council appointed Fons Duckworth to be Morganton's police chief. After the lawsuit was settled, Burleson and Duckworth reconciled, and Broadus Miller's killer rejoined the police force, on which he had previously served years earlier. While on duty, he regularly carried the .45 caliber pistol that he had used to kill Miller; on its wooden handle he had carved "Killed B. Miller. July 3, '27." At some point in the 1930s, the Morganton Klan disbanded, and for years afterward Burleson stored the local klavern's robes and hoods in his attic. He eventually quit the town police and began working in a furniture factory. When he died in 1967, a very brief obituary in the *News-Herald* described the man who had once been hailed as Burke County's hero as merely a "retired furniture worker," but the town's residents had not forgotten him. Among those attending his funeral was his neighbor Sam Ervin Jr., now a US senator. Commodore Burleson's grandson would gain fame among a new generation of hunters, developing and trademarking a camouflage pattern called Trebark that became the bestselling type of camouflage in the United States.[7]

After officially retiring from the bench in 1938, Judge Henry Grady—former Grand Dragon of the North Carolina Ku Klux Klan—continued to serve as a substitute superior court judge. During the early 1950s, now in his eighties, Grady oversaw more superior court sessions than any other judge in North Carolina. In the summer of 1951, he presided over the Hertford County trial of a middle-aged white man accused of raping a fifteen-year-old Black babysitter. The man had been indicted for unlawful carnal knowledge, but an all-white jury refused to convict him on even this lesser charge. The acquittal infuriated the former Klan leader, who from the bench denounced the jury's action as "a disgrace to the white race" that had been "based solely on the fact that the prosecuting witness was a colored girl and the defendant a white man." Judge Grady immediately ordered that the defendant be rearrested and charged with rape, and he told the prosecutor to seek a change of venue for the next trial in order "to get a jury with sense enough and character enough to do the right thing." The following week the judge wrote an open letter criticizing the exclusion of African Americans—who comprised over 60 percent of Hertford County's population—from juries in the county. Judge Grady noted that "the highest courts of the land, state and Federal, have declared in no uncertain terms that jurors must be drawn irrespective of race," and he announced that elsewhere in North Carolina, Blacks had proven to be "very satisfactory jurors."[8]

Long after all other states had abandoned the practice, North Carolina continued outlawing fugitives. Law enforcement officials viewed outlawry proclamations as a highly effective tool, for after being outlawed, many fugitives reversed course: instead of fleeing *from* the police, they came running *to* the police seeking protection. In 1953, after being outlawed in Guilford County for operating an illegal lottery scheme, a man quickly called his attorney and arranged to surrender; newspapers reported that he "was relieved to find sanctuary in the arms of the law." But the arms of the law dispensed death as well as protection. In 1965, a mentally ill Black man in Jones County was outlawed for walking around nude in public and threatening people with a gun. After police raided his house and killed him, a coroner's jury ruled the killing "death by suicidal means." In 1969, the North Carolina Judicial Council called for the repeal of the outlawry statute, warning that it "would not withstand scrutiny for constitutional defects." The recommendation garnered little support among state legislators, but in 1973 they did amend the statute, stripping magistrates of the power to issue outlawry proclamations. Henceforth, only judges could do so.[9]

In 1975, an African American named Arthur Parrish was outlawed for allegedly killing a grocery store owner in Durham. The manhunt for Parrish drew the attention of the nationally syndicated columnist Tom Tiede, who questioned "the propriety of allowing any farmer with a gun the right to plink away with impunity at human beings." Tiede's editorial appeared in newspapers throughout the country. Reacting to the negative publicity, North Carolina officials argued that outlawry proclamations rarely resulted in a fugitive's death. Over the previous decade, nineteen men had been proclaimed outlaws; two of the men had committed suicide, while the remaining seventeen had surrendered. However, the outcome of the Parrish case demonstrated the inherent danger in outlawing accused suspects. Captured by police and put on trial for murder, Arthur Parrish was acquitted; prior to his arrest, he could have been legally killed by any North Carolina citizen.[10]

The year before the manhunt for Parrish, a judge had outlawed Gerald Autry, a fugitive accused of rape, robbery, and assault. Autry promptly surrendered and was then convicted of the charges against him, but the American Civil Liberties Union used his case to challenge the constitutionality of North Carolina's outlawry statute. In October 1976, a federal district court ruled the statute violated the due process clause of the Fourteenth Amendment. No longer legally valid, the statute nevertheless remained on the books. In 1991, the Northampton County sheriff persuaded a district court judge to issue an outlawry proclamation against a jail escapee. The North Carolina attorney general hurriedly intervened and pronounced the proclamation invalid. When informed that the outlawry had been unconstitutional, the sheriff was unapologetic. "I'd do it again," he declared. "They turn themselves in right quick, knowing somebody might shoot them." Six years later, in 1997, the state legislature formally repealed the outlawry statute.[11]

Broadus Miller's native Greenwood County has irrevocably changed over the past century. Cotton is no longer commercially grown in the county, and the wooden shacks of tenant farmers have disappeared. In the mid-twentieth century, as passenger train service declined, the little depot community of Shoals Junction withered and ultimately vanished. Today, even the railroad tracks are gone, having been ripped from the ground and removed. Dunn Creek Baptist Church remains, however, and it continues to be a communal gathering place and the spiritual home of a large congregation. Near the church, spread over a long gentle knoll, is the cemetery where Reverend James Selden Maddox is buried. Next to him lies Emma Walker Maddox, whose first husband, Reverend James Walker, was gunned down and killed by a white mill worker in Ware Shoals. For decades after they moved to North Carolina, Broadus Miller's family maintained ties with the church they left behind. When Miller's adoptive mother Alpha Walker passed away in 1948, her body was returned to Greenwood County and laid to rest at Dunn Creek. In 1991, the last surviving member of Miller's immediate family—his ninety-one-year-old stepbrother Howard Robinson—died in Asheville; almost seventy years after leaving South Carolina, he too was brought back and buried in the Dunn Creek cemetery.[12]

In 1994, South Carolina finally closed the old state penitentiary in Columbia; the prison buildings were demolished and eventually replaced by an exclusive residential and commercial complex. However, a century after

Miller's incarceration, the state's prisons continue to be the dumping ground for mentally ill offenders. In 2005, an advocacy group launched a class action lawsuit on their behalf. For more than eight years, the South Carolina Department of Corrections filed delaying motions and contested all court-ordered evidentiary disclosures. Finally, in January 2014, the case was adjudicated by Judge J. Michael Baxley. In his ruling, the judge described a hellish world in which mentally ill inmates "are exposed to a disproportionate use of force" and are often kept in solitary confinement for years, locked naked in small cells "with the blood and feces of previous occupants smeared on the floor and walls." Judge Baxley ordered South Carolina to begin providing adequate treatment for prisoners suffering from mental illness, emphasizing the danger of discharging "untreated seriously mentally ill individuals from prison into the general population"—a Cassandra-like warning that seems destined to be ignored. Attorneys for the state immediately filed an appeal, and the court case will likely drag on for years to come.[13]

The historic Burke County courthouse remains at the center of present-day Morganton. However, all judicial affairs now take place in a modern courthouse, a drab and unremarkable building a block away—an architectural trend indicative of a greater evolution, from a judicial system that strove to appear imposingly majestic to a modern bureaucracy that has become seemingly mundane. Carefully cleaned and restored in the 1990s, the Confederate monument still stands on the courthouse lawn where Broadus Miller's body was dragged and displayed. Nearly six decades after Miller helped dig its foundations, the Franklin Pierce Tate House was added to the National Register of Historic Places, a proud example of West Union Street's residential mansions. On East Union Street, the hosiery mill in which Gladys Kincaid worked—Garrou Knitting Mill—eventually became Premier Hosiery and remained in operation until the mid-1990s. Renovated in 2001, the former mill now houses the Morganton city hall.[14]

Until her death in 1959, Beatrice Cobb continued to be Morganton's leading civic booster. The *News-Herald* editor maintained her keen interest in politics, serving on the Democratic National Committee from 1934 to 1952. Deeply conservative on many social issues, she remained a generous patron of the local Black community, leaving a will that included an annual legacy to an African American church. Morganton native Sam Ervin Jr. would achieve national fame as a US senator when he chaired the Senate Select Committee investigating Watergate. In 1980, Ervin penned a tribute to a former Burke County law officer in which he briefly described the pursuit of Broadus Miller, calling it "the largest manhunt in western North Carolina's history." Though the manhunt had lasted twelve days, from June 21 to July 3, Ervin inexplicably claimed it had been a three-day affair. He portrayed Miller's alleged possession of a gun as incontestable fact and did not mention the subsequent exhibition of Miller's body.[15]

Rarely discussed in public forums, the events of 1927 were often recounted in private conversations. Over time, these oral histories expanded and exaggerated the horrors of what had occurred, claiming Gladys Kincaid had been raped as well as murdered and that Broadus Miller's body had been dragged by automobile on the streets around the courthouse square—claims that are not supported by any contemporary evidence. In 1977, the local historian Edward Phifer Jr. published a comprehensive history of Burke County that included a three-sentence summary of the Broadus Miller case. Whereas Sam Ervin Jr. grossly understated the length of the manhunt, Phifer wrote that the outlawed fugitive had been hunted "for several weeks." His brief summation of the case was otherwise factually accurate. Phifer's father had been the attending physician for the mortally injured Gladys Kincaid and had performed her autopsy, and the historian noted that Kincaid had been "brutally murdered" but did not state she had been raped. In Phifer's words, Miller had been "shot on sight," his dead body then "exhibited on the south side of the public square as a continuous line of spectators filed by."[16]

Decades after the spectacle on the Morganton courthouse lawn, some residents were still disturbed by what they had witnessed. In 1960, a former schoolteacher named H. Clay Ferree wrote a brief article on the Broadus Miller case for a Winston-Salem newspaper. Ferree had been present when Commodore Burleson and his companions arrived with Miller's body, and the memory of seeing men drag the body across the lawn still haunted him. "I saw the bullet holes in his side, the seared and broken skin where the taut rope had cut his legs, and the blood that smeared his nose and mouth," he recounted. "His work shoes had been completely worn out from constant running and clamoring over the hills and fields, and he had taken old rags and bound them around cracked and bleeding feet." In 1975, the writer John Alex Mull—the son of attorney John Mull—published *Tales of Old Burke*, which included a three-page chapter on the manhunt for Miller. As a seventeen-year-old boy, Mull had been walking home from church "when a car came tearing around the corner at the courthouse, screached [sic] to a halt, and several men jumped out with guns. They opened the back door of the car and dragged a man out by his feet, which were wrapped in bloody rags." Nearly half a century later, Mull still marveled at the fervor of the "angry mob" that had wanted to desecrate a corpse. "It makes me wonder just how thick our veneer of civilization really is," he reflected.[17]

On that Sunday in July 1927, eleven-year-old Harry Wilson Jr. had also been at church, but he left after Sunday school and loitered around the courthouse square, hoping to witness further developments in the ongoing manhunt. His wish was realized with the arrival of the triumphant bounty hunters. In the early 1990s, first as a newspaper article and then as a brief chapter in a privately published memoir, Wilson recorded his still vivid memory of what he had seen. "Deputies and police dragged the black man's body from the car, feet first," recalled Wilson. "He was naked except a small loincloth and enormous wrappings on his feet, evidently made from cutting up his shirt and trousers to protect his feet. . . . His head bounced on the paving stones while being dragged to the courthouse door. His body fluids were draining from his nose and mouth, and the results of shots were plainly seen in the chest." Wilson's graphic description upset some of his fellow townspeople, who grumbled that the way Miller's body had been handled was a contentious and racially inflammatory issue, better ignored than openly addressed.[18]

During the 1970s, the ethnologist Claudia Gould lived in Morganton and interviewed many of the town's residents. She found that the Broadus Miller case was "a famous local event," but African Americans and whites remembered the case in starkly different ways. Whites still recalled the murder of young Gladys Kincaid, citing it as a blunt warning to their daughters to stay away from Black men. African Americans had not forgotten how every Black resident of the town had been targeted in the wake of Kincaid's death. Nor had they forgotten how white churchgoers spent a Sunday afternoon rejoicing over a dead body on the courthouse lawn. "Some people are such good Christians they go to church every Sunday—twice every Sunday and Wednesday go to prayer meeting," a local Black man told Gould. "But they've got so much hate. Now how could you hate somebody and be a Christian?"[19]

Memories of 1927 reverberated into the twenty-first century and continued to be racially divisive. As a ten-year-old child residing on Bouchelle Street, Marjorie Fleming experienced the inflamed anger of local white residents following Kincaid's murder. Eighty years later, she still remembered how frightened and apprehensive her family had felt. One of Fleming's relatives was Will Berry, who spent two weeks in jail threatened by potential lynch mobs, and after his release from custody faced ongoing harassment. "It wasn't right," Fleming plaintively recalled, "the way they treated poor Mr. Berry." Commodore Burleson's son Charles was three years old when

FIGURE E.1 Gravestone of Gladys Kincaid at Catawba Valley Baptist Church. (Photograph by Halley Burleson.)

his father killed Broadus Miller. After a long and successful business career, Charles Burleson retired and moved back to his hometown, where he enjoyed recounting stories about his father's actions as manhunter and Klansman. "Daddy was my hero," he declared in 2007. "He did his duty, that's the way I feel about it."[20]

When Gladys Kincaid's mother died in 1958, her obituary appeared prominently on the front page of the *News-Herald*, but Gladys's name and the reason for Mary Jane Kincaid's prominence were left unstated; longtime Burke

County residents knew and did not have to be reminded. For decades after their sister's murder, Gladys Kincaid's siblings continued living in Morganton. Kincaid's sister Elizabeth was six years old in 1927; eighty years later, she recalled the horrible fear she had experienced in the wake of Gladys's murder. When interviewed in 2007, ninety-year-old Cecil Kincaid still felt a lingering grief over his sister's violent death. He also remembered the lesson Mary Jane Kincaid had taught her surviving children. "My mother told us not to go around hating Black people," he recounted, "because there were good and bad Black people, the same as everybody else."[21]

The farmhouse in which the Kincaids lived has long since disappeared; the area where it stood is now a large municipal park with trails and baseball fields. On a high bluff on the opposite bank of the Catawba, about two miles upriver from the park, is Catawba Valley Baptist Church. The present-day church is a large, modern brick building. Behind the church is a well-kept, unfenced cemetery, and in the corner of the cemetery, next to the church parking lot, is the small gravestone of Gladys Kincaid (see figure E.1). The gravestone's inscription is still legible, but slowly fading, and the passage of time has eroded the face of the lamb carved on top of the stone.

Acknowledgments

I owe special thanks to two people—one at the University of Georgia, the other at Appalachian State University—without whom this book would not have come to fruition. As all his former students know, having John Inscoe as an advisor meant being the recipient of innumerable acts of kindness and generosity, for which I will always be grateful. For many years, Sandy Ballard has been an unfailing source of encouragement, support, and wise counsel, and in several ways her assistance proved essential in completing this project.

In addition, I am indebted to several other people at UGA and App State. In Athens, James Cobb's extensive knowledge and keen critical eye were invaluable. I also received helpful feedback from Kathleen Clark and lynching scholar E. M. Beck. Stephen Berry's emphasis on the art of writing was a continual inspiration, and my cohort of fellow Appalachianists—including Sam McGuire, Luke Manget, James Owen, and Kate Dahlstrand—helped create a collegial atmosphere. Over the course of many years, I have benefited from conversations with and feedback from numerous people in Boone. I started researching the Broadus Miller case in 2006 as a graduate student in a seminar taught by the late Edwin "Chip" Arnold, who was an exemplary professor. Bruce Stewart generously shared research material on the North Carolina Klan, and an essay of mine on the Miller case appeared in a book that he edited, *Blood in the Hills*, for which he provided excellent nuts-and-bolts advice about writing. A good friend and former colleague, Jonathan Bradshaw, was a regular hiking companion on many a trek through the mountains where the 1927 manhunt took place. Several other individuals in Boone assisted my research by sharing information and/or feedback, including Fred Hay, Karl Campbell, and Adam Griffey.

I first learned of the Broadus Miller case from reading Bruce Baker's essay "North Carolina Lynching Ballads," and when I contacted him about it, he kindly sent me a copy of his research notes on the case. Former district attorney Tom Rusher was one of my first sources of information on outlawry in North Carolina and provided me with a copy of the state's outlawry statute. I have presented on various topics relating to this book at conferences of the Appalachian Studies Association and the Society of Appalachian Historians and have enjoyed conversations with and questions posed by many conference participants, including Steve Nash, Tom Lee, Anne Woodford, David Whisnant, Bob Hutton, Richard Starnes, Darin Waters, and Trevor McKenzie.

In many respects this work is a story about Morganton, and I could not have written it without the help of several present-day and former residents of the town. Speaking with Gladys Kincaid's younger brother and sister, Cecil Kincaid and Elizabeth Kincaid Conley, made me keenly aware of the enduring grief caused by their sister's death, and I am grateful to them for talking with me about such a painful episode in their family's history. I am indebted to Commodore Burleson's children—Margaret

Burleson Crumley, Charles Burleson, and Pat Burleson Howell—who were generous with their time and very candid in sharing information about their father. Gail Benfield, Dottie Ervin, and Laurie Johnston of the North Carolina Room in the Burke County Public Library were very helpful with locating research material, and Jeannie Logan arranged and facilitated interviews with Morganton residents. Marjorie Fleming was ten years old in 1927; eighty years later, she still vividly remembered the events of that summer, and speaking with her made an indelible impression on me. Ronald Huffman generously provided me with copies of the photographs taken on the Morganton courthouse square in 1927. (It should be noted that Mr. Huffman did not condone the treatment of Miller's body, but recognized the historical importance of the photos.) Claudia Gould shared with me the ethnographic field notes of her discussions with Morganton residents. Other Burke County residents—including Bobbie Dula-Wakefield, Carl Evans, Willette Chambers, Terry Helton, Charles Tate Jr., and Charles Graham—also provided valuable information, as did members of the Burke County Historical Society. The documentary filmmaker Beth Davison organized a panel discussion of the Miller case at Morganton's historic courthouse, where I participated in a thought-provoking roundtable discussion with Leslie McKesson and Mary Charlotte Safford.

In the summer of 2007, Sandra Coffey of the Collettsville Historical Society interviewed several elderly residents of Caldwell County, North Carolina, preserving the last surviving memories of the large manhunt that had taken place in the county eighty years earlier. She then transcribed these interviews and sent me copies of the transcripts. Within weeks of conducting the interviews, she was diagnosed with cancer and passed away soon thereafter. Her enthusiasm for the project matched my own, and I regret that I never had the chance to meet and thank her personally. In 2014, George Rush III—the former mayor of Ware Shoals, South Carolina—gave me a guided tour of the region around Shoals Junction, which proved essential in reconstructing the story of Broadus Miller's boyhood home. Mr. Rush shared his extensive knowledge of the region's history and arranged interviews with local residents, including present-day members of Dunn Creek Baptist Church, and his kind hospitality was one of the highlights of my research. Lifelong Ashford resident Buford Franklin grew up only a few hundred yards from the scene of Broadus Miller's death; he had a keen memory and was very insightful, and I am glad that I had the opportunity to speak with him before he passed. Ethel Philyaw Crump shared with me her memories of the 1927 manhunt, and Clyde Dula's daughter Brenda Gail Pitts supplied information about her father.

During my research, I have been greatly assisted by various librarians and courthouse clerks. In South Carolina, I was helped by the staff of the following institutions: Greenwood County Public Library; Ware Shoals Public Library; South Carolina Room of the Anderson County Public Library; Anderson County Clerk of Court; Greenwood County Clerk of Court; the Thomas Cooper and South Caroliniana libraries at the University of South Carolina; South Carolina State Archives. In Georgia, the staff of the University of Georgia Libraries, including the Richard B. Russell Library for Political Research and Studies, were very helpful. In North Carolina, the staff of the following institutions facilitated my research: D. H. Ramsey Library at the University of North

Carolina Asheville; Old Buncombe County Genealogical Society; Buncombe County Register of Deeds; Buncombe County Special Collections at Asheville's Pack Memorial Library; Iredell County Public Library; Wilson Library at the University of North Carolina, especially the North Carolina Collection and the Southern Historical Collection; Rubenstein Rare Book and Manuscript Library at Duke University; North Carolina State Archives; North Carolina State Historic Preservation Office; Z. Smith Reynolds Library at Wake Forest University; Charlotte Public Library; Yancey County Public Library; Belk Library at Appalachian State University, especially the W. L. Eury Appalachian Collection; Burke County Historical Society; Burke County Clerk of Court.

I value the fine work done by editor Lucas Church and everyone else at the University of North Carolina Press. As a reader of the manuscript, Dan Pierce offered insightful and encouraging feedback that was much appreciated. I also thank the anonymous second reader for thought-provoking commentary that made me reflect further on the type of book I wished to create. At Appalachian State, Leo Flores and Bethany Mannon helped me find funding from the College of Arts and Sciences for maps to illustrate the book. Cartographer Josh Platt did a stellar job in creating these maps, and photographer Halley Burleson provided a much-needed illustration.

Finally, and most importantly, I am forever indebted to my late parents, Wayne and Helen Young. Born in the Appalachians during the Great Depression, and growing up with circumscribed educational and economic opportunities, they worked hard and never hesitated to sacrifice for the sake of their children.

Notes

Prologue

1. Phifer, *Burke*, 266; Corbitt, *Formation of North Carolina Counties*, 42–48; North Carolina Bar Association, *Centennial Celebration*, 64.

2. Phifer, *Burke*, 266; 1920 and 1930 censuses, Burke County, NC, Morganton township; "The Garrou Mills" and "Garrou Knitting Mills," Industries vertical file, Burke County Public Library, Morganton, NC; "Regarding Will Berry," *News-Herald* (Morganton, NC), July 14, 1927; Baker, "Lynching Ballads in North Carolina," 45.

3. "Negro Attacks White Girl," *News-Herald*, June 23, 1927; Holsclaw and Pennell, "Murder of Gladys Kincaid"; Harry L. Griffin, "Hundreds Join Grim Hunt for Assailant of Girl in Burke," *Charlotte (NC) Observer*, June 23, 1927; "Cupid-Up-to-Date Will Be Presented Tuesday," *News-Herald*, June 23, 1927; "Morganton Negro Attacked Girl in Sight of Three Homes," *Winston-Salem (NC) Journal*, June 28, 1927; A. L. Stockton, "Citizens Continue Hunt for Negro Who Killed Little Morganton Girl," *Greensboro (NC) Daily News*, June 24, 1927.

4. "Negro Attacks White Girl"; "Suspected Slayer of Girl, 15, Caught," *Asheville (NC) Times*, June 22, 1927; Johnston Avery, "Extensive Search Is Being Made for Morganton Slayer," *Hickory (NC) Daily Record*, June 22, 1927; Gladys Kincaid death certificate, July 2, 1927, Burke County, Morganton, #136.

5. "Morganton Negro Attacked Girl"; Cecil Kincaid, telephone interview with author, June 28, 2007; Stockton, "Citizens Continue Hunt"; "Negro Attacks White Girl"; "Suspected Slayer of Girl."

6. "Officials Doubt Negro Taken in Chatham County Is Broadus Miller, Wanted Outlaw," *Winston-Salem Journal*, July 1, 1927; Griffin, "Hundreds Join Grim Hunt"; "Morganton Negro Attacked Girl"; "Young Woman Is Dead following Brutal Attack," *Bee* (Danville, VA), June 22, 1927.

7. Frank Smethurst, "Determined Search for Negro Slayer of Young Morganton Girl Futile," *News and Observer* (Raleigh, NC), June 23, 1927; Griffin, "Hundreds Join Grim Hunt"; "Negro Attacks White Girl"; "Soldiers Hunt for Negro," *Raleigh (NC) Times*, June 23, 1927; "$500 Reward for Capture of Young Girl's Assailant," *Gastonia (NC) Daily Gazette*, June 22, 1927; "Suspected Slayer of Girl"; Mull, *Tales of Old Burke*, 94.

8. Carl Evans, telephone interview with author, July 3, 2007; Marjorie Fleming, personal interview with author, June 26, 2007; Terry Helton, telephone interview with author, May 1, 2007; Smethurst, "Determined Search."

9. Griffin, "Hundreds Join Grim Hunt"; Smethurst, "Determined Search"; Baker, "Lynching Ballads in North Carolina," 46; "Negro Attacks White Girl."

10. Avery, "Extensive Search"; "New Chief of Police," *News-Herald*, May 19, 1927; "Lynching in Prospect in Burke," *Landmark* (Statesville, NC), June 23, 1927; "$500

Reward"; "Young Woman Is Dead"; "Peace Comes after Wild Day at Bridgewater," *Hickory Daily Record*, June 23, 1927.

11. Burke County Historical Society, *Heritage of Burke County*, 312; "Morganton Negro May Be in This County," *Cleveland Star* (Shelby, NC), June 24, 1927; L. J. Hampton, "Manhunt Goes on in Burke," *Winston-Salem Journal*, June 25, 1927; "Broadus Miller Still at Large," *Index-Journal* (Greenwood, SC), June 25, 1927. For national coverage of the case, see, for example, "2,000 Armed Men Search for Negro," *Atlanta Constitution*, June 23, 1927; "Mob of 2,000 Seeks Girl's Negro Slayer," *Washington Post*, June 22, 1927.

Chapter One

1. "Reasons for the Organization of the Proposed New Greenwood County," c. 1897, *Proclamations, Politics, and Commerce: Broadsides from the Colonial Era to the Present*, South Caroliniana Library, Digital Collections, accessed February 2, 2014, https://digital.library.sc.edu/collections/broadsides-from-the-colonial-era-to-the-present-at-the-south-caroliniana-library/; Bowen, *Greenwood County*; 1900 census, Greenwood County, SC. The county's population in 1900 was 28,343, including 18,906 African Americans.

2. Lesh et al., *Soil Survey of Greenwood County*, 1–2; Bowen, *Greenwood County*, 165; Wade, *Greenwood County and Its Railroads*, 16, 118–121, 133; Edgar, *South Carolina*, 448; *Report of the Railroad Commission*, 152; "Store at Shoals Junction Is Robbed," *Daily Journal* (Greenwood, SC), January 28, 1915.

3. 1880 census, Abbeville County, SC, Long Cane township, enumeration district #17, dwelling #128; 1900 census, Greenwood County, SC, Walnut Grove township, enumeration district #71, dwelling #177; 1910 census, Greenwood County, SC, Walnut Grove township, enumeration district #98, dwelling #79; 1920 census, Greenwood County, SC.

4. 1910 census, Greenwood County, SC, Walnut Grove township, enumeration district #98; Mays, *Born to Rebel*, 6–7, 9; Megginson, *African American Life*, 504n14; "Farm Labor Law Unconstitutional," *Progressive Farmer* (Raleigh, NC), June 6, 1907; Paterson, *Wage-Payment Legislation*, 125–126; "Shooting near Greenwood," *Herald and News* (Newberry, SC), April 3, 1908. The 1910 census of the Walkers' district lists a population of 304 whites, 416 Blacks, and 15 "mulattos." Twenty-seven of the 55 white households were tenants, as were 69 of the 78 Black and "mulatto" households. Of the nine African American families who neither rented nor sharecropped, only four of their farms were owned outright; the rest were mortgaged.

5. Wright, *Old South, New South*, 81–123; Tindall, *Emergence of the New South*, 125; South Carolina Department of Archives and History, *African American Historic Places*, 36; Kane and Keeton, *In Those Days*, 18, 23; "Past Monthly Weather Data for Greenwood, SC, 1900–2012," National Weather Service, accessed January 22, 2014, http://weather-warehouse.com; "A Sad Accident in Greenwood," *Keowee Courier* (Pickens, SC), January 2, 1918; Beardsley, *History of Neglect*, 11–41. Greenwood County began recording death certificates in 1915; the next few years show several dozen deaths attributed to pellagra, dysentery, and malnutrition.

6. Mays, *Born to Rebel*, 20–21, 32–33; 1910 census, Greenwood County, SC, Walnut Grove township, enumeration district #98, dwelling #79; 1920 census, Greenwood County, SC, Walnut Grove township, enumeration district #91, dwelling #121; 1930 census, Buncombe County, NC, Asheville township, enumeration district #11-1, #134 Beaumont Street; 1940 census, Buncombe County, NC, Asheville township, ward #1, block #128, #134 Beaumont Street; "Howard Robinson" (obituary), *Index-Journal* (Greenwood SC), February 11, 1991; Hester Lee Walker death certificate, March 9, 1984, Buncombe County, NC, v. 9, #9010.

7. South Carolina General Assembly, *Acts and Joint Resolutions 1904*, 509; Watson, *Greenwood County Sketches*, 130, 355, 357; 1860 census (slave schedule), Abbeville County, SC; 1880 census, Abbeville County, SC, Cokesbury township, dwelling #441; "Algary News," *Index-Journal*, March 21, 1919; "H. L. Rasor Dies at His Home," *Index-Journal*, March 22, 1940; "Clarence Agnew, Shoals Junction Resident, Dies," *Index-Journal*, April 21, 1951; "Tribute Paid W. E. Algary," *Index-Journal*, June 25, 1941.

8. "A Day of Remembrance in Ware Shoals," *Index-Journal*, August 9, 2004; "History of the Dunn Creek Baptist Church," photocopy in possession of the author; Myers and Sharpless, "Of the Least and the Most," 61; Newby, *Black Carolinians*, 146–153; "Howard Robinson"; Caldwell, *History of the American Negro*, 24–26. Caldwell erroneously gives Reverend Maddox's middle name as "Samuel."

9. 1910 census, Greenwood County, SC, Walnut Grove township, district #98, dwelling #79; Mayfield, *School Law of South Carolina*, 5; South Carolina Superintendent of Education, *Forty-Third Annual Report 1911*, 392–405; 1910 census, Greenwood County, SC, Walnut Grove township, enumeration district #98, Bramlett Road, dwelling #8; Hudson, *Entangled by White Supremacy*, 223–241. Walnut Grove township encompassed several school districts; Miller did not live in the school district named Walnut Grove, but in the Algary district, which had two Black schools, both taught by Black women in their early twenties. 1910 census, Greenwood County, SC, Walnut Grove township, enumeration district #98, dwellings #63 and #118. In 1916, the district's two white schools consolidated into a single facility. "Three More Schools Consolidate in County," *Daily Journal* (Greenwood, SC), February 22, 1916.

10. South Carolina Superintendent of Education, *Forty-Third Annual Report 1911*, 115, 398; South Carolina Superintendent of Education, *Forty-First Annual Report 1909*, 57; Newby, *Black Carolinians*, 88–91; Megginson, *African American Life*, 305–306.

11. South Carolina Superintendent of Education, *Forty-Third Annual Report 1911*, 116; "Replies to Taft," *Manning (SC) Times*, January 27, 1909; Holm, *Holm's Race Assimilation*, 121; Simkins, *Pitchfork Ben Tillman*, 402–403; Kantrowitz, *Ben Tillman*, 219; West, *From Yeoman to Redneck*, 180; South Carolina General Assembly, *Report of State Officers, 1910*, 126; Simon, *Fabric of Defeat*, 31; Newby, *Black Carolinians*, 83–85; "Educated People Won't Work, Says Cole Blease," *News-Herald* (Morganton, NC), July 1, 1926.

12. Lesh et al., *Soil Survey of Greenwood County*, 5; Ford, *Origins of Southern Radicalism*, 58–92; Woodward, *Origins of the New South*, 181; Ransom and Sutch, *One Kind of Freedom*, 151–168; Mays, *Born to Rebel*, 6.

13. Brooks, *Cotton*, 130–160; Mays, *Born to Rebel*, 26.

14. 1920 census, Greenwood County, SC, Walnut Grove township, enumeration district #91, dwelling #121; Brooks, *Cotton*, 28–30, 160–166; Mays, *Born to Rebel*, 3, 6, 8; Tindall, *Emergence of the New South*, 430; Kirby, *Rural Worlds Lost*, 68.

15. Mays, *Born to Rebel*, 5; Kane and Keeton, *In Those Days*, 23–25; Brooks, *Cotton*, 258. See also North Carolina State Board of Public Welfare, *Capital Punishment in North Carolina*, 92, which details the history of a Black man who grew up on an upstate South Carolina tenant farm.

16. "Algary News"; Ellenberg, *Mule South to Tractor South*, 63; State Agricultural and Mechanical Society of South Carolina, *State Agricultural Society*, 127, 129; Kane and Keeton, *In Those Days*, 25.

17. Tindall, *South Carolina Negroes*, 88–89, 256–259; R. R. Tolbert, "The Election Tragedy at Phoenix," *Independent* (New York), November 24, 1898; Newby, *Black Carolinians*, 36–42; Finnegan, *Deed So Accursed*, 96–99; Hoyt, *Phoenix Riot*; Mays, *Born to Rebel*, 1; Wells, "Phoenix Election Riot," 58–69; Kleinshmidt, "Phoenix Riot," 27–31; Watson, *Greenwood County Sketches*, 119–122; Bowen, *Greenwood County*, 317–321; "No Negro Domination," "Virtuous Public Sentiment," "A Candid View," "The Closing Chapters," *Greenwood (SC) Index*, November 17, 1898.

18. Wilk, "Phoenix Riot and Memories," 29–55; Wallace Putnam Reed, "Old South on Deck," *Independent* (New York), November 24, 1898.

Chapter Two

1. Carlton, *Mill and Town*, 8–11, 29–31, 50–51, 114–115; South Carolina Department of Agriculture, Commerce and Immigration, *Handbook of South Carolina*, 566; Wade, *Greenwood County and Its Railroads*, 25; Tindall, *Emergence of the New South*, 21; Woodward, *Strange Career of Jim Crow*, 98; "Fugitive Over Two Years, at Last Arrested," *Daily Journal* (Greenwood, SC), January 26, 1916; Kane and Keeton, *In Those Days*, 49; "Ware Shoals," *Evening Index* (Greenwood, SC), May 4, 1916; Flink, *America Adopts the Automobile*, 167.

2. Myers and Sharpless, "Of the Least and the Most," 70; Kane and Keeton, *In Those Days*, 65; "A Warning to Housekeepers," *Press and Banner* (Abbeville, SC), November 17, 1915.

3. Mays, *Born to Rebel*, 14; "A Hanging Postponed," *Times and Democrat* (Orangeburg, SC), July 31, 1908; "Killed at Hot Supper," *Bamberg (SC) Herald*, October 6, 1910; "Quarrel Results in Death of Negro," *Evening Index*, April 29, 1918; "Negro Killing Sunday," *Press and Banner*, March 29, 1920; "Two Negroes Dead, Three in Jail," *Edgefield (SC) Advertiser*, September 13, 1916.

4. Kane and Keeton, *In Those Days*, 65–69; Butterfield, *All God's Children*, 62–63; Abbott and Seroff, *Out of Sight*, 205–210. The term "hot supper" was also used for more formal fundraising dinners held by some churches and civic organizations; see Megginson, *African American Life*, 306.

5. "Hot Suppers," *Daily Journal*, February 6, 1901; "Killed at New Market," *Daily Journal*, October 2, 1901; "The News of Troy," *Daily Journal*, October 5, 1910; "The Hot Supper Season," *Daily Journal*, October 2, 1911; "Negro Hot Suppers," *Daily Journal*, April 16, 1914.

6. "The County Campaign," *Greenwood (SC) Index*, August 23, 1900; "Dispensary Conditions in the State Reviewed," *Daily Journal*, August 2, 1905; Heath and Kinard, "Prohibition in South Carolina," 118–132; "Now Let Laurens Wheel into Line," *Laurens (SC) Advertiser*, January 3, 1906; Christensen, "State Dispensaries of South Carolina," 76; "S.C. Liquor Laws Stand as Are," *Evening Index*, October 18, 1916; "Liquor Too High, Drinks Extracts," *Index-Journal* (Greenwood, SC), November 22, 1920; "Greenwood Negro Killed," *Keowee Courier* (Pickens, SC), April 15, 1903; "George Lark Gets Life Term for Murder," *Daily Journal*, October 31, 1914; "Amos Gets in Bad," *Evening Index*, June 12, 1913; "Officers Got Their Quarry at the Quarry," *Daily Journal*, December 30, 1914; "County Jail about Full of Wouldbes and Hasbeens," *Evening Index*, May 1, 1913; "'Gallon a Month' Bill Will Soon Be a Law," *Daily Journal*, February 23, 1915; "Gallon-a-Month Law Now Enforced in this County," *Daily Journal*, March 13, 1915; "Liquor Measures Not Conflicting," *Watchman and Southron* (Sumter, SC), March 14, 1917; Wade, *Greenwood County and Its Railroads*, 218; South Carolina General Assembly, *Reports and Resolutions*, January 11, 1916, 4:438–446, 462; "Judge Johnson in Favor of Prohibition," *Edgefield Advertiser*, January 24, 1917.

7. "Pistol Toting," *Daily Journal*, June 12, 1907; "Sermon from the Bench," *The State* (Columbia, SC), reprinted in *Anderson (SC) Intelligencer*, April 11, 1900; South Carolina General Assembly, *Acts and Joint Resolutions 1902*, 1093; Bethea, *Code of Laws of South Carolina*, 1912, 2:263; "Big Day's Work in Senate," *The State*, reprinted in *Herald and News* (Newberry, SC), February 15, 1901; "Here Is the Law," *Laurens Advertiser*, August 13, 1902. South Carolina's pistol ban remained in effect until at least the 1970s ("Gun Laws Aren't the Answer," *Morning News* [Florence, SC], June 16, 1972), but any serious effort to enforce the law ended long before then.

8. Mays, *Born to Rebel*, 12–13; "Pistol Toting," *Daily Journal*, June 12, 1907; "Pistol Toting," *Daily Journal*, February 1, 1905; "Grand Jury Presentment," *Evening Index*, February 27, 1908.

9. Cottrol and Diamond, "Second Amendment," 355; West, *From Yeoman to Redneck*, 152–157; "Conspiracy Is the Charge," *Daily Journal*, September 16, 1908; "Rest of Them Out Now," *Evening Index*, October 1, 1908; "12 Negroes Held for Conspiracy," "Negro Conspiracy a Fake?," *Herald and News*, September 18, 1908.

10. "Guilty Go Unpunished," *Edgefield Advertiser*, September 13, 1916; "Will Be Hung," *Times and Democrat*, March 20, 1908; Burke, "Pink Franklin v. South Carolina," 265–302.

11. Newby, *Black Carolinians*, 185–190; Edgar, *South Carolina*, 480–481; Williams, *Torchbearers of Democracy*, 226; "Negro Desperado Captured Friday," *Press and Banner*, April 26, 1920; "Law Enforcement Conference Held," *Edgefield Advertiser*, July 23, 1919; "Causes of Crime Discussed Here," *Press and Banner*, August 12, 1919.

12. "Fight at Greenwood," *Keowee Courier*, July 10, 1918. Sixteen years before the brawl at the fairgrounds, John McLaurin, then a senator, had engaged in a fistfight with fellow South Carolina senator Ben Tillman on the US Senate floor, for which both men were censured. Butler and Wolff, *United States Senate Election*, 269–271.

13. Eichholz, *Red Book*, 594; Greenwood County, SC death certificates, 1915–1920, in *South Carolina, Death Records, 1821–1960*, Ancestry.com; "Charlie Luquire Kills 2, Wounds Another and Takes Own Life," *Daily Journal*, October 9, 1916; "Three Men

Killed, Fourth Is Wounded Saturday Night," *Greenwood Index*, October 11, 1916; "Our Shame and Disgrace," "Dr. Smith Preaches on Saturday's Tragedy," *Daily Journal*, October 9, 1916; "Verdict of Jury in Trout Killing," *Evening Index*, August 1, 1918; "Liquor Quarrel Caused Killing," *Index-Journal*, July 13, 1920; "Killed Wife and Wounded Mother-in-Law," *Keowee Courier*, August 8, 1917; "Young Man Killed at Ware Shoals," *Press and Banner*, December 17, 1920; "Held Killing Justifiable," *Keowee Courier*, December 22, 1920.

14. Greenwood County, SC death certificates, 1915–1920; "Mysterious Murder in Greenwood," *Laurens Advertiser*, May 19, 1915; "Charge Ike Jones Gave Garner Pistol," *Index-Journal*, June 17, 1919; South Carolina General Assembly, *Report of State Officers, January 13, 1920*, 1:130; "T. T. Cromer Fined and Sentenced," *Index-Journal*, October 30, 1919; "Killing of Years Ago Is Recalled," *Index-Journal*, November 1, 1925; "Brief City News," *Index-Journal*, April 18, 1920; "Walter Burns Is Found Guilty of Murder," *Daily Journal*, July 1, 1915; 1910 census, Abbeville County, SC, Long Cane township, enumeration district #19, dwelling #157; South Carolina Attorney General's Office, *Annual Report 1915*, 312–313; "Escaped Murderer Got Lost in Woods and Was Captured," *Index-Journal*, February 3, 1921; "Will Sherard Is Wanted," *Daily Journal*, March 9, 1915; "Will Sherard in Jail," *Daily Journal*, March 10, 1915; "Sessions Court Is Now Sitting," *Greenwood Index*, October 28, 1915; "Albert Tolbert to Die Friday December 10th," *Evening Index*, November 4, 1915. From 1915 through 1920, the only recorded Greenwood County homicide in which the assailant's race is unknown is the May 8, 1920, death of Lula Humphries, a thirty-seven-year-old Black farmworker whose death certificate described her as the gunshot victim of a homicide.

15. Greenwood County, SC death certificates, 1915–1920; "Killing Thursday Afternoon," *Evening Index*, January 21, 1915; "Tragedy Follows a Hot Supper and Cake Walk," *Daily Journal*, March 22, 1915; "Claim Woman Was Killed by Husband," *Daily Journal*, January 31, 1917; "Negro Kills Wife," *Press and Banner*, October 12, 1917; "Another Negro Shooting Scrape in County, Assailant Is Caught," *Press and Banner*, July 4, 1919; "Jealousy Causes a Negro Killing," *Index-Journal*, November 30, 1919.

16. Greenwood County, SC death certificates, 1915–1920; Butterfield, *All God's Children*, 62–63; "Callison Was Scene of Killing on Saturday," *Daily Journal*, November 20, 1916; "Negro Killed at Hot Supper Frolic," *Herald and News*, November 24, 1916; "Oliphant Dead: Man Shot by Ed Gallman Died at Hospital Yesterday," *Evening Index*, August 17, 1918; "Shot by John Oliphant," *Daily Journal*, March 1, 1917; "Palmetto Gleanings," *Yorkville (SC) Enquirer*, November 12, 1915; "Dispute Over 5cts Causes Negro's Death," *Daily Journal*, November 9, 1915; "Negro Charged with Killing Felix Walker About Two Years Ago," *Daily Journal*, December 11, 1916; "John Nelson Held on a Murder Charge," *Daily Journal*, February 11, 1916; "Negro Is Killed with Piece of Steel," *Daily Journal*, November 13, 1916; "Negro Murderer Escapes," *Press and Banner*, November 22, 1916.

17. Butterfield, *All God's Children*, 8; "One Negro Killed Another Wounded in Shooting Scrape," *Press and Banner*, November 28, 1919; "Negro Killing," *Press and Banner*, December 2, 1919. Using the 1920 census figure for Greenwood County's Black residents (21,302 persons), from 1915 through 1920 the annual homicide rate for African Americans was 19.56 per 100,000. In comparison, according to the scholar

Douglas Lee Eckberg, the national homicide rate for the United States in 1920 was 7.8 per 100,000. Eckberg, "Estimates of Homicide Rates," 1–16.

18. Du Bois, *Souls of Black Folk*, 179.

Chapter Three

1. From 1880 to 1947, the South Carolina counties with the most recorded lynching deaths were Barnwell (16), Aiken (14), and Greenwood (14). However, nine of the Barnwell County cases and four of the Aiken County cases occurred prior to the 1897 creation of Greenwood County. See Moore, *Carnival of Blood*, 205–212; Mays, *Born to Rebel*, 1, 17. The six recorded lynching victims within a twenty-mile radius of Shoals Junction are James "Babe" Stuart (1904), Allen Pendleton (1905), Bob "Snowball" Davis (1906), Willis Jackson (1911), Anthony Crawford (1916), and Mark Smith (1919). Because of Shoal Junction's location at the northern edge of Greenwood County, most of these lynchings occurred in Abbeville and Anderson Counties.

2. "Babe Stuart Met His Fate," *Laurens (SC) Advertiser*, September 28, 1904; "Negro Found Dead with His Hands Tied," *Watchman and Southron* (Sumter, SC), September 28, 1904; "Lynched for Attempted Assault," *Edgefield (SC) Advertiser*, October 5, 1904; "Among Our Friends," *Laurens Advertiser*, October 5, 1904; "The Laurens Crime—the Responsibility," *The State* (Columbia, SC), reprinted in *Daily Journal* (Greenwood, SC), September 28, 1904.

3. Carlton, *Mill and Town*, esp. 129–170; United States Bureau of the Census, *Fourteenth Census of the United States 1920*, 3:923–937; Hill, *Men, Mobs, and Law*, 112–161.

4. "Death of J. W. Ashley Occurred Saturday," *Press and Banner* (Abbeville, SC), May 3, 1916; Simkins, *Tillman Movement in South Carolina*, 176; "Citizen Joshua Ashley: Anderson's Famous Legislator and His Political History," *Laurens Advertiser*, February 19, 1902; "Josh Ashley, South Carolina," *Chicago Tribune*, April 10, 1898; 1860 census, Anderson County, SC, Anderson Court House township, 4th Regiment district, dwelling #820; "He Outrivals Ben Tillman," *Inter Ocean* (Chicago), December 31, 1899; McGhee, "Tillman, Smasher of Traditions," 8013–8020.

5. *America's Textile Reporter*, 1122; Kohn, *Cotton Mills of South Carolina*, 54; "Josh Ashley, South Carolina"; Carlton, *Mill and Town*, 207, 233, 246.

6. James Moore, 1900 census, Anderson County, SC, Honea Path township, enumeration district #54, dwelling 150; Robert Monroe, 1900 census, Anderson County, SC, Honea Path township, town of Honea Path, enumeration district #55, dwelling #109; "Murder and Lynching in Abbeville County," "Coroner's Inquest," *Press and Banner*, September 20, 1905; West, *From Yeoman to Redneck*, 161.

7. "Murder and Lynching in Abbeville County," "Coroner's Inquest," *Press and Banner*, September 20, 1905; "Coroner's Inquest," *Press and Banner*, September 27, 1905; "No Conclusion but Foul Murder," "Governor to Mr. Cooper," *Herald and News* (Newberry, SC), September 22, 1905; "Mob Murder Again," "Murder and Lynching," *Watchman and Southron*, September 20, 1905; West, *From Yeoman to Redneck*, 161–163.

8. "No Conclusion but Foul Murder."

9. "Governor to Mr. Cooper"; "South Carolina's Shameful Murder," "Public Sentiment against Lynching Growing More and More Intense," *Charlotte (NC) News*, September 22,

1905; "White Bandits Sent to Jail," *Keowee Courier* (Pickens, SC), September 27, 1905; "Slayers of Allen Pendleton Get Bail," *Anderson (SC) Intelligencer*, October 4, 1905; West, *From Yeoman to Redneck*, 162.

10. "Honea Path Is Serene after Trying Ordeal," "Honea Path's Vigilantes," *Anderson Intelligencer*, March 14, 1906; "Ashley's Son Tells of Killing of His Father," "Acquitted of Killing Ashley," *Herald-Journal* (Spartanburg, SC), May 15, 1906.

11. "McGaha's Career" (reprinted from *Anderson Daily Mail*), *Keowee Courier*, September 30, 1908; "McGaha Arrested," *Press and Banner*, June 10, 1908; "The Granting of Bail," *Press and Banner*, July 1, 1908.

12. "Desperado McGaha Killed," "McGaha's Career," *Keowee Courier*, September 30, 1908; "McGaha Buried at Night," *Daily Journal*, September 30, 1908; "Death of John McGaha," Greenwood, SC *Evening Index*, October 1, 1908; "A Bully Killed," *Press and Banner*, October 7, 1908; "Three Homicides in Anderson," *Watchman and Southron*, September 30, 1908; "McGaha Murder," *Spartanburg (SC) Herald*, September 12, 1909; "McGaha Murderers Freed," *Watchman and Southron*, September 22, 1909; "One Negro Found Guilty of Killing M'Gaha," *Spartanburg Herald*, May 5, 1911; South Carolina General Assembly, *Report of State Officers, 1911*, 1078.

13. "'Josh' Ashley Indicted," *Herald and News*, January 22, 1909; "Citizen Joshua Ashley," *Times and Democrat* (Orangeburg, SC), January 23, 1909; "May Be Hung Jury in Ashley's Case," *Spartanburg Herald*, April 25, 1909; "'Citizen Josh' Will Be Tried Tuesday," *Spartanburg Herald*, April 26, 1910; "Begin Arguments in the Ashley Peonage Case," *Spartanburg Herald*, April 28, 1910; "Ashley Acquitted of Peonage Charge by Jury," *Spartanburg Herald*, April 29, 1910.

14. Carlton, *Mill and Town*, 207, 233, 246; Simon, *Fabric of Defeat*, 11–35; West, *From Yeoman to Redneck*, 181–182.

15. "Negro Rapist Was Lynched after Confessing His Crime," *Anderson Daily Mail*, October 11, 1911; "100 Years Later, Notorious Honea Path Lynching Remembered," *Independent Mail* (Anderson, SC), October 9, 2011; Finnegan, *Deed So Accursed*, 40; 1900 census, Abbeville County, SC, Donaldsville township, enumeration district #11, dwelling #410; 1910 census, Abbeville County, SC, Donalds township, enumeration district #14, dwelling #2; "Algary School Open," *Evening Index*, January 12, 1918; L. F. Agnew death certificate, February 23, 1919, Anderson County, SC, Anderson city, file #3286.

16. "Negro Rapist Was Lynched"; "All Quiet at Honea Path," "Lynched at Honea Path for the Usual Crime," *Herald and News*, October 13, 1911; "Negro Captured after Mad Chase," *Bamberg (SC) Herald*, October 19, 1911.

17. Moore, *Carnival of Blood*, 75–76; National Association for the Advancement of Colored People, *Thirty Years of Lynching*, 18–19; West, *From Yeoman to Redneck*, 181–182; Tolnay and Beck, *Festival of Violence*, 26–27; "Negro Rapist Was Lynched"; "All Quiet at Honea Path"; "Lynched at Honea Path"; "Negro Captured after Mad Chase"; "100 Years Later"; "Negro Brute Is Lynched after Long Auto Chase by Determined Citizens," *Greenwood (SC) Index*, October 12, 1911; "Lynching of Willis Jackson," *Sentinel* (Pickens, SC), October 19, 1911; "Mob Unknown to Jury," *Bamberg Herald*, October 19, 1911; "'Unknown Parties' Lynched Jackson," *Herald and News*, October 13, 1911.

18. Tolnay and Beck, *Festival of Violence*, 26–27; "Mob Riddled Coon's Body," *Bamberg Herald*, October 19, 1911; "'Lynch-Law' Governor," 964–965; Pope, *History of Newberry County*, 2:106; West, *From Yeoman to Redneck*, 181–182; Carlton, *Mill and Town*, 247.

19. "When a human brute. . . . ," untitled editorial, *Herald and News*, October 13, 1911.

Chapter Four

1. 1900 census, Greenwood County, SC, Verdery township, enumeration district #75, dwelling #174; "Fresh Posse Pursues Fiend in Greenwood," *Herald and News* (Newberry, SC), August 17, 1906; "Negro Cut's Lady's Throat," *Watchman and Southron* (Sumter, SC), August 22, 1906; "Negro Lynched for Assault," *Keowee Courier* (Pickens, SC), August 22, 1906; "Negro Brute Lynched," *Watchman and Southron*, August 22, 1906; "He Plead in Vain," "The Closing Scene," *Edgefield (SC) Advertiser*, August 22, 1906; "Fiend Lynched," *Marlboro Democrat* (Bennettsville, SC), August 24, 1906; Dray, *Hand of Persons Unknown*, 146–149; Finnegan, *Deed So Accursed*, 146–149; West, *From Yeoman to Redneck*, 166–167; Moore, *Carnival of Blood*, 73–75.

2. "State Fair: Southern Railway," *Herald and News*, October 18, 1910; 1910 census, Abbeville County, SC, Abbeville city; Abbeville County Historical Society, *Abbeville County*; Roy Nash, "The Lynching of Anthony Crawford," *Independent* (New York), December 11, 1916; "Abbeville Has a Quick Lynching," *Index-Journal* (Greenwood, SC), October 26, 1916; Dray, *Hand of Persons Unknown*, 226–229; Finnegan, *Deed So Accursed*, 103–110; Hudson, *Entangled by White Supremacy*, 161–163; Moore, *Carnival of Blood*, 78–80; Ancestry.com, *U.S., World War I Draft Registration Cards, 1917–1918*, Ancestry.com; 1920 census, Abbeville County, SC, Abbeville city, Fourth Ward, enumeration district #6, dwelling #17 (161 North Main St.).

3. "Sons of Man Lynched Asked to Leave Town," *Index-Journal*, October 26, 1916; "Five Men Charged with Whipping Negro," *Press and Banner* (Abbeville, SC), November 8, 1916; "Abbeville Man to Be Tried Here?," *Daily Journal* (Greenwood, SC), December 14, 1916; "Abbeville Takes Action," *The State* (Columbia, SC), reprinted in *Press and Banner*, November 15, 1916.

4. 1910 census, Abbeville County, SC, Abbeville township, Abbeville city, ward 1, enumeration district #3, dwelling #27; Abbeville County Historical Society, *Abbeville County*, 44–46; National Park Service, "Burt-Stark Mansion"; "Mass Meeting of Citizens Pledge Support to Officers in Discharge of Their Duties," *Press and Banner*, November 8, 1916; "Abbeville to Enforce Law," *Watchman and Southron*, November 11, 1916; "South Takes Stand against Mob Rule and Lynching of Negroes," *Indianapolis Recorder*, December 2, 1916; Dray, *Hand of Persons Unknown*, 229.

5. Ellen Barry, "Service Atones for Past Racial Strife," *Los Angeles Times*, July 13, 2005; Lau, *Democracy Rising*, 15–16; Hudson, *Entangled by White Supremacy*, 163–167; Finnegan, *Deed So Accursed*, 108–109; "The Departed Negroes," *Charlotte Observer*, June 24, 1917.

6. "Abbeville Men under Arrest," *The State*, reprinted in *The Crisis* 13, no. 3 (January 1917): 147; Dray, *Hand of Persons Unknown*, 227; 1910 census, Abbeville County, SC, Cedar Springs township, enumeration district #10, dwelling #36; "Lester Cann Wounded," *Press and Banner*, February 4, 1919; "News from Mr. Cann," *Press and Banner*, February 7, 1919; "Held in Washington," *Watchman and Southron*, February 19, 1919; "Mark Smith Captured," "Mr. Cann Out," *Press and Banner*, February 18, 1919; "Mark Smith in Jail," *Press and Banner*, February 21, 1919.

7. "Criminal Court Now in Session," *Press and Banner*, February 25, 1919; "Court News," *Press and Banner*, February 28, 1919; South Carolina to the General Assembly, *Constitution of the State of South Carolina*, 8 (Article 1, Section 16); South Carolina to the General Assembly, *Reports January 11, 1916*, 4:439. In 1926, when examining a similar invasion of an African American home by white officers, the South Carolina supreme court affirmed Black homeowners' right to defend themselves: "The defendants had a right to use so much force as was necessary in keeping the officers from entering the house, or in expelling them from it and protecting themselves in their home, until the authority of the officers was made known." Quoted in Robeson, "Ominous Defiance," 78.

8. 1910 census, Abbeville County, SC, Abbeville township, Abbeville city, enumeration district #3, dwelling #27; Mark Smith death certificate, June 7, 1919, Abbeville County, SC, file #10891; "Mark Smith Foully Murdered near This City Saturday Night," *Press and Banner*, June 10, 1919; "Body of Negro Found in Savannah River," *Press and Banner*, June 13, 1919; "Body of Smith Been Identified," *Press and Banner*, June 17, 1919.

9. "Mark Smith Foully Murdered"; "Capital News and Gossip," *Herald and News*, June 17, 1919; "Abandoning State Rights," *The State*, reprinted in *Press and Banner*, June 10, 1919; "Will Lynchers Save Themselves?," *The State*, reprinted in *Press and Banner*, June 13, 1919; "A Brutal Murder," *Press and Banner*, June 10, 1919; "What Others Think," *Press and Banner*, June 13, 1919; "No New Developments in Case of Negro Smith Murdered Near Here," *Press and Banner*, June 20, 1919; "Verdict Rendered in Mark Smith Case," *Press and Banner*, September 12, 1919; 1920 census, Abbeville County, SC, Abbeville township, Abbeville city (part 2), ward 1, enumeration district #3, Ralph Davenport. In November 1921, while drunk at the Abbeville Opera House, Deputy Lester Cann shot two town policemen, killing one and injuring the other, and was himself fatally wounded in the encounter. "Bail Is Granted to T. L. Cann," *Press and Banner*, November 16, 1921; "Shot Week Ago T. L. Cann Dies," *Press and Banner*, November 18, 1921.

10. 1870 census, Laurens P.O. 636 [?], Laurens County, SC, dwelling #284; 1880 census, Sullivan township, Laurens County, SC, enumeration district #105, dwelling #202; 1880 census, McBee Avenue, Greenville city, Greenville County, SC, enumeration district #80, dwelling #86; 1900 census, Greenville city and township, Greenville County, SC, enumeration district #34, dwelling #123; 1920 census, Ware Shoals, Walnut Grove township, Greenwood County, SC, enumeration district #90, Briar Hollow 315, dwelling #275; James H. Walker death certificate, June 21, 1920, Ware Shoals, Walnut Grove township, Greenwood County, SC, file #11615; Caldwell, *History of the American Negro*, 26; Newby, *Black Carolinians*, 112–114; Davis, *Enduring Dream*, 285; *From Hill to Dale*, 38.

11. "Plead Temporary Insanity in Case of Pope McCarty," *Index-Journal*, June 29, 1921; James H. Walker death certificate. The attack on Reverend Walker recalls the historian Edward Ayers's observation about the late nineteenth-century South: "Accounts of the violence directed at Blacks often spoke of well-dressed clergymen and well-dressed women as the objects of white anger." Ayers, *Promise of the New South*, 139.

12. "Negro Is Killed at Ware Shoals," *Index-Journal*, June 22, 1920; "White Man Kills Negro Minister," *Pittsburg Press*, June 23, 1920; "Crime," *The Crisis* 20, no. 5 (September 1920): 242; "General Sessions Court Convenes," *Index-Journal*, June 30, 1920; "Pope McCarty Gets Sentence of 7 Years," *Index-Journal*, June 30, 1921.

13. "Plead Temporary Insanity"; "Pope McCarty Gets 7 Years"; 1910 census, Anderson County, South Carolina, Williamston township, Pelzer town, enumeration district #71, square #21, dwelling #150, and Goodrich street #7, dwelling #180; 1920 census, Anderson County, South Carolina, Williamston township, enumeration district #63, dwelling #466; U.S., *World War I Draft Registration Cards, 1917–1918*, Ancestry.com; South Carolina Attorney General's Office, *Annual Report of the Attorney General December 31, 1921*, 165; Pope McCarty death certificate, November 2, 1922, SC State Penitentiary, Columbia, Richland County, SC, file #17839. The year after McCarty's conviction, he died of pneumonia in the state penitentiary.

14. Trotti, "What Counts," 380; "Plead Temporary Insanity"; "Pope McCarty Gets Sentence"; Caldwell, *History of the American Negro*, 26; "Emma Maddox Building," archived January 18, 2015, at the Wayback Machine, http://web.archive.org/web/20150118013640/http://ms.gwd51.org/about_us/emma_maddox_building.

Chapter Five

1. Tindall, *Emergence of the New South*, 60, 111; South Carolina Commissioner of Agriculture, Commerce and Industries, *Year Book and Seventeenth Annual Report 1920*, 130.

2. "Broadus Miller Still at Large," *Index-Journal* (Greenwood, SC), June 25, 1927; "Biracialism a Product of a Class Society," Folder 17, Arthur Franklin Raper Papers, Southern Historical Collection, Manuscripts Department, Wilson Library, University of North Carolina at Chapel Hill (hereafter cited as SHC); Hilton and Due, *Electric Interurban Railways*, 331; South Carolina General Assembly, *Reports of State Officers, January 14, 1919*, 1:96; "State Fair," *Herald and News* (Newberry, SC), October 18, 1910; "Excursion," *Herald and News*, August 22, 1916; 1900 and 1920 federal censuses, Anderson County, SC, Anderson City; South Carolina Commissioner of Agriculture, Commerce and Industries, *Year Book and Seventeenth Annual Report 1920*, 209; Woody, *South Carolina Postcards*, 9:12, 26–27.

3. Anderson, SC City Directory, Vol. 8, 1920–1921, accessed February 6, 2014, https://archive.org; Megginson, *African American Life*, 335–353; Lau, *Democracy Rising*, 53–54; United States Bureau of the Census, *Negro Population, 1790–1915*, 773; United States Bureau of the Census, *Fourteenth Census of the United States 1920*, 3:928; South Carolina Commissioner of Agriculture, Commerce and Industries, *Year Book and Seventeenth Annual Report 1920*, 209; 1920 census, Anderson County, SC, Anderson City, ward #4, 122 West Market Street and 404½ South Main Street; Cooper and Terrill,

American South, 2:527; Marks, *Farewell, We're Good and Gone*, 61. For the Great Migration as a gradual relocation from countryside to southern towns, and then to northern cities, see, for example, Trotter, *Great Migration in Historical Perspective*, 22.

4. 1920 census, Anderson County, SC, Anderson City, ward #4, 122 West Market Street and 404½ South Main Street; Sanborn Fire Insurance Map, Anderson, SC, February 1918 (New York: Sanborn Map and Publishing), University of South Carolina, South Caroliniana Library, Digital Collections, accessed February 1, 2014, http://www.sc.edu/library/digital/collections/sanborn.html; 1900 census, Anderson County, SC, Broadway township, enumeration district #42, dwelling #104; 1910 census, Anderson County, SC, Anderson City, ward #3, 1307 South Fant Street; "Negro Confesses to Killing Negress at House in Anderson," *Greenville (SC) News*, May 3, 1921; Essie Walker death certificate, Anderson County, SC, May 1, 1921, file #6249, South Carolina State Archives, Columbia, SC. Press accounts state that Walker's body was discovered by her son; however, census records indicate Walker's only living child was a daughter and the Walkers raised their daughter's son. These press accounts also state that Broadus Miller had relatives in Anderson, and Essie Walker's shared surname with Miller's uncle suggests some possible kinship.

5. Anderson County, SC, death certificates, January 1–December 31, 1921, *South Carolina, Death Records, 1821–1960*, Ancestry.com; Brearley, "Study of Homicides," 24–25, 28–35; Florence Bowers death certificate, Anderson County, SC, January 28, 1921, file #64; Eliza Wakefield death certificate, Anderson County, SC, April 24, 1921, file #4366; 1920 census, Centerville township, Anderson County, SC, dwelling #196. In 1921, 292 homicides were recorded in South Carolina. Brearley, "Study of Homicides," 24, 28. Of the seventeen homicide victims in Anderson County in 1921, seven were white men, seven were African American men, and three were Black women. Sixteen of the death certificates for Anderson County homicides list gunshot as a cause of death; the seventeenth states the cause of death as "homicidal." Among South Carolina towns, only Florence had a higher homicide rate than Anderson.

6. "Negro Confesses"; "Former Anderson Negro Is Killed," *Anderson (SC) Daily Mail*, July 4, 1927; Records of General Sessions of Anderson County Court, 1921, Anderson County Clerk of Court's Office, Anderson, SC.

7. "Negro Confesses"; "Former Anderson Negro Is Killed"; Records of General Sessions of Anderson County Court, 1921; "Murdered Negro Woman," *Press and Banner* (Abbeville, SC), May 4, 1921; Sanborn Fire Insurance Map, Anderson, SC, February 1918; "Murdered Negro Woman," *Index-Journal*, May 3, 1921; "Negro Boy Slays Aged Negro," *Keowee Courier* (Pickens, SC), May 4, 1921.

8. Records of General Sessions of Anderson County Court, 1921; Brooks, "Judge George E. Prince," 1:302–304; Snowden and Cutler, *History of South Carolina*, 3:14–15; "George E. Prince, Esq.," *Anderson (SC) Intelligencer*, September 30, 1896; West, *From Yeoman to Redneck*, 130; "The New Judges," *Laurens (SC) Advertiser*, February 22, 1905; Simkins, *Pitchfork Ben Tillman*, 185; McKissick, *Men and Women of Carolina*, 40–41; Vandiver, *Traditions and History*, 125, 280; Dickson, *Journeys into the Past*, 169–171. For the "town people" whom Judge Prince epitomized, see Carlton, *Mill and Town*; West, *From Yeoman to Redneck*, 101–168.

9. "The New Judges"; "Judge's Letters in S. K. Williams Case," *Herald and News*, December 9, 1913; "Many Plead Guilty in Court Yesterday," *Anderson Daily Intelligencer*, May 9, 1916; "Anderson Jurist Made Impression," *Anderson Daily Intelligencer*, October 8, 1914.

10. West, *From Yeoman to Redneck*, 163; "Court," *Manning (SC) Times*, September 25, 1907.

11. "Judge Prince Passes after Long Illness," *Anderson Daily Mail*, March 31, 1923; "Impressive Services Mark Prince Funeral," *Anderson Daily Mail*, April 2, 1923; "Excellent Opening at Lander College," *Greenwood (SC) Index*, September 21, 1905; Records of General Sessions of Anderson County Court, 1921; Klosky, *Daring Venture*, 99–114, 122–123; "Broadus Miller Still at Large." Dr. Young later became one of South Carolina's leading obstetricians, delivering several thousand babies over the course of a long career.

12. Records of General Sessions of Anderson County Court, 1921; Johnson, "Negro and Crime," 97; 1920 census, Anderson County, SC, Anderson township, enumeration district #21, 518 Greenville Street; "Solicitor—10th Circuit," *Keowee Courier*, June 9, 1920; "Other Election News," *Press and Banner*, September 1, 1920; "To the Democratic Voters of Oconee County," *Keowee Courier*, August 25, 1920; Kemp, *Alumni Directory*, 343; South Carolina Secretary of State, *Report January 1, 1920 and Ending December 31, 1920*, 18; Beaney, *Right to Counsel*, 17–19, 25; Tomkovicz, *Right to Assistance of Counsel*, 12; McAninch, "Criminal Procedure," 180; 1920 census, Anderson County, SC, Anderson township, enumeration district #21, 501 North McDuffie Street.

13. Records of General Sessions of Anderson County Court, 1921; Anderson, SC City Directory, Vol. 8, 1920–1921; Essie Walker death certificate, Anderson County, SC, May 1, 1921, file #6249; 1920 census, Anderson County, SC, Anderson City, ward #4, 122 West Market Street, and ward #2, 578 South Fant Street.

14. Records of General Sessions of Anderson County Court, 1921; Hart, *Southern South*, 199; Brearley, "Study of Homicides," 21; Dollard, *Caste and Class*, 282–283.

15. 1920 census, Greenwood County, SC, Walnut Grove township, enumeration district #91, dwellings #31, 55, and 65; "Killing Resulted from Lack of Rain," *Anderson Daily Intelligencer*, July 28, 1914; "Causes of Crime Discussed Here," *Press and Banner*, August 12, 1919; Dollard, *Caste and Class*, 282–283.

16. South Carolina Superintendent of Education, *Forty-Third Annual Report 1911*, 392–405; Watson, *Greenwood County Sketches*, 130, 355, 357; Church records, Turkey Creek Baptist Church, Ware Shoals, SC; "H. L. Rasor Dies at His Home," *Index-Journal*, March 22, 1940; "Clarence Agnew, Shoals Junction Resident, Dies," *Index-Journal*, April 21, 1951; "Tribute Paid W. E. Algary," *Index-Journal*, June 25, 1941; Records of General Sessions of Anderson County Court, 1921; 1920 census, Abbeville County, SC, Donalds township, enumeration district #10, dwelling #115; "Broadus Miller Still at Large."

17. Records of General Sessions of Anderson County Court, 1921; "Sentence of Ten Years for Ashley," *Laurens Advertiser*, June 1, 1921. The following jurors are found on the 1920 Anderson County census: Thomas L. Webb—Hopewell township,

enumeration district #49, dwelling #176; J. Otto Banister—Martin township, enumeration district #42, dwelling #225; Samuel S. McMahan—Hall township, enumeration district #45, dwelling #164; Robert H. Tripp—Brushy Creek township, enumeration district #33, dwelling #305; J. N. Harris—Savannah township, Starr town, enumeration district #59, dwelling #244; Furman E. Burris—Centerville township, enumeration district #87, dwelling #212; Daniel Patterson—Corner township, Iva town, enumeration district #38, dwelling #285.

Chapter Six

1. Williamson, *Crucible of Race*, 115–118, 127–130.
2. Bethea, *Code of Laws*, 1912, 2:254–255, 260; South Carolina Supreme Court, *Reports of Cases Heard*, 79:224–225; Wolfe, *Code of Laws* 1922, 2:9.
3. South Carolina Governor's Office, *Statement of Pardons*, 1921, 13–14, 33–34; South Carolina Attorney General's Office, *Report of the Attorney General* 1916, 255; "Convict Pardoned," *Index-Journal* (Greenwood, SC), June 6, 1921; "Paroled during Good Behavior," *Watchman and Southron* (Sumter, SC), June 8, 1921.
4. South Carolina General Assembly, *Report of State Officers*, 1915, 656–674.
5. "Greenwood Rogers Goes to the Chair," *Laurens (SC) Advertiser*, March 10, 1915; "Greenwood Rogers Saved from Chair," *Laurens Advertiser*, July 14, 1915. For life sentences of Blacks convicted of interracial murder, see also "Negro Gets Life Sentence for Murder of Magistrate," *Gaffney (SC) Ledger*, October 5, 1920. Nearly a quarter of a century after the Laurens County solicitor's attempt to secure the death penalty by bringing the arson charge, his action prevented the by now seventy-five-year-old Black man from receiving parole. As he left office in early 1939, Governor Olin Johnston signed parole papers for the man, but because the prisoner was serving concurrent life sentences—one for murder and one for arson—and the parole specified only one of the two sentences, prison officials refused to release him. "Convict to Stay in Prison in Spite of Parole," *Spartanburg (SC) Herald*, July 20, 1939.
6. "A Case in Anderson," *The State* (Columbia, SC), reprinted in *Gaffney Ledger*, April 5, 1921; "Several Negroes Were Badly Beaten," *Anderson (SC) Intelligencer*, December 28, 1915; "Anderson Murder Cases," *Anderson (SC) Daily Mail*, reprinted in *Keowee Courier* (Pickens, SC), February 23, 1916; Moses Shanks death certificate, December 30, 1915, Anderson County, SC, Abbeville city, file #22737; South Carolina Governor's Office, *Statement of Pardons*, 1920, 5. In 1919, a white Greenville County farm laborer shot and killed a young Black man. A coroner's jury ruled the killing a "justifiable homicide," but in 1921 the killer was convicted of manslaughter; sources do not indicate the sentence imposed, which the farm laborer immediately announced he would appeal. "Jury's Deliberation Long," *Gaffney Ledger*, March 29, 1921; "Suspects Picked Up Prove Nothing; Negro Still Free," *Asheville (NC) Citizen*, October 8, 1919; 1920 census, Greenville County, SC, Bates township, enumeration district #4, dwelling #152, Ernest Batson. When examining scores of upstate South Carolina homicides from 1915 through 1921, the author identified four cases in which whites were convicted of manslaughter for killing African Americans, but no murder convictions for such killings. Three of the four manslaughter convictions occurred in 1921.

7. "Reach Verdict against Todd," *Index-Journal*, March 29, 1921; "Gets Two Years for Killing Negro," *Press and Banner* (Abbeville, SC), April 13, 1921; "Solicitor Leon Harris Tells *New York Herald* That Our Courts Do Justice to the Negroes," *The Piedmont* (Greenville, SC), April 27, 1921, reprinted in *Keowee Courier*, May 4, 1921; "Case in Anderson."

8. "Jury's Deliberation Long"; "Reach Verdict against Todd"; "Gets Two Years"; South Carolina Governor's Office, *Statement of Pardons, 1918*, 11; South Carolina Governor's Office, *Statement of Pardons, 1920*, 5.

9. Brearley, "Study of Homicides," 41, 57; "South Carolina Is World's Bloodiest Spot," *Gastonia (NC) Daily Gazette*, August 15, 1925; Carlton, *Mill and Town*, 145.

10. "Jury Fails to Agree," *Gaffney Ledger*, May 14, 1921; "Anderson Defendants Given Sentences," *Index-Journal*, May 15, 1921; "Gets Three Years for Killing Man," *Sentinel* (Pickens, SC), May 19, 1921.

11. "Court Adjourns Sine Die Saturday," *Press and Banner*, September 13, 1920; 1920 census, Abbeville County, SC, Donalds township, enumeration district #10, dwelling #219; "State Rests in the Ernest Ashley Trial," *Press and Banner*, May 25, 1921; "Sentence of Ten Years for Ashley," *Laurens Advertiser*, June 1, 1921. Ernest Ashley appealed his ten-year manslaughter conviction to the South Carolina supreme court, which granted him a new trial; Ashley was again convicted of manslaughter, and, in a rare departure from the typical pattern, a court then imposed an even harsher sentence of twelve years. "Twelve Years for Ashley," *Watchman and Southron*, September 23, 1922. Ernest Ashley was a great-nephew of John Marion Ashley, while the man who tried to engage the policeman in a wrestling match was Will Moore—the brother of Jim Moore, who fifteen years earlier had attacked the hapless Allen Pendleton.

12. "Court of General Session Ended Today," *Press and Banner*, March 2, 1921; South Carolina Supreme Court, *Reports of Cases Heard*, 121:17; Kotch, "Unduly Harsh," 100; "Life Sentences for Four Negroes," *Laurens Advertiser*, June 18, 1919; "Robert Burdette Cleared by Jury," *Laurens Advertiser*, March 23, 1921; "Life Sentence for Killing Wife," *Keowee Courier*, May 4, 1921; "Gets Life Sentence," *Press and Banner*, May 4, 1921.

13. "First Gallows Here Ready for Its Victim," *Greenwood (SC) Index*, March 21, 1907; "Joe Evans Hanged," *Greenwood Index*, April 18, 1907; "A Hanging Postponed," *Times and Democrat* (Orangeburg, SC), July 31, 1908; "Two Hangings in South Carolina," *Sentinel-Journal*, October 22, 1908; "Murderers To Be Hanged," *Manning (SC) Times*, October 25, 1911; "First Execution in 20 Years," *Herald and News* (Newberry, SC), December 22, 1911; Wood, *Lynching and Spectacle*, 29; Hearn, *Legal Executions*, 153–175; Espy and Smykla, *Executions in the United States*. For the decades prior to 1912, Hearn documents several more executions in South Carolina than are listed by Espy. However, Espy documents one 1921 execution that is not included in Hearn.

14. Hearn, *Legal Executions*, 153–175; Espy and Smykla, *Executions in the United States*. The charge of attempted rape was sometimes levied against—and resulted in the execution of—African American men who had attempted to burglarize a home in which a white woman lived, especially if there was no white man present in the household. See the 1912 case of William Reed in Anderson County and the 1918 case of Aaron Walker in Greenwood County. "Attempted Assault at Dean," *Anderson*

Intelligencer, reprinted in *Keowee Courier,* March 6, 1912; "Electric Chair for Reed," *Keowee Courier,* April 3, 1912; "First Electrocution in This State Today," *Herald and News,* August 6, 1912; "Attempted Assault or Robbery by Aaron Walker of County Gang," *Greenwood Index,* September 18, 1918; "Court Adjourned after Short Session," *Greenwood Index,* March 7, 1918; "Death Sentence Passed in Court" *Greenwood Index,* December 18, 1918; "Aaron Walker Given More Time To Live," *Greenwood Index,* February 21, 1919; "Aaron Walker Given Another Reprieve," *Index-Journal,* February 22, 1919; "Greenwood Negro Electrocuted," *Keowee Courier,* March 12, 1919.

15. Banner, *Death Penalty,* 155; Wood, *Lynching and Spectacle,* 29; "Negro Hanged at Georgetown," *Lexington (SC) Dispatch,* August 18, 1909; West, *From Yeoman to Redneck,* 182; "Blease's Clemency Extended to 70 More," *County Record* (Kingstree, SC), January 7, 1915; Blackmon, *Slavery by Another Name,* 305. For the local dynamics in judicially punishing Black-on-Black violence, see, for example, "Negroes Try to Lynch a Negro," *Bamberg (SC) Herald,* August 23, 1906; "There are a goodly number of people . . . ," untitled editorial, *Manning Times,* March 29, 1905; "Justice Is Asked," *Manning Times,* April 5, 1905.

16. "Tobe Abercrombie," *Yorkville (SC) Enquirer,* September 2, 1919; South Carolina Attorney General's Office, *Annual Report of the Attorney General 1919,* 128; South Carolina Attorney General's Office, *Annual Report of the Attorney General 1921,* 159; South Carolina Governor's Office, *Statement of Pardons, 1921,* 3; "Death Day Fixed," *Watchman and Southron,* November 13, 1920; "Will Be Electrocuted Friday," *Keowee Courier,* November 17, 1920; "Greenville Negro Is Granted a Reprieve," *Index-Journal,* November 19, 1920; "Greenville Negro Given a Third Reprieve," *Press and Banner,* January 24, 1921; "Will Lomax Pays Penalty," *Watchman and Southron,* February 9, 1921; "Will Lomax Executed," *Gaffney Ledger,* February 7, 1921. The execution of Lomax is omitted from Hearn, *Legal Executions,* but is included in Espy and Smykla, *Executions in the United States.*

17. "Greenville Negro Is Granted a Reprieve"; "Greenville Negro Given a Third Reprieve"; "Will Lomax Pays Penalty."

Chapter Seven

1. Central Register of Prisoners, May 27, 1913–May 2, 1925, SC Department of Corrections, South Carolina Department of Archives and History, Columbia, SC (hereafter cited as SCDAH); "South Carolina Is World's Bloodiest Spot," *Gastonia (NC) Daily Gazette,* August 15, 1925; South Carolina General Assembly, *Report of State Officers, 1921,* 38–42; South Carolina Attorney General's Office, *Annual Report 1921,* 47; South Carolina General Assembly, *Special Joint Legislative Committee,* 23–24, 130. See also the photograph of the administrative building in Trinkley and Hacker, *Penitentiary Cemetery,* 11.

2. Trinkley and Hacker, *Penitentiary Cemetery,* 7–10; South Carolina General Assembly, *Special Joint Legislative Committee,* 142. For the penitentiary's history, see Oliphant, *Evolution of the Penal System,* 4; Mancini, *One Dies, Get Another,* 198–212.

3. 1920 census, Richland County, SC, Columbia city, dwelling #1515; South Carolina State Board of Public Welfare, *First Annual Report 1920,* 44; South Carolina Gen-

eral Assembly, *Special Joint Legislative Committee*, 2–11, 138; South Carolina General Assembly, *Reports of the State Officers, 1918*, 2:37–40; South Carolina State Board of Public Welfare, *Third Annual Report 1922*, 3.4:42; Williams, "Crime and Its Treatment," 3–6; South Carolina Governor's Office, *Statement of Pardons, 1921*, 10. Official population figures for the penitentiary sometimes included the population of the state work farms, while at other times they referred only to those inmates housed in Columbia. South Carolina General Assembly, *Special Joint Legislative Committee*, 2, 138.

4. "White Criminals Outnumber Negro," *Laurens (SC) Advertiser*, June 22, 1921; Kirchwey, "Prison's Place," 13; "Able-Bodied Male Convicts to Work on County Chain Gangs," South Carolina Criminal Code, Chapter 8, Section 104, in Bethea, *Code of Laws 1912*, 2:244–245; South Carolina General Assembly, *Reports of State Officers Boards 1920*, 2:134.

5. Williams, "Crime and Its Treatment," 4–6; South Carolina General Assembly, *Special Joint Legislative Committee*, 23; Central Register of Prisoners, May 27, 1913–May 2, 1925, SCDAH. Throughout the South Carolina penal system, a larger percentage of white prisoners than Blacks were diagnosed as mentally ill. In 1921, the National Committee on Mental Hygiene surveyed South Carolina county jails and found that 19 percent of Black inmates—and 30 percent of whites—were mentally ill or psychopathic. Williams, "Crime and Its Treatment," 4.

6. South Carolina General Assembly, *Special Joint Legislative Committee*, 27–32, 245, 258, 259, 286, 287, 348; South Carolina General Assembly, *Reports of the State Officers, January 8, 1918*, 2:37–38; "Columbia Journal: Prison Lures Them In (as Tourists)," *New York Times*, February 22, 1994; "Facts vs. Theory in Prison Management," *Watchman and Southron* (Sumter, SC), December 16, 1922. In the 1930s a separate dining hall was built for Black inmates. Trinkley and Hacker, *Penitentiary Cemetery*, 10. Inmates' testimony about food contradicts statements by state inspectors (e.g., South Carolina General Assembly, *Report of State Officers, 1921*, 2:38–42); officials apparently served better meals when inspectors visited.

7. South Carolina General Assembly, *Special Joint Legislative Committee*, 13, 183, 213–214, 232–233, 285; "Able-Bodied Male Convicts"; South Carolina General Assembly, *Report of State Officers, 1921*, 2:38–42. According to testimony before the Special Joint Legislative Committee, laborers who exceeded the quota typically earned $3.50 a month; however, the *Report of State Officers* gives a figure of "from three to nine cents a day."

8. South Carolina General Assembly, *Report of State Officers, 1921*, 2:38–42.

9. Crawford, *Who's Who in South Carolina*, 165–166; "Arthur Sanders New Superintendent," *Watchman and Southron*, March 3, 1917; 1920 census, Richland County, SC, Columbia city, dwelling #165; Witherspoon, "Social Legislation in South Carolina," 232; South Carolina Penitentiary Superintendent's Office, *Annual Report of the Board 1921*, 6; "Captain of the Guard," *Watchman and Southron*, December 3, 1921; South Carolina General Assembly, *Reports and Resolutions 1909*, 2:996; South Carolina General Assembly, *Reports and Resolutions 1912*, 1:874; South Carolina General Assembly, *Special Joint Legislative Committee*, 145–146; 1880 census, Lexington County, SC, Lexington Township, dwelling # 181; 1903 Columbia, SC, City Directory; 1910 census, Richland County, SC, Columbia City, South Carolina Penitentiary; 1920 census,

Lexington County, SC, Congaree township, family #354; "Capt. Clay Roberts Will Resign Job," *Index-Journal* (Greenwood, SC), March 30, 1923.

10. South Carolina General Assembly, *Special Joint Legislative Committee*, 14, 25.

11. South Carolina General Assembly, *Special Joint Legislative Committee*, 20, 147, 149, 192, 223, 225, 230, 246, 263–266; "Facts vs. Theory"; Tannenbaum, *Darker Phases of the South*, 196–197; Robeson, "Ominous Defiance," 78–79.

12. South Carolina General Assembly, *Special Joint Legislative Committee*, 331; "Spartanburg Jury Convicts Chaingang Man," *Edgefield (SC) Advertiser*, November 2, 1921; Tannenbaum, *Darker Phases of the South*, 109–112; Holt, "Men, Women and Children," 141–152; Carper, "Martin Tabert," 115–131; Mancini, *One Dies, Get Another*, 115, 197; Hart, *Social Progress of Alabama*, 31; "Message of Governor Thomas W. Hardwick to the General Assembly of Georgia, June 29, 1923," Folder 18, Box 2, Georgia Governors' Messages, Richard B. Russell Library for Political Research and Studies, University of Georgia Libraries, Athens, Georgia; Corbitt, *Cameron Morrison*, 317. According to the North Carolina State Board of Public Welfare, Governor Morrison completely abolished whipping in the state prisons, which seems to overstate Morrison's action. North Carolina State Board of Public Welfare, *Capital Punishment in North Carolina*, 92. For a general discussion of whipping in penal systems, see Mancini, *One Dies, Get Another*, 75–77.

13. South Carolina General Assembly, *Special Joint Legislative Committee*, 12, 106, 136; *Report of the Joint Legislative Committee to Investigate the State Penitentiary—Appointed by the General Assembly Session of 1925*, quoted in Trinkley and Hacker, *Penitentiary Cemetery*, 7; "State Penitentiary Is a Medieval Prison Out of Place in Present Day," *Aiken (SC) Standard*, August 14, 1925.

14. Tannenbaum, *Darker Phases of the South*, 82–83; South Carolina State Board of Charities and Corrections, *First Annual Report*, 68–72; South Carolina General Assembly, *Reports of the State Officers*, 1918, 2:41–44; South Carolina General Assembly, *Reports of State Officers*, 1921, 2:49–51; Oliphant, *Evolution of the Penal System*, 9; 1920 census, Sumter County, SC, Rafting Creek township, dwelling #260.

15. Tannenbaum, *Wall Shadows*, 143; South Carolina General Assembly, *Reports of the State Officers*, 1918, 2:42–43; South Carolina General Assembly, *Special Joint Legislative Committee*, 121, 11, 118. As Tannenbaum noted, South Carolina was unusual in having more prisoners in the penitentiary than on farms; other southern states sent most inmates to prison farms (142).

16. South Carolina General Assembly, *Special Joint Legislative Committee*, 102, 68, 330, 58–59, 6, 330, 340.

17. Oliphant, *Evolution of the Penal System*, 4, 6; Tindall, *South Carolina Negroes*, 267–271; Cooper, *Conservative Regime*, 114; Mancini, *One Dies, Get Another*, 207–208; Eelman, *Entrepreneurs in the Southern Upcountry*, 239–241.

18. Mancini, *One Dies, Get Another*, 199; Oliphant, *Evolution of the Penal System*, 7, 13.

19. South Carolina General Assembly. Senate, *Journal of the Senate 1913*, 27; Oliphant, *Evolution of the Penal System*, 8, 13; South Carolina General Assembly, *Special Joint Legislative Committee*, 12, 106; "Hosiery Mill Case," *Watchman and Southron*, October 1, 1921; South Carolina General Assembly. Senate, *Journal of the Senate 1915*, 889; South Carolina General Assembly, *Reports of the State Officers*, 1918, 2:37–40. Following the mill's closing, Columbia Hosiery sued the state for breach of contract and was

eventually awarded over $4,000. South Carolina Attorney General's Office, *Annual Report 1921*, 7–8. For the various ways that states utilized penitentiary labor, see Jackson, "Prison Labor," 218–268.

20. Du Bois, *Some Notes on Negro Crime*, 61; Hart, *Southern South*, 201; Oliphant, *Evolution of the Penal System*, 7; South Carolina General Assembly, *Special Joint Legislative Committee*, 20, 244.

21. South Carolina General Assembly, *Special Joint Legislative Committee*, 23, 128, 176, 177, 284, 285, 291.

22. South Carolina General Assembly, *Special Joint Legislative Committee*, 208, 251, 291, 299. The racial composition of the striking prisoners is suggested by the denouement of the incident: all thirteen of the prisoners struck by gunfire were white.

23. South Carolina General Assembly, *Special Joint Legislative Committee*, 191–192, 222, 254, 292, 313, 315; "Investigation of Prison Mutiny," *Watchman and Southron*, May 13, 1922.

24. South Carolina General Assembly, *Special Joint Legislative Committee*, 192, 279–280, 290. In March 1923, following a critical report by legislators, Roberts announced his resignation. "Capt. Clay Roberts." Roberts later became an assistant marshal at the University of South Carolina; following his death, the university newspaper eulogized his "strict performance of duty." "Roberts Dies after Illness," *The Gamecock* (Columbia, SC), October 28, 1932.

25. Central Register of Prisoners, May 27, 1913–May 2, 1925, SCDAH; Oliphant, *Evolution of the Penal System*, 13.

Chapter Eight

1. South Carolina General Assembly, *Special Joint Legislative Committee*, 26.

2. Mark Robert Schneider, "We Return Fighting," 21–22; Lange, Olmstead, and Rhode, "Impact of the Boll Weevil," 685–718; Higgs, "Boll Weevil," 337, 345, 350; Wright, *Old South, New South*, 122, 204–205; Giesen, *Boll Weevil Blues*, 35; "Cotton Men Hope to Conquer Weevil," *New York Times*, September 25, 1921; "$700,000,000 Loss from Boll Weevil," *New York Times*, November 16, 1921; Edgar, *South Carolina*, 485; Gordon, *Sketches of Negro Life*, 166. Estimates for Great Migration numbers vary greatly, ranging from 300,000 to more than 1 million people. In later years, popular opinion exaggerated the role of the boll weevil in overall emigration of African Americans from the South. Only Georgia and South Carolina in the early 1920s fit the model of heavy infestation, dramatically lowered cotton yields, and subsequent large-scale out-migration that has sometimes been misleadingly portrayed as typical of the entire South. Higgs, "Boll Weevil," 345.

3. John B. Culbertson, interviewed by R. V. Williams, January 27, 1939, Campobello, SC, and J. Thomas Metz, interviewed by John L. Dove, January 24, 1939, Chapin, SC, National Digital Library Program, Library of Congress, *American Life Histories*; Kane and Keeton, *In Those Days*, 22–25; Ransom and Sutch, *One Kind of Freedom*, 13, 174–176; Lesh et al., *Soil Survey of Greenwood County*, 7; B. R. Thomas, interviewed by John L. Dove, March 3, 1939, Columbia, SC, National Digital Library Program, Library of Congress, *American Life Histories*.

4. "Where We Are," *Index-Journal* (Greenwood, SC), August 1, 1922; "Wheat Planting Is Urged by W. A. Collins," *Index-Journal*, August 25, 1921; "Thinks Damage Estimate Too Low," *Index-Journal*, August 23, 1921; Lesh et al., *Soil Survey of Greenwood County*, 6; Mays, *Main Street United Methodist Church*, 113–114; Bethel, *Promiseland*, 114.

5. "Weather Ideal for Weevil," *Index-Journal*, August 13, 1922; "Andrew Chapel," *Index-Journal*, August 13, 1922; "Description of Destruction," *Index-Journal*, August 7, 1922; "Suggests Giving Supply of Corn to Hail Sufferers," *Index-Journal*, August 9, 1922.

6. "Asks Prayer for Pest," *New York Times*, June 8, 1923; Edgar, *South Carolina*, 485; Newby, *Black Carolinians*, 200–201; "50,000 Negroes Have Left South Carolina," *News-Herald* (Morganton, NC), June 28, 1923. On the 1920 census, Tom and Alpha Walker were enumerated in Walnut Grove township; during Broadus Miller's 1921 trial, Tom Walker appeared as a witness with other Shoals Junction residents. The Walkers' next appearance in the written record came in late 1923, when they were listed for the first time in the annually compiled Asheville, NC, city directory. *Asheville City Directory: 1924* (Asheville, NC: Commercial Service Company, 1923), Buncombe County Special Collections, Pack Memorial Library, Asheville, NC.

7. For sharecropping as a mutual compromise between landlord and laborer, see Ransom and Sutch, *One Kind of Freedom*, 94.

8. Carlton, *Mill and Town*, 8–11, 29–31, 50–51, 114–115; South Carolina Department of Agriculture, Commerce and Immigration, *Handbook of South Carolina*, 566; Wade, *Greenwood County and Its Railroads*, 25; Tindall, *Emergence of the New South*, 21; Woodward, *Strange Career of Jim Crow*, 98; Edgar, *South Carolina*, 448; United States Bureau of the Census, *Fourteenth Census of the United States*, 1:604; United States Bureau of the Census, *Fifteenth Census of the United States*, 3.2:809; Lesh et al., *Soil Survey of Greenwood County*, 2. In 1900, Walnut Grove had 1,356 residents; by 1930, the number had grown to 4,843.

9. Johnson and Campbell, *Black Migration in America*, 74–77; Kirby, *Rural Worlds Lost*, 316; Bethel, *Promiseland*, 115; Finkelman, *Encyclopedia of African American History*, 346. Among the African Americans from the Greenwood/Abbeville area who moved to Pittsburgh were the grandparents of writer John Edgar Wideman; see Wideman, *Fatheralong*, 87–128.

10. Clodfelter, "Saluda," 26–39; Cox, *Rails across Dixie*, 383–384; Sakowski, *Touring the Backroads*, 122–124; Mays, *Born to Rebel*, 25; Starnes, *Creating the Land of the Sky*, 9, 23–24, 43, 84; 1920 and 1930 censuses, Buncombe County, NC, Asheville township.

11. *Asheville City Directory: 1924*; Waters, "Life beneath the Veneer," 152–168; Erline L. McQueen, interviewed by Dorothy Joynes, in Voices of Asheville Oral History Collection, Ramsey Library Special Collections, University of North Carolina at Asheville; Chase, *Asheville*, 136–160; Tessier, *Asheville*, 198.

12. *Asheville City Directory*, 7 vols. (Asheville, NC: Commercial Service Company, 1921–27), Buncombe County Special Collections, Pack Memorial Library, Asheville, NC; 1910 census, Fairfield County, SC, township #13, dwelling #221; 1930 census, Fairfield County, SC, township #15, dwelling #203; "Weather," *Asheville Citizen*, June 30, 1924; Broadus Miller / Mamie Wadlington marriage license and certificate, June 30, 1924, Buncombe County Register of Deeds, Asheville, NC.

13. Turnbull, *Thomas Wolfe*, 16; Wolfe, *Welcome to Our City*, 11–12; Wolfe, *Look Homeward, Angel*, 250–251.

Chapter Nine

1. Beeby, *Revolt of the Tar Heels*; Gilmore, *Gender and Jim Crow*, 105–117, 121–126; Craig, *Josephus Daniels*, 146–191; H. Leon Prather, "The Red Shirt Movement," 174–184; 1898 Wilmington Race Riot Commission, *Final Report*; Cecelski and Tyson, *Democracy Betrayed*; "White Men, Take Warning," *News-Herald* (Morganton, NC), September 22, 1898; Perman, *Struggle for Mastery*, 148–172. For the historiographical argument on whether legally sanctioned measures served as mere window dressing for the fait accompli of disfranchisement of African Americans by force, or whether legal disfranchisement represented an attempt by white elites to suppress the votes of lower-class whites, see Key, *Southern Politics*; Kousser, *Shaping of Southern Politics*; Woodward, *Origins of the New South*, 321–349; Feldman, *Disfranchisement Myth*, 1–12. In North Carolina, advocates of African American disfranchisement strove to ensure that few whites would be affected by the new voting requirements. The constitutional amendment included a provision delaying implementation of the literacy test until 1908; elected governor in 1900, disfranchisement advocate Charles Aycock promptly launched a vigorous campaign for public education that dramatically increased literacy rates among the state's white population. Christensen, *Paradox of Tar Heel Politics*, 43–45.

2. Craig, *Josephus Daniels*, 146–191; Phillips, "Exploring Relations," 372; Daniels, *Tar Heels*, 207; Cash, "Paladin of the Drys," 139–147; Cash, "Jehovah of the Tar Heels," 313; Richardson, "No More Lynchings!," 403–404; "Governor Warns Lynchers," *New York Times*, December 9, 1923.

3. "Tar Heel of the Week: J. Van B. Metts," *News and Observer* (Raleigh, NC), April 22, 1951; John V. B. Metts to "Elizabeth," November 12, 1898, Hinsdale Family Papers (1712–1973), Box 3: Correspondence, 1892–1901, Rubenstein Rare Book and Manuscript Library, Duke University, Durham, NC.

4. E. C. Branson to J. R. Brown, February 8, 1921, Folder 188, E. C. Branson Papers, SHC; "Goss Will Go on Trial for His Life Today," *News and Observer*, October 22, 1923; "John Gross [sic] Writes His Religious Faith," *News-Herald*, December 13, 1923; John Goss death certificate, December 7, 1923, State Prison, Raleigh, Wake County, NC, #332, register #699; Corbitt, *Cameron Morrison*, 255; Jaspin, *Buried in the Bitter Waters*, 201–218; Newkirk, *Lynching in North Carolina*, 100–105. The escaped chain gang prisoner, John Goss, was recaptured, tried and convicted for rape, and then executed at the state penitentiary in December 1923.

5. Waldrep, "War of Words," 75–100; Trotti, "What Counts," 375–400; National Association for the Advancement of Colored People, *Thirty Years of Lynching*, 32; Tolnay and Beck, *Festival of Violence*, 112, 232; Newkirk, *Lynching in North Carolina*, 167–170; Phillips, "Exploring Relations," 361–374; Dray, *Hands of Persons Unknown*, 262; "Lynching Outlawed," *Wilmington Morning Star*, July 4, 1927; Richardson, "No More Lynchings!," 403–404; Cash, "Paladin of the Drys," 144.

6. MacLean, *Behind the Mask*, xiii. For the violence of the Reconstruction-era Klan in North Carolina, see Trealease, *White Terror*, 189–225, 336–348.

7. "'Fiery Cross' Is Once More Raised in Durham," *Landmark* (Statesville, NC), January 3, 1921; Chalmers, *Hooded Americanism*, 93; "Imperial Officers," Subseries 1.4, Folder 440, 1920-1921, Bryan Family Papers, SHC; Ku Klux Klan, *Constitution and Laws*, 23, 59. During the World War, Handy had overseen the Justice Department's operations in North and South Carolina, pursuing draft evaders and deserters and investigating persons suspected of subversion. Corbitt, *Clyde Roark Hoey*, 423; United States Provost Marshal General's Bureau, *Final Report July 15, 1919*, 287; United States Congress. Senate, *Brewing and Liquor Interests*, 2:2147; "Old North State Had Much," *Keowee Courier* (Pickens, SC), June 2, 1920; Waldrep, "National Policing," 605-606; "Fred C. Handy Resigns Office," *Watauga Democrat* (Boone, NC), September 21, 1922. A primary target of Handy's investigations was Rev. Cary Wilmer, the progressive rector of St. Luke's Episcopal Church in Atlanta and implacable foe of the Klan. Fuller, *Visible of the Invisible Empire*, 41-45, 87-88. For the actions of the Louisiana Klan, see Pegram, *One Hundred Percent American*, 172-174.

8. "Gen. Julian S. Carr," 204; Webb, *Jule Carr*, 195-196; "Klan Views Avowed by Confederates," *New York Times*, April 13, 1923; "Carr Says He's Rebel and Ku Kluxer, Too," *News-Herald*, April 19, 1923; Address to Confederate Memorial Association, New Orleans, April 10, 1923, and untitled/undated speech, both in Folder 29 (Addresses 1923), Julian Shakespeare Carr Papers #141, SHC; Rable, "Politics of Antilynching Legislation," 201-220; Dray, *Hands of Persons Unknown*, 258-272; Schneider, *We Return Fighting*, 123, 172-173. In contrast to the UCV, the Grand Army of the Republic—the Union veterans' organization—had unanimously adopted a resolution at its 1921 reunion condemning the Ku Klux Klan "as a standing menace to constitutional government and the open and impartial administration of the law." Grand Army of the Republic, *Journal of the Fifty-Fifth National Encampment*, 82-83.

9. Chalmers, *Hooded Americanism*, 95; Powell, *Dictionary of North Carolina Biography*, 2:325-326; Wilson, *Makers of America*, 2:243; Grady, *South's Burden*, vii; "Agreement Negotiated and Entered into by, among, and between William Joseph Simmons, H. W. Evans, et al.," John Quincy Jett Papers, Box 2, Legal Documents, Richard B. Russell Library for Political Research and Studies, University of Georgia Libraries, Athens. In the secondary literature, Henry A. Grady has sometimes been confused with New South spokesman Henry W. Grady; see, for example, MacLean, *Behind the Mask*, 133.

10. "Grady Admits He Is Grand Dragon of Klan in State," *Robesonian* (Lumberton, NC), January 24, 1924; Grady, "Klan and the Negro"; Gilmore, "False Friends and Avowed Enemies," 225-226; Powell, *Dictionary of North Carolina Biography*, 4:71. Ten years later, Judge Parker's comments came back to haunt him when the NAACP, in one of its first manifestations of political power, helped defeat his nomination to the United States Supreme Court. Goings, *NAACP Comes of Age*; Kluger, "Story of John Johnston Parker," 124-125; Powell, *Dictionary of North Carolina Biography*, 5:17; United States Congress, Senate, *Nomination of Frank A. Linney*, 7-8, 24, 43; Haley, *Charles N. Hunter*, 235-245.

11. "Grady Defends Klan," *Robesonian*, July 12, 1926; Grady, *South's Burden*, vii; "Grady Admits He Is Grand Dragon"; Grady, "Klan and the Negro"; "Lynching #12," *Time*, September 1, 1930. Some present-day scholars have reclassified a handful of

killings in early 1920s North Carolina as "lynchings," sometimes without clearly defining the term; see, e.g., Newkirk, *Lynching in North Carolina*, 170.

12. Lawrence Froneberger's death certificate, June 10, 1950, Buncombe County, NC, Asheville township, #12436; 1900 census, Gaston County, NC, Crowder Mountain township, district #76, dwelling # 225; 1910 census, Duval County, FL, Jacksonville city, ward #2, precinct #16, dwelling # 821; "Three Chinamen Captured in Raid and Opium Found," *Atlanta Constitution*, August 16, 1915; "Fight against Sale of Drugs Continued," *Atlanta Constitution*, August 17, 1915; "Loo Sang Is Held for Federal Jury by Commissioner," *Atlanta Constitution*, August 18, 1915; "F. M. Elliot Arrested, Charged with Forging of Orders for Dope," *Atlanta Constitution*, August 18, 1915; "Doctors and Druggists to Help Government in Fight on Drugs," *Atlanta Constitution*, September 11, 1915; "Drug Law Violations Flagrant in Columbus," *Atlanta Constitution*, October 11, 1915; "Government Drug Law Explained at Meeting," *Atlanta Constitution*, October 14, 1915; *U.S. World War I Draft Registration Cards, 1917-1918*, Ancestry.com; 1920 census, Mecklenburg County, NC, Charlotte, ward #8, district #152, dwelling #511½.

13. "Deposed Kleagle," *Asheville Citizen*, September 29, 1922; Powell, *Dictionary of North Carolina Biography*, 1:4; "Commissioner Defends Action in Naming Special Officers," *Asheville Citizen*, November 23, 1921; "Grand Jury Urge Audit of Books of Magistrates," *Asheville Citizen*, November 19, 1921; Pleasants, *Buncombe Bob*, 7.

14. "Return of Women Still Wrapped in Complete Mystery," *Asheville Citizen*, November 3, 1921; "Carolina Jury to Investigate Ku Klux Klan," *Washington (DC) Times*, November 10, 1921; H. E. C. Bryant, "Ku Klux Klan Is Blamed," *Charlotte Observer*, reprinted in *Landmark*, November 7, 1921; "Eugene Garlington Given Two Years on Road," *Asheville Citizen*, November 20, 1921; Ohio Adjutant General's Office, *Official Roster of Ohio Soldiers*, 16:5922; Scott, *Scott's Official History*, 136-137, 146, 149-153, 161, 173, 187, 286-291; 1920 census, Buncombe County, NC, Asheville township, ward #4, subdivision #3, dwelling #182 (24 Goodlake Avenue); *U.S. City Directories, 1821-1989*, Ancestry.com; *U.S. Department of Veterans Affairs Beneficiary Identification Records Locator Subsystem (BIRLS) Death File, 1850-2010*, Ancestry.com; *U.S. World War I Draft Registration Cards, 1917-1918*, Ancestry.com; 1940 census, Cuyahoga County, OH, Cleveland, ward #16, block#11, household #134.

15. "Find True Bill in Case against Four," *Asheville Citizen*, November 8, 1921; "Grand Jurors to See If Ku Klux Are Active Here," *Asheville Citizen*, November 10, 1921; "To Continue Grand Jury Probe Today," *Asheville Citizen*, November 11, 1921; "Grand Jury Probe Nears Completion," *Asheville Citizen*, November 12, 1921; "Ku Klux Klan's Organizer Here Is Under Arrest." *Asheville Citizen*, November 13, 1921; "Ku Klux Leader Will Plead Not Guilty In Trial," *Asheville Citizen*, November 14, 1921; "Ku Klux Organizer Is Special Officer," *Asheville Citizen*, November 17, 1921; "Courts or Chaos," *Asheville Citizen*, November 13, 1921; "Expect Indictments Today in Grand Jury Probe," *Asheville Citizen*, November 15, 1921; Hapgood, "New Threat," 58; "Voice of the People: Anent the Two White Girls and Negro Men," *Asheville Citizen*, November 4, 1921.

16. "Lawyers Engage in Sharp Verbal Clash," *Asheville Citizen*, November 19, 1921; Duncan and Burns, *National Parks*, 221-223; "An Ugly Slander Proved False," *Asheville*

Citizen, November 20, 1921; "Ask 'Bill of Particulars' in Massa Case," *Asheville Citizen*, November 20, 1921; "Judge Wells Orders Solicitor to File 'Bill of Particulars' in Case against George Massa," *Asheville Citizen*, November 22, 1921; "Ku Klux Sought to Use Services of Young Citizen," *Asheville Citizen*, November 23, 1921; "Bill of Particulars Is Filed by O.K. Bennett in Case against Massa," *Asheville Citizen*, November 24, 1921; "Sought to Buy Evidence to Convict in Massa Case," *Asheville Citizen*, November 27, 1921; "A Case in Equity," *Asheville Citizen*, November 28, 1921; "Probe of Charges involving High School Girls Ordered," *Asheville Citizen*, November 29, 1921; "Hearing to Fix Blame for High School Slander," *Asheville Citizen*, November 30, 1921; "'No Truth in Alleged Charge against School Girls' Is the Verdict," *Asheville Citizen*, December 1, 1921; "Roberts Moves to End False Reports," *Asheville Citizen*, December 2, 1921.

17. "Deposed Kleagle," *Asheville Citizen*, September 29, 1922; *Asheville City Directory*, 7 vols. (Asheville, NC: Commercial Service Company, 1921–27), Buncombe County Special Collections, Pack Memorial Library, Asheville, NC; *Meeting of Grand Dragons*, 70.

18. "Color Line on the Square," *Asheville Times*, July 20, 1924; Tindall, *Emergence of the New South*, 146.

Chapter Ten

1. Theodore Harris, "Negroes Present Their Side of the Situation," *Asheville Citizen*, October 30, 1925; "Negro Assailant of a White Woman Hunted by Police," *High Point (NC) Enterprise*, August 18, 1925; "Sheriff Takes Negro from the City as Big Crowd Begins to Form," *Asheville Citizen*, September 20, 1925; North Carolina State Board of Public Welfare, *Capital Punishment in North Carolina*, 96–103.

2. North Carolina State Board of Public Welfare, *Capital Punishment in North Carolina*, 96–103.

3. "Sheriff Takes Negro from the City."

4. "Neely and Mansel to Face Trial at Once," *Asheville Citizen*, October 28, 1925; "Asheville," *Times Picayune* (New Orleans), October 28, 1925; "Asheville, N.C., Scene of Another Attack," *Bee* (Danville, VA), October 27, 1925; "To Asheville Negroes," *Asheville Citizen*, October 29, 1925; "A Warning Repeated," *Asheville Citizen*, October 30, 1925.

5. "To Asheville Negroes"; "Warning Repeated"; "Negro Citizens of Asheville Call Huge Mass Meeting for Sunday to Consider Situation," *Asheville Citizen*, October 31, 1925.

6. Theodore Harris, "Negroes Present Their Side of the Situation," *Asheville Citizen*, October 30, 1925.

7. "Neely and Mansel to Face Trial"; "Solicitor Will Relentlessly Prosecute the Negroes Held on Criminal Assault Counts," *Asheville Citizen*, October 29, 1925.

8. *Report of the Adjutant General 1925 to 1926*, 9; "Troops Ordered to Guard Trials Here If Needed," *Asheville Citizen*, October 31, 1925; "Local Briefs in and around Town," *News-Herald* (Morganton, NC), November 11, 1925; "With Troops Guarding Jail Negroes Await Their Trial," *News and Observer* (Raleigh, NC), November 3, 1925; "Woman Accuser of Alvin Mansel Placed on Stand," *News and Observer*, November 4, 1925.

9. "Woman Accuser of Alvin Mansel"; North Carolina State Board of Public Welfare, *Capital Punishment in North Carolina*, 96–103; "Found Guilty of Attack," *California Eagle* (Los Angeles), November 27, 1925; "Preston Neely Goes on Trial for His Life," *Asheville Citizen*, November 6, 1927; "Preston Neely Is Acquitted and Rushed to South Carolina under Guard," *Asheville Citizen*, November 8, 1925; "Troops Again Ordered to Report in Armory," *Asheville Citizen*, November 8, 1925.

10. North Carolina State Board of Public Welfare, *Capital Punishment in North Carolina*, 98–102.

11. Corbitt, *Angus Wilton McLean*, xvi; Underwood, *Scotsman from Lumber River*; Daniels, *Tar Heels*, 64; "McLean Is Timber for Presidential Seat," *Independent* (Elizabeth City. NC), reprinted in *Hickory (NC) Daily Record*, June 25, 1927; Lewis, "North Carolina," 43; "Machine Has Decreed Wilton M'Lean Shall Succeed Mr. Morrison," *Greensboro Daily News*, July 11, 1921; North Carolina State Board of Public Welfare, *Capital Punishment in North Carolina*, 102; "Both of Them Are Happy," *Pittsburgh Courier*, November 15, 1930.

12. Corbitt, *Angus Wilton McLean*, 528–529.

13. Lewis, "North Carolina"; "Wrong Man May Be Serving Time," *News and Observer*, June 25, 1927; "Seek Pardon for N.C. Life Termer," *Afro-American* (Baltimore), May 26, 1928.

14. Records of General Sessions of Greenwood County Court, 1926, Clerk of Court's Office, Greenwood County, SC; "More True Bills," *Index-Journal* (Greenwood, SC), March 3, 1926; "Liquor Comes High in Sessions Court," *Index-Journal*, March 3, 1926; 1930 census, Greenwood County, SC, Greenwood city, enumeration district #24-10, 247 Pressley Street; Waronker, "Dillon's Ohav Shalom," 17; Form N-315, US Department of Justice, Immigration and Naturalization Service, *South Carolina, Naturalization Records, 1868-1991*, Ancestry.com.

15. Kirby, *Rural Worlds Lost*, 217–221; Steiner and Brown, *North Carolina Chain Gang*, 177. As Steiner and Brown note, Virginia and Maryland were exceptions to the county-operated chain gang system; in both Virginia and Maryland, state authorities managed the chain gangs.

16. Steiner and Brown, *North Carolina Chain Gang*, 3–7; "Buddy Boyd Goes to Gang," *Index-Journal*, September 18, 1926; 1930 census, Greenwood County, SC, Callison township, dwelling #35; Department of Commerce, Bureau of the Census, *Prisoners and Juvenile Delinquents*, 88; "Report for 1st. Quarter of 1926 of Disbursements by J. A. Marshall, Supervisor," *Index-Journal*, April 14, 1926; "Report for 2nd. Quarter of 1926 of Disbursements by J. A. Marshall, Supervisor," *Index-Journal*, July 8, 1926; South Carolina General Assembly, *Report of State Officers, 1920*, 2:119–120; "'Hot Stuff' Caught at Greenville," Greenwood *Index-Journal*, August 18, 1926; South Carolina General Assembly, *Special Joint Legislative Committee*, 26; "A Cross-Country Road Is Improved," *Index-Journal*, June 23, 1926; "Levelling Ridlehuber Hill," *Index-Journal*, October 26, 1926.

17. South Carolina General Assembly, *Report of State Officers, January 13, 1920*, 2:119–120; South Carolina State Board of Public Welfare, *Second Annual Report of the State Board of Public Welfare of South Carolina, 1921*, 102; "Prisoner Voices Grave

Accusation against Officers," *Index-Journal*, March 8, 1926; "Spartanburg Jury Convicts Chaingang Man," *Edgefield (SC) Advertiser*, November 2, 1921; Tannenbaum, *Darker Phases of the South*, 80.

18. "Broadus Miller Still at Large," *Index-Journal*, June 25, 1927; "Suspected Slayer of Girl, 15, Caught," *Asheville Times*, June 22, 1927; National Park Service, "Franklin Pierce Tate House"; 1930 census, Buncombe County, NC, Leicester township, 132 County Home Road; Petition for Naturalization, US Department of Labor, Naturalization Service, *North Carolina, Naturalization Records, 1868-1991*, Ancestry.com.

Chapter Eleven

1. "Mr. and Mrs. Frank Tate to Build Stone House," *News-Herald* (Morganton, NC), May 5, 1927; Phifer, *Burke*, 162, 165; "Garrou Knitting Mills"; Betts, *North Carolina School for the Deaf*, 101; "Thomason-Tate Engagement Announced," *News-Herald*, May 25, 1922; "Local Briefs in and around Town," *News-Herald*, June 22, 1927; "A Tale of a Ford, Two Negroes and a Mule," *News-Herald*, December 14, 1922; "Franklin Pierce Tate House"; "Suspected Slayer of Girl, 15, Caught," *Asheville Times*, June 22, 1927.

2. Evans, *Confederate Military History*, 4:486–487; Powell, *Dictionary of North Carolina Biography*, 6:3; Phifer, *Burke*, 97, 130, 463–465; Betts, *North Carolina School for the Deaf*, 103; Inscoe, *Mountain Masters*, 66, 79–81, 161–176; Brown, *State Movement*, 191–214; Jeffrey, "Unclean Vessel," 389–431; Morris, "Western North Carolina Railroad," 256–282; Arthur, *Western North Carolina*, 472–478; Summers, *Railroads, Reconstruction*, 110.

3. Mancini, *One Dies, Get Another*, 207; "North Carolina Legislature," *Charlotte Southern Home*, March 10, 1873; "Captions of the Acts and Resolutions," *Weekly Era* (Raleigh, NC), March 13, 1873; "Legislature of North Carolina," *Charlotte Democrat*, March 1, 1875; "Railroad Matters," *Raleigh News*, March 4, 1875; Abrams, "Western North Carolina Railroad"; Starnes, *Creating the Land of the Sky*, 24. For a sampling of the stockaded convict laborers, see 1880 census, McDowell County, NC, Old Fort township, enumeration district # 1411, dwelling # 215, which lists a prisoner contingent of 167 African American men, 5 white men, and 3 African American women.

4. Phifer, *Burke*, 463; 1870, 1880, 1900, and 1910 censuses, Burke County, NC; United States Bureau of the Census, *Fourteenth Census of the United States 1920*, 3:736. From 1870 through 1920, the African American (Black and "mulatto") population of Burke County fluctuated between 2,300 and 2,700 people. "The Negro Exodus," *Blue Ridge Blade* (Morganton, NC), October 11, 1879; "Burke County," *Carolina Mountaineer* (Morganton, NC), January 2, 1884; William Cohen, "Negro Involuntary Servitude," 39.

5. "New Census Needed," *News-Herald*, April 8, 1926; "Big Paving Program on for Next Year," *News-Herald*, December 13, 1923; "Morganton Has a New Lighting System," *News-Herald*, September 20, 1923; "Good Impressions," *News-Herald*, May 26, 1927; "Burke County Confederate Monument, Morganton," DocSouth: Commemorative Landscapes of North Carolina, accessed July 17, 2022, https://docsouth.unc.edu/commland/monument/259/; Gill Billings, "Confederate Statue," photocopy in

Confederate—Monument vertical file, Burke County Public Library, Morganton, NC; "Children Took Big Part in Memorial Exercises," *News-Herald*, May 12, 1927.

6. "Military Company Is Probable for Town," Morganton *News-Herald*, November 9, 1922; "Local Briefs in and around Town," *News-Herald*, November 30, 1922; "Formal Opening of Armory on June 26," *News-Herald*, June 7, 1923; "Rumors," "Morganton Boys Are at Spruce Pine," *News-Herald*, October 4, 1923; "Morganton Boys Return from Spruce Pine," *News-Herald*, October 11, 1923; "It Is Capt. Connelly and Lieut. Sam Ervin," *News-Herald*, February 21, 1924; "Company B 105 Engineers Are Praised by Major," *News-Herald*, November 1, 1923; "Young Men Wanted," *News-Herald*, September 17, 1925; "Local Guardsman on Duty in Asheville," *News-Herald*, November 5, 1925; "Local Briefs in and around Town," *News-Herald*, November 11, 1925.

7. "Union Meeting for Law Enforcement," *News-Herald*, January 18, 1923; "Mr. J. Gilmore Mabe Died Early Yesterday," *News-Herald*, May 4, 1922; "Klansmen Appear at Burial of Member," "Resolutions," *News-Herald*, May 11, 1922; "Prominent Clansman to Speak Here Tonight," *News-Herald*, May 18, 1922; "Ku Klux Klan Holds Open Forum Meeting," *Charlotte Observer*, May 21, 1922; "Ku Klux Klanism Is Practical Religion," *News-Herald*, May 25, 1922; "Anarchy or Patriotism Subject of Dialogue," *News-Herald*, July 26, 1923; "Tent Meeting Is Attracting Crowds," *News-Herald*, July 6, 1922; "Triplett Campaign Very Successful," "Klansmen Appear at Triplett Meeting," *News-Herald*, July 20, 1922; "Ku Kluxers Appear at Revival Service," *News-Herald*, September 14, 1922. The money given to Triplett and Eastes was small change compared to the vast sums earned by the major stars of the evangelical circuit. During a six-week revival in Charlotte in early 1924, Billy Sunday raked in $26,000 in donations—including $225 from the Mecklenburg County Klan. "30,000 Hear Billy Sunday in Farewell Sermon," *News-Herald*, February 14, 1924.

8. "Ku Klux Klan on Hunt for Burke Booze Violations," *News-Herald*, November 9, 1922; "Burke Kounty Klan Objects to Communication," *News-Herald*, November 23, 1922; Charles Burleson, personal interview with author, April 13, 2007.

9. "Koming Klansmen," Folder 125, Guy Benton Johnson Papers, SHC; "To Organize Patriotic Sons of America," *News-Herald*, August 2, 1923; Lichliter, *History of the Junior Order*, 1–3, 107, 121, 328, 330, 532, 719; Briggs, *Immigration and American Unionism*, 46–47; Gilman, Peck, and Colby, *New International Encyclopaedia*, 14:619; Clawson, *Constructing Brotherhood*, 83; Preuss, *Secret and Other Societies*, 208, 530–533, 542; Bennett, *Party of Fear*, 452; Powell, *Dictionary of North Carolina Biography*, 3:158–159, 5:204–205; "Junior Order Orphanage Dedicated at Lexington," *News-Herald*, June 9, 1927; "Junior Order Proposes Uniform School Taxes," *News-Herald*, October 21, 1926; "Junior Order to Have Flag Raising in Hickory Sunday," *News-Herald*, October 1, 1925; "Oak Hill Presented with Flag and Bible," *News-Herald*, December 9, 1926; "New School Building Dedicated Last Sunday," *News-Herald*, June 2, 1927; "North Virginia Flooded with Klux Posters," *Washington (DC) Times*, February 25, 1922. "Mr. S. S. Lane Buried on Sunday Afternoon," *News-Herald*, September 17, 1925; "Resolutions of Respect," *News-Herald*, September 24, 1925; United States Congress. House of Representatives, *Ku-Klux Klan*, 76, 90; Sweeney, "Great Bigotry Merger," 9; Shotwell, "Crystallizing Public Hatred," 113. In the words of Grand Dragon Henry Grady, the Klan

and the Junior Order were "almost as one" in their attitudes toward "the Jew, the negro and the Roman Catholic." "Grady Admits He Is Grand Dragon of Klan in State," *Robesonian* (Lumberton, NC), January 24, 1924.

10. Lichliter, *History of the Junior Order*, 540; Burke County Historical Society, *Heritage of Burke County*, 145; Parker. "Beatrice Cobb"; "Miss Beatrice Cobb," 6; "A Question of Usefulness to the County," *News-Herald*, October 26, 1922.

11. "Why Not?," *News-Herald*, August 30, 1923; Burke County Historical Society, *Heritage of Burke County*, 145; "Observations in Florida," *News-Herald*, February 18, 1926; "S. J. Ervin, Jr. Named Democratic Chairman," *News-Herald*, July 17, 1924; "Looking in on the Democratic National Convention," *News-Herald*, July 3, 1924; "The Campaign," *News-Herald*, September 25, 1924; Burke County Historical Society, *Heritage of Burke County*, 145; "It Pays to Boost," *News-Herald*, September 13, 1923; "Burke County Rich in History and Attractions," *News-Herald*, Prosperity and Publicity edition, spring 1924; "Comments on Special Edition," *News-Herald*, April 3, 1924.

12. "Uncle Howard Passed Away Last Sunday," *News-Herald*, February 16, 1922; "Uncle Calvin Smith," *News-Herald*, October 15, 1925; "An Old Timer at Morganton," *News-Herald*, August 23, 1923; "'Uncle Jones' Erwin Gets Letter from His Friend," *News-Herald*, September 13, 1923; "Good Colored Woman Dies," *News-Herald*, July 3, 1924; "The Negro Problem," *News-Herald*, August 26, 1926; Dollard, *Caste and Class*, 282–283; "Among the Home Folks," *News-Herald*, March 17, 1927.

13. "The Seating of Mrs. Felton," untitled editorial, *News-Herald*, November 23, 1922; Burke County Historical Society, *Heritage of Burke County*, 145; Williamson, *Crucible of Race*, 124–130; "Negro Tom Gwynn Found Guilty in Ten Minutes," *News-Herald*, May 29, 1919; "Negro Barely Escapes Vengeance of a Mob," "Outwitting a Mob," *News-Herald*, June 12, 1919; "Praise for Burke Officers," *Landmark* (Statesville, NC), reprinted in *News-Herald*, June 19, 1919; Kotch, "Unduly Harsh and Unworkably Rigid," 118–119. Within six weeks of his arrest, Gwynn was tried, convicted, and executed by the state.

14. 1900 census, Pierce County, Georgia, Blackshear district, dwelling #108; 1910 census, Pierce County, Georgia, Blackshear district, dwelling #62; Puckett, *Memories of a Georgia Teacher*, 12–13.

15. "Montague Must Die Friday for His Crime," *News-Herald*, January 21, 1926; "Negroes Fall Out over Cards, One Dead," *News-Herald*, June 12, 1924; Register of Deeds, Burke County, North Carolina, marriage records, Book 16, p. 296; 1920 census, Burke County, North Carolina, Morganton township, precinct # 2, dwellings # 38 through #60; Fleming, *Summer Remembered*, 11. The 1920 census lists the head of Louise Avery's household as her grandmother, but the woman was actually her great-aunt; see "Annie Corinna Avery Grimes," in Burke County Historical Society, *Heritage of Burke County*, 208.

16. Betts, *North Carolina School for the Deaf*, 11; "School for the Deaf, N.C.," Series 2, Box 3, Post-1920 Burke County, N.C., Edward William Phifer Papers, SHC; Phifer, *Burke*, 97; "'Old Hurrygraph' Visits Morganton," *News-Herald*, July 12, 1923; 1920 and 1930 censuses, Burke County, NC, Morganton township #2, North Carolina School for the Deaf.

17. "Atrocious Crime at N.C. School for Deaf," *News-Herald*, April 30, 1925; "Montague Must Die"; "Found Asleep in Girl's Room after Assault," *Charlotte Observer*, April 25, 1925; Kotch, "Unduly Harsh and Unworkably Rigid," 121; "Montague Negro Is Sentenced to Die," *News-Herald*, May 14, 1925. The Morganton newspaper stated the alleged victim was fourteen years old, while the *Charlotte Observer* reported that she was twelve.

18. North Carolina Adjutant General's Office, *Report January 1, 1925 to June 30, 1926*, 7–8; "Atrocious Crime"; "Found Asleep"; "Montague Negro Sentenced to Die"; "In Fairness to Our Negroes," *News-Herald*, May 14, 1925; 1920 census, Burke County, NC, Morganton township, dwelling #68, and Morganton township, precinct # 2, dwelling #19.

19. "Delay a Dangerous Element," *News-Herald*, November 5, 1925; "When Patience Has Ceased to Be a Virtue," *News-Herald*, November 26, 1925; "Arthur Montague Dies in Chair for His Crime," Morganton *News-Herald*, January 28, 1926; North Carolina State Board of Public Welfare, *Capital Punishment in North Carolina*, 39.

20. "Pageant Tonight Promises to be Instructive—Entertaining; Many Visitors Expected," *News-Herald*, May 15, 1924; "'The Birthright' Presented Scenes in Burke County History in Inspiring Way," *News-Herald*, May 22, 1924; "Burke County History Effectively Presented in Pageant Form in 'The Birthright,'" *News-Herald*, May 22, 1925; John A. Livingstone, "'The Birthright' Was an Artistic Triumph and a Review of Burke's Wonderful History," *News and Observer*, reprinted in *News-Herald*, May 28, 1925.

Chapter Twelve

1. "Atrocious Crime"; "Precaution Well Enough," *News-Herald* (Morganton, NC), April 30, 1925; "Special Court Term Closed on Wednesday," "In Fairness to Our Negroes," *News-Herald*, May 14, 1925; "Speaking for the Negroes," *News-Herald*, May 21, 1925. The grand jury's recommendation was not followed, and African Americans continued to be employed at the School of the Deaf. 1930 census, Burke County, NC, Morganton township #2, North Carolina School for the Deaf.

2. "Negro Dependency in the Southern Community," Folder 20, Arthur Franklin Raper Papers, SHC; Moore and Freeman, *History of First Baptist Church*, 22; "Burke Tannery and Big Shoe Co. Merge," *News-Herald*, May 5, 1921; Burke County Historical Society, *Heritage of Burke County*, 209; "Local Briefs in and around Town," *News-Herald*, June 30, 1927; "News, Personals, and Other Things from Fonta Flora," *Burke County News* (Morganton, NC), March 17, 1899; Minchin, *Hiring the Black Worker*, 23; Woodward, *Origins of the New South*, 222–225; Gilmore, *Gender and Jim Crow*, 23; Byerly, *Hard Times Cotton Mill Girls*, 44–50; Thompson, *From the Cotton Field*, 249.

3. Hall, *Like a Family*, 66–67, 238, 255–266; McGregor, *Hosiery Manufacturing Industry*, 5; Brown, *Upbuilding Black Durham*, 92–93; Newby, *Plain Folk in the New South*, 462–466, 474–481; United States Department of Labor, *Wages and Hours of Labor*, 7–8, 30.

4. North Carolina Department of Labor and Printing, *Thirty-Second Report 1919–1920*, 78; Burke County Historical Society, *Heritage of Burke County*, 198; Phifer, *Burke*, 245–247, 267–268; "The Garrou Mills" and "Garrou Knitting Mills," Industries vertical file, Burke County Public Library, Morganton, NC.

5. Johnston Avery, "Extensive Search Is Being Made for Morganton Slayer," *Hickory (NC) Daily Record*, June 22, 1927; C. K. Avery to Jess Byrd, March 5, 1969, Folder 1, Andrew Dunn Kincaid Papers, SHC; Hood, "The Tale of Crooked Neck John"; 1860 census (slave schedule), Burke County, NC; "Glen Alpine Has Lost Three Leading Citizens," *News-Herald*, June 23, 1927; Kirby, *Rural Worlds Lost*, 293; 1920 census, Burke County, NC, Lower Creek township, enumeration district #16, dwelling #93; James Kincaid death certificate, January 4, 1923, Burke County, NC, Quaker Meadow township. Among the numerous Kincaids in Burke County was Beatrice Cobb's mother. The *News-Herald* editor was thus a distant cousin of the young mill worker, but it is unlikely that Cobb would have known who the girl was before the fatal attack. Burke County Historical Society, *Heritage of Burke County*, 145.

6. 1930 census, Burke County, NC, Morganton township, enumeration district #19, dwelling #20; Avery, "Extensive Search"; Cecil Kincaid (Gladys Kincaid's younger brother), telephone interview with author, June 28, 2007; Cecil Kincaid and Mae Fleming Wellman, interviewed in *Let the Dead Speak*. For a general description of the living conditions of individuals like Gladys Kincaid, see Byerly, *Hard Times Cotton Mill Girls*, esp. 44–50.

7. Marjorie Fleming, personal interview with author, June 26, 2007; Frank Smethurst, "Determined Search for Negro Slayer of Young Morganton Girl Futile," *News and Observer* (Raleigh, NC), June 23, 1927; "Troops Trail Negro on M'Lean Order," *Asheville Times*, June 23, 1927; "Morganton Negro Attacked Girl in Sight of Three Homes," *Winston-Salem Journal*, June 28, 1927; Baker, "Lynching Ballads in North Carolina," 45; Harry L. Griffin, "Hundreds Join Grim Hunt for Assailant of Girl in Burke," *Charlotte Observer*, June 23, 1927; "Negro Attacks White Girl," *News-Herald*, June 23, 1927; "A Trying Week," Morganton *News-Herald*, June 30, 1927; "Funeral Today Is Burke's Sadest [sic]," *Hickory Daily Record*, 23 June 1927; "Young Woman Is Dead Following Brutal Attack," *Bee* (Danville, VA), June 22, 1927; "Can't Afford a Lynching," *Twin City Sentinel* (Winston-Salem, NC), June 24, 1927.

8. "Sleepless Searchers for Negro Slayer Find No Clue," *Hickory Daily Record*, June 24, 1927; "Morganton Negro Attacked Girl"; "Hopes of Capturing Man Back to Low Ebb Again," *News and Observer*, June 27, 1927; Smethurst, "Determined Search"; Harry L. Griffin, "Net Tightens about Negro Sought for Attacking Girl," *Charlotte Observer*, June 24, 1927; Griffin, "Hundreds Join Grim Hunt"; L. J. Hampton, "Hickory Reports Say Murderer Has Been Caught," *Winston-Salem Journal*, June 24, 1927 (morning edition); H. Clay Ferree, "The Day the Mob Took Over," Crime and Criminals vertical file, Burke County Public Library; Mae Fleming Wellman, interviewed in *Let the Dead Speak*.

9. Mae Fleming Wellman and Cecil Kincaid, interviewed in *Let the Dead Speak*; Cecil Kincaid, telephone interview with author, June 28, 2007; "Suspected Slayer Caught."

10. "Troops Trail Negro"; Ownby, *Subduing Satan*, 122–123; Catawba River Baptist Association, *Minutes of the Ninety-Eighth Annual Session*, 28–29; "First Baptist Church Calls Mr. Bradshaw," *News-Herald*, November 26, 1925; Holsclaw and Pennell, "Murder of Gladys Kincaid"; "Final Tribute Saturday for Rev. W. R. Bradshaw," *News-Herald*, March 31, 1942; "Funeral Today."

11. "Monument for Gladys Kincaid Has Been Ordered," *News-Herald*, July 28, 1927.

Chapter Thirteen

1. "Negro Is Declared an Outlaw," *News-Herald* (Morganton, NC), June 23, 1927; North Carolina General Assembly, *Public Laws 1866*, 125–126.

2. "New Officers Take Over Affair of the County," *News-Herald*, December 9, 1926. For the wording of the statute as in effect in the 1920s, see Fugitives from Justice, North Carolina Consolidated Statutes, Article 6, Section 4549: Outlawry for Felony, in North Carolina General Assembly, *Consolidated Statutes of North Carolina*, 1:1846–1847.

3. Johnston Avery, "Extensive Search Is Being Made for Morganton Slayer," *Hickory (NC) Daily Record*, June 22, 1927; Harry L. Griffin, "Hundreds Join Grim Hunt for Assailant of Girl in Burke," *Charlotte (NC) Observer*, June 23, 1927; "Statement from Mr. Taylor," *News-Herald*, July 7, 1927; "To My Friends," *News-Herald*, July 14, 1927.

4. Great Britain Privy Council, "Order of the Privy Council." For outlawry's origins in English common law, see Pollard and Maitland, *History of English Law*, 459–461.

5. Kay and Cary, *Slavery in North Carolina*, 61–66. Colonial authorities compensated the owners of slaves killed as the result of outlawry, but in 1753 the General Assembly stipulated that in order to receive compensation, an owner must certify the slave had "been sufficiently cloathed, and . . . constantly received, for the preceding Year, an Allowance not less than a Quart of Corn per Diem." Five years later, noting "the High Valuation of Slaves . . . killed by Virtue of an Outlawry," legislators decreed that a slaveholder would receive no more than sixty pounds in compensation, approximately one-third of a male slave's potential monetary value. Clark, *State Records of North Carolina*, 23:389–390, 489. For an example of a colonial-era proclamation of outlawry against a fugitive slave, see "State of North Carolina, Craven County," *North Carolina Gazette* (New Bern), March 6, 1778 (reprinted March 27, 1778). Colonial Virginia also outlawed fugitive slaves and compensated owners if the slaves were killed; see Cleve, *Slaveholders' Union*, 53. However, the Virginia law authorizing the outlawing of fugitive slaves was apparently revoked in 1792. *African Observer*, October 1827, 198.

6. "Outlawry," *Cape Fear Reporter* (Wilmington, NC), April 14, 1821; "Outlawry," "Fifty Dollars Reward," *Franklyn Herald* (Greenfield, MA), May 22, 1821; *New-York Post*, May 10, 1821; "From the N.Y. Daily Advertiser," *Western Carolinian* (Salisbury, NC), June 12, 1821; Stowe, *Key to Uncle Tom's Cabin*, 85–86; British and Foreign Anti-Slavery Society, *Slavery and the Internal Slave Trade*, 176–177. For other examples of printed outlawry proclamations, see, for example, *Wilmington (NC) Gazette*, January 1, 1807; *Edenton (NC) Gazette*, September 17, 1821; *Newbern (NC) Sentinel*, August 11, 1827. In 1831, when the state legislature incorporated the existing slave code into a new "Act concerning Slaves and Free Persons of Color," the process for outlawing fugitive slaves remained unchanged. North Carolina General Assembly, "Slaves and Free Persons of Color."

7. Bowditch, *Slavery and the Constitution*, 104–105; Watson, *Wilmington, North Carolina*, 125, 153; 1850 census, New Hanover County, NC, Wilmington city, dwelling #5; Campbell, *Southern Business Directory*, 399; "Notice," *Wilmington (NC) Chronicle*, November 2, 1842; "Ranaway," *Wilmington Chronicle*, May 4, 1842; "Notice," *Wilmington (NC) Commercial*, March 16, 1849; "$50 Reward for London," *Wilmington (NC)*

Journal, August 31, 1849. For other examples of slaveholders who offered greater rewards for outlawed slaves' deaths than for their return, see "Fifty Dollars Reward for Aaron," *Wilmington Journal*, April 5, 1850; "State of North Carolina," *Wilmington Journal*, September 20, 1850.

8. Hamilton, *Reconstruction in North Carolina*, 147, 313; Du Bois, *Black Reconstruction in America*, 470; North Carolina General Assembly, *Public Laws 1866*, 98–105; "Captions of the Acts and Resolutions," *Daily Progress* (Raleigh, NC), February 10, 1866; North Carolina General Assembly, *Public Laws 1866*, 125–126. In 1905, the legislature made minor revisions to the outlawry statute, adding criminal court judges to those empowered to issue outlawry proclamations and clarifying that if the proclamation were issued by a judge, as opposed to two justices of the peace, then the judge did not have to be from the county where the alleged felony had occurred. Moreover, judges could authorize the sheriff of any county in the state to organize a posse, while justices of the peace could do so for only their own county. Womack, Gulley, and Rodman, *Revisal of 1905 of North Carolina*, 1:953.

9. Sider, *Living Indian Histories*, 157–176; Bailey, "How Scuffletown Became Indian Country," 18–69; Evans, *To Die Game*; Evans, "Native Americans in the Civil War," 187–212; Dial and Eliades, *Only Land I Know*, 45–87; Blu, *Lumbee Problem*, 50–61; Lee, *Claiming the Union*, 129–131; United States Congress. Senate, *Testimony Taken*, 283, 286–287, 297. The process by which the Lowries were outlawed was complex and murky, stretching over several years and involving multiple proclamations. Press accounts often and erroneously asserted that they had been outlawed by the North Carolina governor; even the Robeson County sheriff and the North Carolina adjutant general made statements to this effect.

10. "House of Representatives," *Daily Journal* (Wilmington, NC), January 27, 1872; North Carolina General Assembly, *Public Laws 1871–72*, 166; Evans, *To Die Game*, 221, 234–235, 240–241; "The Lowry Gang," *Wilmington (NC) Morning Star*, July 21, 1872; "The Outlaws," *Daily Journal*, July 23, 1872; "Paid Up," *Raleigh News*, August 9, 1872; Lowery, *Lumbee Indians*, 15–17; Image SF-P-4624/1, Wishart Family Papers #4624, SHC; Norment, *Lowrie History*, 141–142; "The Dead Outlaw," *Wilmington Journal*, January 3, 1873; Battle, *Battle's Revisal of the Public Statutes*, 80–81; "Act for Amnesty and Pardon," *Daily Era* (Raleigh, NC), March 6, 1873; "North Carolina," *Raleigh News*, March 27, 1873; "Stephen Lowery Killed," *North Carolina Gazette* (Fayetteville), February 26, 1874.

11. Gerth and Mills, *From Max Weber*, 78.

12. "A Negro Desperado," *Wilmington (NC) Sun*, November 28, 1878; "Proclamation of Outlawry against Tom Johnston," *Wilmington Sun*, December 5, 1878; "Shooting Affray," *Wilmington Sun*, December 6, 1878; "Cape Fear Ripples," "Kidnapped in the City," *Wilmington Sun*, December 11, 1878; "Load Your Gun," *Durham (NC) Daily Globe*, October 20, 1892; "A Highway Robber!," *Durham Daily Globe*, October 17, 1892; "Burglars at Work!," *Durham Daily Globe*, October 24, 1892; "Rogers Outlawed!," *Durham Daily Globe*, October 26, 1892; "$25 Reward," *Durham Daily Globe*, November 4, 1892; "A Foul Murder," "The Jones Murder," "That 'Inaccessible' Swamp," *Wilmington Morning Star*, June 7, 1895; "Murder in House's Creek," *News and Observer* (Raleigh, NC), August 30, 1896; "Booker Is Outlawed," *News and Observer*, September 10, 1896.

For the demographics of outlawed fugitives, see "Appendix: Known Cases of Outlawry Proclamations in North Carolina, March 1866–June 1927," in Young, "World of Broadus Miller," 366–377. North Carolina's approval of statewide prohibition in 1908 caused a major demographic change; over the next twenty years, the majority of outlawry proclamations would be issued against white men, in most cases bootleggers who had shot law officers.

13. "Negroes Jailed, Charge of Arson," *Charlotte (NC) News*, October 15, 1901; "Harris Has Gone," *Charlotte News*, October 18, 1901; "Bad Negro Again on the Rampage," *Charlotte News*, December 26, 1902; "Will Harris Again," *Charlotte News*, January 10, 1903; "Desperado Harris Caught," *Charlotte Observer*, April 2, 1903; "Will Harris, Desperado, Gets 25 Years," *Charlotte News*, April 25, 1903; "Negro Desperado, Will Harris, Is Now at Large," *Charlotte News*, August 11, 1903; "Harris Outlawed," *Charlotte Observer*, August 15, 1903; "Was This Harris?," *Charlotte News*, August 15, 1903; "Is Negro Harris Highwayman?," *News and Observer*, September 1, 1903; Terrell, *Will Harris Murders*; Olson, "Race Relations in Asheville," 153–157; "Mob Is Pursuing Harris, Asheville Negro Murderer," *Daily Industrial News* (Greensboro, NC), November 15, 1906; "Proclamation of Outlawry," *News and Observer*, November 17, 1906; "Bloodhound on the Track of Harris, the Atrocious Murderer," *Raleigh Times*, November 14, 1906.

14. Mauldin, *Thomas Wolfe*, 19–20; Kennedy, *Window of Memory*, 316–318; Wolfe, *Complete Short Stories*, 340, 345.

15. "Hundreds of Men Searching Country Near Greenville for Escaped Felons," *Wilmington (NC) Dispatch*, February 17, 1916; "Convict Guard Dies from His Injuries," *Greensboro (NC) Daily News*, February 18, 1916; "Dave Evans Gets Another Victim," *News and Observer*, March 2, 1916; "Throngs View Body of Dale Evans in Street," *Wilmington Morning Star*, March 4, 1916; "Relief in Pitt," *Greenville Reflector*, reprinted in *Hickory Daily Record*, March 7, 1916; "Local and Personal," *Washington (NC) Progress*, March 9, 1916; "State and Foreign," *Graphic* (Nashville, NC), March 9, 1916.

16. "Mrs. Charles Mace Shot through Head," *News-Herald*, February 24, 1916; "Charles Mace, Burke Outlaw, Is Captured," *Marion (NC) Progress*, March 30, 1916; "Charles Mace Is Captured," *News-Herald*, March 30, 1916; "The Mace Murder Trial," *News-Herald*, May 11, 1916; "Charles Mace Sentenced to Thirty Years in Pen," *Charlotte News*, May 12, 1916.

17. "Get the Criminal, but Save the State," *Winston-Salem Journal*, June 23, 1927; "Mob Violence," *Hickory Daily Record*, June 25, 1927; "No Cause for Alarm," *Hickory Daily Record*, June 29, 1927; "A Trying Week," *News-Herald*, June 30, 1927.

Chapter Fourteen

1. "Thousands in Burke Hunt Negro," *Charlotte (NC) Observer*, June 22, 1927; Frank Smethurst, "Determined Search for Negro Slayer of Young Morganton Girl Futile," *News and Observer* (Raleigh, NC), June 23, 1927; "Morganton Once More Breathes Sigh of Relief," *Landmark* (Statesville, NC), July 4, 1927; Raper, *Tragedy of Lynching*, 15–16; Harry L. Griffin, "Net Tightens about Negro Sought for Attacking Girl," *Charlotte Observer*, June 24, 1927; Frank Smethurst, "Troops Now Taking Part in Search at Morganton," *News and Observer*, June 24, 1927; "Ask Troops to Curb Man-Hunters'

Fury," *Washington Post*, June 24, 1927; "Morganton Is Quiet but Disappointed over Failure," *Greensboro (NC) Daily News*, June 26, 1927; L. J. Hampton, "Hickory Reports Say Murderer Has Been Caught," *Winston-Salem (NC) Journal*, June 24, 1927 (morning edition); Marjorie Fleming, interview by author, June 26, 2007.

2. "Sleepless Searchers for Negro Slayer Find No Clue," *Hickory (NC) Daily Record*, June 24, 1927; "Manhunt Goes on in Burke," *Winston-Salem Journal*, June 25, 1927; Hampton, "Hickory Reports"; "Militia Patrols Seat of Burke," *The State* (Columbia, SC), June 24, 1927; "Still No Trace of Negro Is Found by N.C. Searchers," *Thomasville (GA) Times-Enterprise*, June 24, 1927.

3. "Knob Surrounded in Man-Hunt," *Charlotte Observer*, June 25, 1927; "A Trying Week," *News-Herald*, June 30, 1927; "Morganton Once More Breathes"; "Wrong Man May Be Serving Time," *News and Observer*, June 25, 1927; North Carolina Adjutant General's Office, *Report July 1, 1926 to December 31, 1927*, 5.

4. Marjorie Fleming, interviewed by author, June 26, 2007; "Resolutions Adopted by Negro Mass Meeting," *News-Herald*, June 30, 1927; Burke County Historical Society, *Burke County Heritage*, 2:271.

5. "Resolutions Adopted"; "An Outsider," *News-Herald*, June 23, 1927; "Posse Closes in upon Negro Killer of Girl," *Asheville Times*, June 26, 1927; "Morganton Negro May Be in This County," *Cleveland Star* (Shelby, NC), June 24, 1927.

6. "The Difference," *News-Herald*, June 23, 1927; "There Must Not Be Mob Rule," *Charlotte (NC) News*, June 25, 1927; "The Lynch Law Spirit Must Go," *Charlotte News*, June 28, 1927; "Get the Criminal but Save the State," *Winston-Salem Journal*, June 23, 1927, reprinted in *Hickory (NC) Daily Record*, June 23, 1927, and *Statesville (NC) Daily*, July 2, 1927; "Why Mob Law Pays Not," *Cleveland Star*, July 1, 1927; Phifer, *Burke*, 347; Mull, *Tales of Old Burke*, 91; "Hung from a Railroad Bridge," *Morganton (NC) Star*, September 12, 1889. In the words of the historian George C. Rable, the rhetorical question that Beatrice Cobb posed to her readers was "the perennial clincher" of lynching apologists. Rable, "Politics of Antilynching Legislation," 202. For the 1889 lynchings in Morganton, see Gardner, *Further Tales of Murder*. According to the NAACP, in March 1897 a Native American doctor and a young girl were lynched in Morganton, but this claim seems a misidentification of a Cabarrus County case from November 1895. NAACP, *Thirty Years of Lynching*, 84; *Marion (OH) Daily Star*, November 15, 1895.

7. Smethurst, "Troops Now Taking Part"; "Suspect Held in Odd Tangle," *Charlotte Observer*, July 1, 1927; "New Hunt for Negro Slayer Is Started in Adako Section Today," *Asheville Times*, June 25, 1927; "Seeking Negro in Wide Area," *Charlotte Observer*, June 26, 1927; "Morganton Officers Come to Gaffney to See 'Broadus Miller,'" *Index-Journal* (Greenwood, SC), June 25, 1927; "National Guard Troops Aid Search for Negro," *Hickory Daily Record*, June 23, 1927; "Miller May Have Hopped Off the Train at Spencer," *News and Observer*, July 2, 1927; "Think Slayer of Morganton Girl Captured," *Charlotte Observer*, July 3, 1927; "Bridges Tells of Slaying of Miller," *Charlotte News*, July 4, 1927.

8. "Seeking Negro in Wide Area"; Hampton, "Hickory Reports"; "Citizens Calm at Morganton," *Charlotte Observer*, June 23, 1927; "National Guard Troops"; "Arrest 3 New Suspects in Burke Slaying," *Asheville Times*, June 24 1927; "Local Negroes Believe Wrong Person Hunted," *Hickory Daily Record*, June 27, 1927; "Suspect Held in Odd

Tangle"; "Gene Martin Was in Gaston Jail For Few Days," *Gastonia (NC) Daily Gazette*, July 5, 1927.

9. "Search for Negro Outlaw Renewed with New Enthusiasm as Trail Seems to Lead Nearer," *News-Herald*, June 30, 1927; Bobbie Wakefield, email to author, July 4, 2007; Marjorie Fleming, interview by author, June 26, 2007. As Sam Ervin Jr. later remarked, people had "a superstitious awe about bloodhounds and any testimony of bloodhounds tracking a suspect." In a detailed study of lynchings in 1930, three years after the Miller case, the sociologist Arthur Raper noted that the "the only evidence against several of the persons lynched" was "the bloodhounds' halting trails," which Raper considered "symbolic of the primitive elements in man-hunts." The high regard for "bloodhound evidence" was not limited to lynch mobs. Under North Carolina law, prosecutors could present such evidence in court—provided the hound was "of pure blood," "of a stock characterized by acuteness of sense and power of discrimination," and had "been trained in the exercise of tracking human beings." However, identification by bloodhounds could be used only to corroborate more substantial proof, and though juries in North Carolina sometimes convicted defendants based solely on "bloodhound evidence," these convictions were consistently overturned on appeal. In the fall of 1927, a Wake County grand jury indicted an African American man based entirely on "bloodhound evidence," but a superior court judge then dismissed the indictment. Wise, *Wisdom of Sam Ervin*, 61; Raper, *Tragedy of Lynching*, 10; Jerome and Jerome, *Jerome's Criminal Code*, 107; North Carolina State Board of Public Welfare, *Capital Punishment in North Carolina*, 57.

10. "Phantom Negro Eludes Dogs and Officers in Several Days Chase," *Lenoir (NC) News-Topic*, June 30, 1927; "Search for Negro Outlaw Renewed"; "Hopes of Capturing Man Back to Low Ebb Again," *News and Observer*, June 27, 1927; "Morganton Negro Attacked Girl in Sight of Three Homes," *Winston-Salem Journal*, June 28, 1927; "Knob Surrounded in Man-Hunt"; "Man Hunt Started Again Today in Adako Section," *Hickory Daily Record*, June 25, 1927; Hampton, "Manhunt Goes on in Burke." For the eligibility of law enforcement officers to claim reward money in 1920s North Carolina, see, for example, "Officer Gets Large Reward," *Charlotte Observer*, April 24, 1925. Four years earlier, in October 1923, Lentz had captured John Goss, the escaped convict whose alleged assault of a white woman had sparked the expulsion of Black workers from Mitchell County. When Lentz attempted to claim a $200 reward offered for Goss by the town of Spruce Pine, officials there refused to give him the money, preferring to reward Mitchell County citizens who had been involved in the pursuit, not the Catawba County police chief who actually made the capture. Rusher, *Until He Is Dead*, 17, 40.

11. "Man Hunt Started Again Today"; "Seeking Negro in Wide Area"; "Now Believe Capture of Negro Fugitive Is Near," *News and Observer*, June 26, 1927; "Trail of Slayer of 15 Year Old Morganton Girl Is Lost," *Lenoir News-Topic*, June 27, 1927.

12. "Pursuers Fag in Man-Hunt; Negro Escapes Sight Race," *Charlotte Observer*, June 27, 1927; "Local Negroes Believe"; "Trail of Slayer."

13. "Hunt in Vain for Broadus Miller," *News and Observer*, June 27, 1927; "Trail of Slayer"; "Local Negroes Believe." As Arthur Raper noted, "The man-hunt provides an

opportunity for carrying and flourishing firearms with impunity, a privilege which appeals strongly to the more irresponsible elements." Raper, *Tragedy of Lynching*, 9.

14. "Dense Forests Hide Fugitive," *Charlotte Observer*, June 29, 1927; "Hunt in Vain."

15. The only newspaper account of the intruder in the Ingrams' home ("Search for Negro Outlaw Renewed") appeared in the *News-Herald* and alleged that canned fruit, shoes, and a shotgun had been taken from the home; an article in the *Charlotte Observer* ("Posse Hot on Negro's Trail," June 30, 1927) claimed that these same three items (canned fruit, shoes, and a shotgun) were stolen during the Tuesday night burglary of a store near Piney, a small community a dozen miles south of the Ingram residence. In the summer of 2007, Sandra Coffey of the Collettsville Historical Society interviewed several elderly Caldwell County residents who had firsthand knowledge of the manhunt (Sandra Coffey, emails to the author, August 4, 13, 17, and 20, 2007). None of the interviewees claimed that the fugitive had stolen a shotgun during any of the local burglaries; the only items they described as being taken were food and clothing.

16. "Posse Hot on Negro's Trail"; "Phantom Negro Eludes Dogs"; "7 Bloodhounds Aid in Search for Negro Now," *Hickory Daily Record*, June 29, 1927.

17. "Posse Hot on Negro's Trail"; Frankenberg, *Exploring North Carolina's Natural Areas*, 293–95; "Negro Suspect in Custody of Law at Newton," *Hickory Daily Record*, June 30, 1927.

Chapter Fifteen

1. "M'Lean Sends Pardon Chief on Man Hunt," *Asheville (NC) Times*, July 3, 1927; Underwood, *Scotsman from Lumber River*, 80; Winfield Scott Downs, ed., *Encyclopedia of American Biography*, s.v. "Edwin Breathed Bridges"; Edwin B. Bridges to Sam Ervin Jr., May 24, 1924 and February 19, 1926, Sam J. Ervin Papers, Manuscripts Department, Library of the University of North Carolina at Chapel Hill; Corbitt, *Angus Wilton McLean*, 861; Edwin B. Bridges to Governor A. W. McLean, July 5, 1927, McLean Governor Papers, Correspondence, 500–526, North Carolina State Archives, Raleigh; "Boys Off to Camp," *News-Herald* (Morganton, NC), July 7, 1927; North Carolina Adjutant General's Office, *Report July 1, 1926 to December 31, 1927*, 90.

2. Ben Dixon MacNeill, "Broadus Miller Meets His Doom in Gun Battle," *News and Observer* (Raleigh, NC), July 7, 1927; Frank W. Bicknell Photograph Collection, North Carolina State Archives, Raleigh; "Special Court Term Closed on Wednesday," *News-Herald*, May 14, 1925. Primary information on Commodore Burleson comes from interviews with his children: Charles Burleson, personal interview with author, April 13, 2007; Pat Burleson Howell, personal interview with author, June 26, 2007; Margaret Burleson Crumley, telephone interview with author, June 27, 2007. See also "Young Man from the Mountains," *Hickory (NC) Daily Record*, July 4, 1927; "Bears Are Fat," 555. White Southerners often viewed African Americans and black bears in a similar fashion—almost, but not fully, human, with potentially dangerous strength. This perceived similarity caused a single term to be used for both; the word "Cuffy" had a long and infamous history as a racial epithet and was a widely used nickname for bears. A nineteenth-century visitor to the American South reported that

black bears were sometimes kept as pets, but "if bruin misbehaves or grows rough and restive, they kill him and get another." "'Cuffy,' so they style the black bear, is often led into fatal mishaps," the visitor noted. "Sportsman Abroad," 39. For use of the term "Cuffy" to refer to African Americans, see Mencken, *American Language*, 523. For the term "Cuffy" used in reference to bears, see, for example, "Cuff, Jonas Ridge Pet," *News-Herald*, July 7, 1927.

3. "Negro Brought Here for Safe-Keeping," *Asheville Times*, July 3, 1927; "Long Hunt for Negro Outlaw Ended Sunday When He Was Shot Down near Linville Falls," *News-Herald*, July 7, 1927.

4. "Long Hunt for Negro Outlaw"; "Those Who Searched," *News-Herald*, July 7, 1927; "Citizen's Ticket," *News-Herald*, March 24, 1927; "Burkemont Council Installs New Officers," *News-Herald*, January 7, 1926; Burke County Historical Society, *Heritage of Burke County*, 160; "The *News-Herald* believes . . . ," untitled editorial, *News-Herald*, January 21, 1926; MacNeill, "Broadus Miller Meets His Doom"; "Negro Brought Here."

5. "Leaves from a Notebook," *News-Herald*, July 21, 1927; "Long Hunt for Negro Outlaw"; "Young Man from the Mountains"; "Negro Outlaw Slain at End of Long Trail in Mountains," *Charlotte (NC) Observer*, July 4, 1927; "Broadus Miller, Outlaw, Is Killed," *Marion (NC) Progress*, July 7, 1927. According to the *Marion Progress*, farmer George Ollis glimpsed the fugitive. However, Ashford resident Buford Franklin, who grew up a few hundred feet from the scene and knew the Ollis family personally, remembered Ollis's daughter Tressie as the person who claimed to have spotted the outlaw. Buford Franklin, personal interview with author, June 11, 2007.

6. Lewis, "Costliest Railroad in America"; "Broadus Miller, Outlaw"; "Long Hunt for Negro Outlaw."

7. "Broadus Miller, Outlaw"; "Long Hunt for Negro Outlaw."

8. "Vain Effort Being Made to Discredit Burleson," *News-Herald*, July 21, 1927; "Posse Hot on Negro's Trail," *Charlotte Observer*, June 30, 1927; "Claims Broadus Miller Shot While Asleep beside Stump," *Lenoir (NC) News-Topic*, July 14, 1927; "Broadus Miller, Negro Outlaw, Is Killed," *Lenoir News-Topic*, July 4, 1927.

9. Buford Franklin, interview with author, June 11, 2007. Franklin's account is corroborated by a description given by H. Clay Ferree, who later saw Miller's body in Morganton: "I saw . . . the seared and broken skin where the taut rope had cut his legs." Ferree, "The Day the Mob Took Over," in Crime and Criminals vertical file, North Carolina Room, Burke County Public Library, Morganton, NC; "Man Slaying Negro Killer Is Hero of the Day," *Asheville Times*, July 4, 1927.

10. Margaret McMahan, "Early Years of Ben Dixon MacNeill," *News and Observer*, August 13, 1967; "To Unveil Monument at Historic Gillespie Gap," *Raleigh Times*, June 24, 1927; MacNeill, "Broadus Miller Meets His Doom"; Margaret Burleson Crumley, telephone interview with author, June 27, 2007.

11. MacNeill, "Broadus Miller Meets His Doom"; "Negro Outlaw Slain"; "Burke County Confederate Monument, Morganton," DocSouth: Commemorative Landscapes of North Carolina, accessed July 17, 2022, https://docsouth.unc.edu/commland/monument/259/; Confederate Monument vertical file, North Carolina

Room, Burke County Public Library, Morganton, NC. A photograph of the scene on the courthouse lawn appeared on the front page of the *Charlotte Observer*, July 5, 1927, and the *Raleigh Times*, July 6, 1927.

12. MacNeill, "Broadus Miller Meets His Doom"; "Long Hunt for Negro Outlaw"; "Young Man from the Mountains"; "Negro Outlaw Slain."

13. MacNeill, "Broadus Miller Meets His Doom"; "Long Hunt for Negro Outlaw"; "Young Man from the Mountains"; "Negro Outlaw Slain."

14. "Negro Outlaw Slain"; Edwin B. Bridges to Governor A. W. McLean, July 5, 1927, McLean Governor Papers, Correspondence, 500–526, North Carolina State Archives, Raleigh, NC; "Burleson's Deed," *Hickory Daily Record*, July 15, 1927; "Along Comes a Hero," *Cleveland Star* (Shelby, NC), July 6, 1927. As Amy Louise Wood has noted, there is often an "uncanny resemblance" between lynching photography and photographs of hunters with their prey. Wood, *Lynching and Spectacle*, 94.

15. MacNeill, "Broadus Miller Meets His Doom"; "L. E. Webb Relates Experience When Negro Was Killed," *Hickory Daily Record*, July 13, 1927. Copies of the photographs of Broadus Miller's corpse are in the author's possession.

16. MacNeill, "Broadus Miller Meets His Doom"; "Young Man from the Mountains"; "Long Hunt for Negro Outlaw"; "Negro Outlaw Slain"; Beatrice Cobb, "Indignant," *News-Herald*, July 7, 1927; Cecil Kincaid, telephone interview with author, June 28, 2007.

17. "Says Morganton Wild When Broadus Miller Was Slain," *Winston-Salem (NC) Journal*, July 4, 1927; "Long Hunt for Negro Outlaw"; MacNeill, "Broadus Miller Meets His Doom"; "Young Man from the Mountains"; "Negro Outlaw Slain"; "Man Slaying Negro Killer"; "Broadus Miller's Body Buried Here," *Landmark* (Statesville, NC), July 4, 1927; Mull, *Tales of Old Burke*, 95–96.

18. "Young Man from the Mountains"; "Bridges Tells of Slaying of Miller," *Charlotte (NC) News*, July 4, 1927; "Long Hunt for Negro Outlaw"; "Man Slaying Negro Killer."

Chapter Sixteen

1. "Man Slaying Negro Killer Is Hero of the Day," *Asheville (NC) Times*, July 4, 1927; Angus Wilton McLean to Bailey Groome, June 27, 1927, Angus W. McLean General Correspondence, 1924–28, North Carolina State Archives, Raleigh.

2. Chalmers, *Hooded Americanism*, 95; Evans, "Preserving the American Home," 3–5, 10, 13; Booth, *Mad Mullah of America*, 269; "Anti Klan Bill Having Rough Sailing in House," *Burlington (NC) Daily Times*, February 25, 1927; 1920 U.S. Federal Census, Montgomery County, AL, ward 3, enumeration district #101, dwelling #117; "Klan Planning War to Block Atheist Move," *Charlotte (NC) Observer*, July 5, 1927.

3. "Several Thousand Klansmen in City," *Landmark* (Statesville, NC), July 4, 1927; "Horse Show Very Successful Event," *Landmark*, July 7, 1927; "Klan Parade Draws Immense Crowd," *Statesville (NC) Daily*, July 5, 1927.

4. "Several Thousand Klansmen in City," *Landmark* (Statesville, NC), July 4, 1927; "Horse Show Very Successful Event," *Landmark*, July 7, 1927; "Klan Parade Draws Immense Crowd," *Statesville (NC) Daily*, July 5, 1927; Smith, "Hooded Crusaders," 18; Brooks, *History of the First Baptist Church*, 13.

5. Ben Dixon MacNeill, "Broadus Miller Meets His Doom in Gun Battle," *News and Observer* (Raleigh, NC), July 7, 1927; "Morganton Church-Goers Applaud a Gory Matinee," *Raleigh Times*, July 4, 1927; "Needless Atrocity," *News and Observer*, July 5, 1927; "On a Sunday Afternoon," *Greensboro (NC) Daily News*, July 5, 1927; "The Veneer Is Thin," *Durham (NC) Morning Herald*, July 6, 1927. Debate over the events in Morganton reverberated far beyond North Carolina. In a front-page article titled "Lynch Man, Let Public View Body: Church Goers Take Part in Celebration," the *Chicago Defender*—the most widely read Black-owned newspaper in the United States—excoriated the town's residents. *Chicago Defender*, July 9, 1927.

6. "Morganton Warm over Paper Story," *Hickory (NC) Daily Record*, July 7, 1927; "Sheriff Resents Unfair Reports Affair Sunday," *News-Herald* (Morganton, NC), July 7, 1927; "Why the Fuss?," *Hickory Daily Record*, July 12, 1927; "Morganton and Burke," *Lenoir (NC) News-Topic*, July 18, 1927; "Some of the newspapers . . . ," untitled editorial, *Charlotte News*, July 6, 1927; "A Defense of Morganton," *Charlotte Observer*, July 14, 1927; "The Morganton Affair," *Cleveland Star* (Shelby, NC), July 11, 1927; "Six Girls Victims of an Automobile Wreck," *News-Herald*, August 5, 1926; "Five Killed, One Injured, When Southern Train Hit Ford Truck at Crossing," *Gastonia (NC) Daily Gazette*, August 2, 1926.

7. Hearn, *Legal Executions in New England*, 352; "Three Men Electrocuted at Boston Prison Today for a Single Murder," *Lancaster (PA) Daily Eagle*, January 6, 1927; "Car-barn Bandits Put to Death," *Fitchburg (MA) Sentinel*, January 6, 1927; "Three Massachusetts Bandits Die in Chair For Killing of Watchman in Car Barn Hold-Up," *New York Times*, January 6, 1927; Brisbane, "This Week," *News-Herald*, January 27, 1927.

8. "Morganton Warm"; "Sheriff Resents Unfair Report"; "Too Severely Criticized," *News-Herald*, July 14, 1927; Sandra Coffey, emails to the author, August 4, 13, 17, and 20, 2007.

9. "Long Hunt for Negro Outlaw," *News-Herald*, July 7, 1927; Waldrep, "War of Words," 75–100; Tolnay and Beck, *Festival of Violence*, 78; C. T. Jr., telephone interview with author, May 21, 2007. As Waldrep notes, anti-lynching activists were not consistent when drawing the distinction between "lynching" and "non-lynching." Though the NAACP did not classify Broadus Miller as a lynching victim, six years later—in August 1933—the organization would list as a lynching the North Carolina case of Doc Rogers, an African American killed in a gunfight with Pender County police whose corpse was subsequently desecrated by a mob. Waldrep, "War of Words," 87; Ames, *Changing Character of Lynching*, 46.

10. "Nash Negro Who Assaulted Girl Dies of Wounds," *News and Observer*, August 3, 1927. The historian Vann R. Newkirk has categorized Broadus Miller's death as a "lynching," but he does not define the term. Newkirk, *Lynching in North Carolina*, 106.

11. "A Matter of Definition," *Greensboro Daily News*, January 10, 1928.

12. "Nash Negro."

13. "Claims Broadus Miller Shot While Asleep beside Stump," *Lenoir News-Topic*, July 14, 1927; "New Light on Miller Slaying," *Charlotte Observer*, July 19, 1927.

14. "What Is the Truth?," *Charlotte Observer*, July 20, 1927; "Vain Effort Being Made to Discredit Burleson," *News-Herald*, July 21, 1927; "Blame the Newspapers," *News-Herald*,

July 28, 1927; "Gragg and Dula Are Sued by Commodore Burleson," *Lenoir News-Topic*, July 28, 1927; "A Show-Down Called," *Durham Morning Herald*, reprinted in *News-Herald*, August 4, 1927; "Gragg Offers Apologies to Commodore Burleson," *Lenoir News-Topic*, August 1, 1927; Commodore Burleson v. C. L. Dula, Superior Court of Burke County, August 29, 1927, Records of Burke County Superior Court, Burke County Clerk of Court Office, Morganton, NC. Laurel thickets in the North Carolina mountains were notoriously difficult to navigate. In the early 1900s, the writer Horace Kephart related the experience of two "powerful mountaineers" who had taken two days to traverse a laurel thicket that was only three or four miles wide. "I asked one of them how they had managed to crawl through the thicket," recounted Kephart. The man replied, "We couldn't crawl, we swum." Kephart, *Book of Camping and Woodcraft*, 212.

15. North Carolina State Board of Public Welfare, *Capital Punishment in North Carolina*, 133–138.

16. Ben Dixon MacNeill, "Judge Grady, Pistol in Hand, Foils Attempt to Lynch Negro Murderer," *News and Observer*, December 12, 1927.

17. MacNeill, "Judge Grady"; North Carolina Adjutant General's Office, *Report July 1, 1926 to December 31, 1927*, 10–11. Because of the unprecedented circumstances of the court proceedings in Goldsboro, defense attorneys for Newsome filed an appeal and he received a new trial, but within nine months of Judge Grady's original death sentence, he had once again been found guilty and electrocuted by the state. Kotch, *Lethal State*, 39.

18. "Deserved Commendation," *News-Herald*, December 15, 1927.

19. North Carolina Department of Public Safety, "Persons Executed in North Carolina"; "Negro Says Stewart Admit Killing George and Lilly," *Robesonian* (Lumberton, NC), August 14, 1924; "C. W. and Elmer Stewart Plead Not Guilty," *Landmark*, October 2, 1924; "Stewart and Son Are Sentenced to Electric Chair," *Kingsport (TN) Times*, October 13, 1924. In addition to Arthur Montague, the other nine African Americans who had moved to North Carolina and were then executed were Kenneth Hale (WV), John Leak (SC), Willie Williams (SC), Thomas Robinson (SC), William Dawkins (SC), Fred Jones (GA), John Williams (GA), Robert Lumpkin (GA), and Ernest Walker (SC). For the birthplaces of these men, see the following: Kenneth Hale: death certificate, January 5, 1925, State Prison, Raleigh, Wake County, NC, register #134; John Leak: death certificate, January 5, 1925, State Prison, Raleigh, Wake County, NC, register #133, and 1920 census, Laurens County, SC, Cross Hill township, enumeration district #48, dwelling #140; Willie Williams: death certificate, June 12, 1925, State Prison, Raleigh, Wake County, NC, #12, register #326; Thomas Robinson: death certificate, October 2, 1925, State Prison, Raleigh, Wake County, NC, #107, register #532; William Dawkins: death certificate, January 8, 1926, State Prison, Raleigh, Wake County, NC, #20, register #15; Fred Jones: death certificate, June 11, 1926, State Prison, Raleigh, Wake County, NC, #67, register #346; John Williams: death certificate, September 21, 1926, State Prison, Raleigh, Wake County, NC, #11, register #548; Robert Lumpkin: death certificate, March 11, 1927, State Prison, Raleigh, Wake County, NC, Raleigh, 141, 466; Ernest Walker: 1920 census, Greenville County, SC, Greenville township, enumeration district #22, dwelling #63.

20. "Two Arrests at Winston," *Landmark*, April 23, 1925; "Taxi Driver Is Murdered"; "Negro Found with License Number," *Landmark*, August 11, 1924; "Lexington Citizen Brutally Murdered," *News-Herald*, August 14, 1924; "Hale and Leak Are Electrocuted at Prison," *News-Herald*, January 8, 1925; Kenneth Hale's death certificate, January 5, 1925, State Prison, Raleigh, Wake County, NC, register #134; John Leak's death certificate, January 5, 1925, State Prison, Raleigh, Wake County, NC, register #133; 1920 census, Laurens County, SC, Cross Hill township, enumeration district #48, dwelling #140.

21. Baker, *Following the Color Line*, 178.

Epilogue

1. "Too Severely Criticized," *News-Herald* (Morganton, NC), July 14, 1927; "Regarding Will Berry," *News-Herald*, July 14, 1927.

2. "Negro Men Held on Serious Charges," *Landmark* (Statesville, NC), July 25, 1927; "A Show Negro Shot by Deputy Sheriff at Depot," *News-Herald*, October 20, 1927.

3. Baker, "Lynching Ballads in North Carolina," 47–49; Mae Fleming Wellman, interviewed in *Let the Dead Speak*; Gould, "Fear and Truth in America," 222. Present-day Morganton residents have shown the author yellowing newspaper clippings of the poem from the *News-Herald* (unfortunately missing the date).

4. Baker, "Lynching Ballads in North Carolina," 50–54; Baker, "North Carolina Lynching Ballads," 219–246; White, *Frank C. Brown Collection*, 2:687–688; Henry, *Songs Sung*, 57.

5. "Demand Is Made That Reward Be Divided," *News-Herald*, September 15, 1927; "Civil Term of Court Will Open on Monday," *News-Herald*, September 20, 1928; "Civil Court in Second Week Moving Slowly," *News-Herald*, October 4, 1928; Records of Burke County Civil Court, 1928 and 1929, Burke County Clerk of Court Office, Morganton, NC; Charles Burleson, personal interview with author, April 13, 2007; Margaret Burleson Crumley, telephone interview with author, May 15, 2007.

6. "Man-Hunters Hunt Gold," *Landmark*, June 25, 1928; Margaret Burleson Crumley, telephone interview with author, May 15, 2007.

7. "Town Board Names a New Police Force," *News-Herald*, May 9, 1929; "C.V. Burleson," *News-Herald*, December 29, 1967; Pat Burleson Howell, personal interview with author, June 26, 2007; Charles Burleson, personal interview with author, April 13, 2007; Margaret Burleson Crumley, telephone interview with author, June 27, 2007; John E. Phillips, "Where Did Trebark® Come From?," accessed June 29, 2007, http://www.outfittertuff.com/history.htm.

8. Powell, *Dictionary of North Carolina Biography*, 2:326; "Busiest Judge Is 83 Today," *News and Observer* (Raleigh, NC), September 19, 1954; "White Man Accused by Negro Girl Acquitted," *New York Times*, August 4, 1951; Henry A. Grady, "Jury Demands Men of Character, Intelligence," *Daily Independent* (Kannapolis, NC), August 14, 1951.

9. "Proclamation of Outlawry Brings Quick Surrender," *Florence (AL) Times*, February 7, 1953; "Murder, Suicide or a Legal Lynching? 1965 Death Still Raises Questions," *News and Record* (Greensboro, NC), May 21, 1994; Henderson, *Death by Suicidal Means*; "N.C. Assembly Advised to Rewrite Death Law," *High Point (NC) Enterprise*, January 30, 1969. In New York and Pennsylvania, outlawry statutes remained on the

books until the 1970s, but had not been used for several decades prior to their repeal. Prassel, *Great American Outlaw*, 107–108.

10. Tom Tiede, "North Carolina Still Employs 'Outlaw Law,'" *Sarasota (FL) Journal*, August 13, 1975; State v. Carrington, 240 S.E.2d 475 (1978), 35 N.C. App. 53, http://www.leagle.com/decision/1978715240SE2d475_1693.Obie Carrington Jr., the defendant in *State v. Carrington*, had been charged as an accessory after the fact in the Durham murder. In their original indictment of Carrington, prosecutors had listed "Arthur Parrish" as the culprit, but following Parrish's acquittal, this listing was changed to "unknown black male." Carrington unsuccessfully appealed his conviction, citing the revised indictment.

11. "'Outlaw' Statute Not Valid," *Herald-Journal* (Spartanburg, NC), October 16, 1976; "N.C. Outlawry Statute Challenged," *Wilmington (NC) Morning Star*, December 17, 1975; Autry v. Mitchell, 420 FSupp. 967 (1976), https://www.leagle.com/decision/19761387420fsupp96711221; "Fed. Court Cuts Down State's Outlaw Rule," *Robesonian* (Lumberton, NC), October 15, 1976; "Declared an Outlaw," *Times-News* (Hendersonville, NC), June 2, 1991; "Outlaw Declaration Invalid; Hunt for Escapee Continues," *Dispatch* (Lexington, NC), June 3, 1991; Chong, "Targeting the Outlaw," 750. According to the 1976 court decision, North Carolina's outlawry statute "was procedurally deficient under the due process clause of the Fourteenth Amendment in four respects. First, it did not require a probable cause determination by a neutral judicial officer. Second, the statute did not require an arrest warrant or grand jury indictment. Third, the statute did not require an arrest warrant or other process to be served and returned, showing that the accused was not to be found within the jurisdiction. Finally, the outlawry proclamation was issued ex parte and did not require notice and an opportunity for the fleeing felon to be heard." Chong, 769–770. Chong asserts that the North Carolina legislature could have rewritten the statute to make it compliant with the judicial determination, but it is difficult to see how revising the statute could have eliminated these inherent procedural deficiencies: providing "an opportunity for the fleeing felon to be heard" would necessarily preclude shooting the fleeing fugitive on sight.

12. Alpha Walker death certificate, April 7, 1948, Buncombe County, NC #4684; "Howard Robinson," *Index-Journal* (Greenwood SC), February 11, 1991. In the summer of 2014, George Rush III—a former mayor of Ware Shoals—gave the author a guided tour of the region around Shoals Junction, including the Dunn Creek church and cemetery.

13. "Columbia Journal: Prison Lures Them In (as Tourists)," *New York Times*, February 22, 1994; "Columbia's Vista Was Once Home to the 'Prison from Hell," *The State* (Columbia, SC), November 8, 2017; Cohen, "When Good People Do Nothing"; Cohen, "South Carolina Is Still Defending"; T. R., P. R., K. W., et al. v. South Carolina Department of Corrections, et al. Court of Common Pleas, Fifth Judicial District, C/A No: 2005-CP-40-2925, https://www.mentalhealth4inmates.org/resources/downloads/T_R_et_al_v_SCDC_final_order_and_judgment_for_Plaintiffs_(Richland)_01-08-14.pdf.

14. Bill Poteat, "New Video Oral History Recalls Death of Gladys Kincaid," May 13, 1997, Crime and Criminals vertical file, Burke County Public Library, Mor-

ganton, NC; Confederate Monument vertical file, Burke County Public Library, Morganton, NC; National Park Service, "Franklin Pierce Tate House."

15. Burke County Historical Society, *Heritage of Burke County*, 145, 312; Parker, "Beatrice Cobb"; Burke County Historical Society, *Heritage of Burke County*, 2:309.

16. Phifer, *Burke*, 348.

17. H. Clay Ferree, "The Day the Mob Took Over," Crime and Criminals vertical file, Burke County Public Library, Morganton, NC; Mull, *Tales of Old Burke*, 93–95.

18. Wilson, "1927," in *Lazarus Bros*. The description of public reaction to Wilson's work is based on the author's private conversations with Morganton residents in 2006 and 2007.

19. Claudia Gould, email to author, March 3, 2013; Gould, "Fear and Truth in America," 222. Gould later included a fictionalized retelling of the Broadus Miller case in one of her short stories. Gould, *Jesus in America*, 50.

20. Marjorie Fleming, personal interview with author, June 26, 2007; Charles Burleson, personal interview with author, April 13, 2007.

21. "Mrs. Kincaid Dies at 75," *News-Herald*, March 20, 1958; Elizabeth Kincaid Conley, telephone interview with author, June 28, 2007; Cecil Kincaid, telephone interview with author, June 28, 2007.

Bibliography

Primary Sources

Interviews

Charles Burleson
Elizabeth Kincaid Conley
Margaret Burleson Crumley
Ethel Philyaw Crump
Carl Evans
Marjorie Fleming
Buford Franklin
Charles Graham
Terry Helton
Pat Burleson Howell
Cecil Kincaid
Brenda Gail Pitts
Charles Tate

Court Records, Manuscript Collections, and Archival Material

Anderson County Clerk of Court, Anderson, SC
   Records of General Sessions of Anderson County Criminal Court, May 1921
Buncombe County Register of Deeds, Asheville, NC
   Marriage records, 1924
Burke County Clerk of Court, Morganton, NC
   Records of General Sessions of Burke County Superior Court, 1927–1929
Burke County Public Library, Morganton, NC
   North Carolina Reading Room: "Industry," "Crime and Criminals," and "Confederate—Monument" vertical files
Greenwood County Clerk of Court, Greenwood, SC
   Records of General Sessions of Greenwood County Criminal Court, 1926
North Carolina Department of Archives and History, Raleigh, NC
   Angus W. McLean General Correspondence, 1924–28
Pack Memorial Library, Asheville, NC
   Buncombe County Special Collections: Asheville city directories, 1921–1927, "Race Relations" vertical file
Ramsey Library Special Collections, University of North Carolina at Asheville
   Voices of Asheville Oral History Collection
Richard B. Russell Library for Political Research and Studies, University of Georgia, Athens
   Georgia Governors' Messages
   John Quincy Jett Papers
Rubenstein Rare Book and Manuscript Library, Duke University, Durham, NC
   Hinsdale Family Papers
South Carolina Department of Archives and History, Columbia, SC
   Department of Corrections, Central Register of Prisoners, May 27, 1913–May 2, 1925
   South Carolina State Death Certificates

South Caroliniana Library, University of South Carolina, Columbia, SC
Southern Historical Collection, University of North Carolina, Chapel Hill, NC
  E. C. Branson Papers
  Bryan Family Papers
  Julian Shakespeare Carr Papers
  Sam J. Ervin Papers
  Guy Benton Johnson Papers
  Andrew Dunn Kincaid Papers
  Edward William Phifer Papers
  Arthur Franklin Raper Papers
  Wishart Family Papers

Federal Census Records

1850: New Hanover County, NC
1860 (both population and slave schedules): Abbeville County, SC; Anderson County, SC; Burke County, NC
1870: Burke County, NC; Laurens County, SC
1880: Abbeville County, SC; Burke County, NC; Laurens County, SC; Lexington County, SC; McDowell County, NC; Wake County, NC
1900: Abbeville County, SC; Aiken County, SC; Anderson County, SC; Buncombe County, NC; Burke County, NC; Gaston County, NC; Greenville County, SC; Greenwood County, SC; Pierce County, GA
1910: Abbeville County, Anderson County, SC; Buncombe County, NC; Burke County, NC; Durham County, NC; Duval County, FL; Greenwood County, SC; Pierce County, GA; Richland County, SC
1920: Abbeville County, SC; Anderson County, SC; Buncombe County, NC; Burke County, NC; Greenwood County, SC; Greenville County, SC; Lexington County, SC; Mecklenburg County, NC; Randolph County, NC; Richland County, SC; Sumter County, SC; Wake County, NC
1930: Buncombe County, NC; Burke County, NC; Greenwood County, SC
1940: Buncombe County, NC; Cuyahoga County, OH

Newspapers

NORTH CAROLINA
Asheville Citizen
Asheville Times
Blue Ridge Blade (Morganton)
Burke County News (Morganton)
Burlington Daily Times
Cape Fear Reporter (Wilmington)
Carolina Mountaineer (Morganton)
Charlotte Democrat
Charlotte News
Charlotte Observer
Charlotte Southern Home
Cleveland Star (Shelby)
Daily Era (Raleigh)
Daily Independent (Kannapolis)
Daily Industrial News (Greensboro)
Daily Journal (Wilmington)

Daily Progress (Raleigh)
Daily Times (Wilson)
Dispatch (Lexington)
Durham Daily Globe
Durham Morning Herald
Edenton Gazette
Fayetteville Index
Gastonia Daily Gazette
Graphic (Nashville)
Greensboro Daily News
Greenville Reflector
Hickory Daily Record
High Point Enterprise
Landmark (Statesville)
Lenoir News-Topic
Morganton Star
Morning Post (Raleigh)
Newbern Sentinel
News and Observer (Raleigh)
News and Record (Greensboro)
News-Herald (Morganton)
North Carolina Gazette (Fayetteville)
North Carolina Gazette (New Bern)
Progress (Marion)
Progressive Farmer (Raleigh)
Raleigh News
Raleigh Times
Robesonian (Lumberton)
Statesville Daily
Times-News (Hendersonville)
Twin City Sentinel (Winston-Salem)
Washington Progress
Watauga Democrat (Boone)
Weekly Era (Raleigh)
Western Carolinian (Salisbury)
Wilmington Chronicle
Wilmington Commercial
Wilmington Dispatch
Wilmington Gazette
Wilmington Journal
Wilmington Morning Star
Wilmington Sun
Winston-Salem Journal

SOUTH CAROLINA
Aiken Standard
Anderson Daily Mail
Anderson Intelligencer
Bamberg Herald
County Record (Kingstree)
Daily Journal (Greenwood)
Edgefield Advertiser
Evening Index (Greenwood)
Gaffney Ledger
The Gamecock (Columbia)
Greenville News
Greenwood Index
Herald and News (Newberry)
Herald-Journal (Spartanburg)
Independent Mail (Anderson)
Index-Journal (Greenwood)
Keowee Courier (Pickens)
Laurens Advertiser
Lexington Dispatch
Manning Times
Marlboro Democrat (Bennettsville)
Morning News (Florence)
Piedmont (Greenville)
Press and Banner (Abbeville)
Sentinel (Pickens)
Sentinel-Journal (Pickens)
Southern Indicator (Columbia)
Spartanburg Herald
The State (Columbia)
Times and Democrat (Orangeburg)
Watchman and Southron (Sumter)
Yorkville Enquirer

OTHER STATES
African Observer (Philadelphia)
Afro-American (Baltimore)
Atlanta Constitution
Bee (Danville, VA)
California Eagle (Los Angeles)
Chicago Defender

Chicago Tribune
Fiery Cross (Indianapolis)
Fitchburg (MA) Sentinel
Florence (AL) Times
Franklyn Herald (Greenfield, MA)
Independent (New York)
Indianapolis Recorder
Inter Ocean (Chicago)
Kingsport (TN) Times
Lancaster (PA) Daily Eagle
Los Angeles Times

Marion (OH) Daily Star
New-York Post
New York Times
Pittsburg Press
Pittsburgh Courier
Sarasota (FL) Journal
Thomasville (GA) Times-Enterprise
Times Picayune (New Orleans)
Washington Post
Washington Times

Online Databases

North Carolina, Naturalization Records, 1868–1991. Online database. Ancestry.com. 2013.

Sanborn Fire Insurance Maps of South Carolina. Online database. South Caroliniana Library Digital Collections. University of South Carolina. Accessed February 1, 2013. https://digital.library.sc.edu/collections/sanborn-fire-insurance-maps-of-south-carolina/.

South Carolina, Death Records, 1821–1960. Online database. Ancestry.com. 2008.

South Carolina, Naturalization Records, 1868–1991. National Archives and Records Administration. Online database. Ancestry.com. 2013.

U.S. City Directories, 1821–1989. Online database. Ancestry.com. 2011.

U.S. Department of Veterans Affairs Beneficiary Identification Records Locator Subsystem (BIRLS) Death File, 1850–2010. Online database. Ancestry.com. 2011.

U.S. World War I Draft Registration Cards, 1917–1918. Online database. National Archives and Records Administration. Ancesty.com. 2005.

Government Documents

Bethea, Andrew J. *Code of Laws of South Carolina, 1912.* Vol. 2. Charlottesville, VA: Michie, 1912.

Butler, Anne M., and Wendy Wolff. *United States Senate Election, Expulsion, and Censure Cases, 1793–1990.* Washington, DC: Government Printing Office, 1995.

Corbitt, David Leroy, ed. *Addresses, Letters and Papers of Clyde Roark Hoey, Governor of North Carolina, 1937–1941.* Raleigh, NC: Council of State, 1944.

———. *Public Papers and Letters of Angus Wilton McLean, Governor of North Carolina, 1925–1929.* Raleigh, NC: Edwards and Broughton, 1931.

———. *Public Papers and Letters of Cameron Morrison, Governor of North Carolina, 1921–1925.* Raleigh, NC: Edwards and Broughton, 1927.

Grand Army of the Republic. *Journal of the Fifty-Fifth National Encampment of the Grand Army of the Republic.* Washington, DC: Government Printing Office, 1922.

Great Britain Privy Council. "Order of the Privy Council of Great Britain concerning an Act of the North Carolina General Assembly concerning Riots." April 22, 1772. Accessed May 22, 2015. http://docsouth.unc.edu/csr/index.html/document/csr09-0104.

Jerome, Edward C., and Thomas J. Jerome. *Jerome's Criminal Code and Digest of North Carolina*. 4th ed. Atlanta: Harrison, 1916.

Lesh, F. R., et al. *Soil Survey of Greenwood County, South Carolina*. Washington, DC: United States Department of Agriculture, 1929.

Mayfield, W. D. *The School Law of South Carolina*. Columbia, SC: Bryan, 1896.

National Archives. "Reports of Outrages." Records of the Assistant Commissioner for the State of North Carolina Bureau of Refugees, Freedmen and Abandoned Lands. National Archives Publication M843, Roll 33. 1973.

National Park Service. "Burt-Stark Mansion." National Historic Landmark Nomination. United States Department of the Interior, National Park Service, NRHP Registration Form (Rev. 8–86), 1992.

———. "Franklin Pierce Tate House." National Register of Historic Places Inventory—Nomination Form. United States Department of the Interior, National Park Service, Form 10–900, 1985.

North Carolina Adjutant General's Office. *Report of the Adjutant General of the State of North Carolina: January 1, 1925 to June 30, 1926*. Raleigh, NC: Edwards and Broughton, 1927.

———. *Report of the Adjutant General of the State of North Carolina: July 1, 1926 to December 31, 1927*. Raleigh, NC: Edwards and Broughton, 1928.

North Carolina Bar Association. *Centennial Celebration of the Supreme Court of North Carolina, 1819-1919*. Raleigh, NC: Mitchell, 1919.

North Carolina Department of Labor and Printing. *Thirty-Second Report of the Department of Labor and Printing of the State of North Carolina, 1919-1920*. Raleigh, NC: Edwards and Broughton, 1921.

North Carolina Department of Public Safety. "Persons Executed in North Carolina, 1921–1930." Accessed December 17, 2013. https://www.ncdps.gov/adult-corrections/prisons/death-penalty/list-of-persons-executed/executions-1921-1930/

North Carolina General Assembly. *Consolidated Statutes of North Carolina*. Vol. 1. Raleigh, NC: Commercial Printing, 1920.

———. *Public Laws of the State of North-Carolina, Passed by the General Assembly at the Session of 1866*. Raleigh, NC: William E. Pell, 1866.

———. *Public Laws of the State of North-Carolina, Passed by the General Assembly at Its Session 1871-72*. Raleigh, NC: Theo. N. Ramsay, 1872.

———. "Slaves and Free Persons of Color: An Act Concerning Slaves and Free Persons of Color." North Carolina Revised Code-No. 105. 1831 (1741 c 35 s 40). Accessed May 20, 2015. http://docsouth.unc.edu/nc/slavesfree/slavesfree.html.

North Carolina General Assembly. Senate. *Journal of the Senate of the General Assembly of the State of North Carolina at Its Session of 1865-66*. Raleigh, NC: William E. Pell, 1865–1866.

North Carolina State Board of Public Welfare. *Capital Punishment in North Carolina*. Raleigh, NC: North Carolina State Board of Charities and Public Welfare, 1929.

North Carolina Supreme Court. *North Carolina Reports: Cases Argued and Determined in the Supreme Court of North Carolina*. Vol. 123, September Term, 1898. Goldsboro, NC: Nash Brothers, 1899.

Ohio Adjutant General's Office. *Official Roster of Ohio Soldiers, Sailors and Marines in the World War, 1917–1918*. Vol. 16. Columbus, OH: F. J. Heer, 1928.

Paterson, Robert Gildersleeve. *Wage-Payment Legislation in the United States*. Washington, DC: Government Printing Office, 1917.

South Carolina Attorney General's Office. *Annual Report of the Attorney General for the State of South Carolina to the General Assembly for the Fiscal Year Ending December 31, 1919*. Columbia, SC: Gonzales and Bryan, 1920.

———. *Annual Report of the Attorney General for the State of South Carolina to the General Assembly for the Fiscal Year Ending December 31, 1921*. Columbia, SC: Gonzales and Bryan, 1922.

———. *Annual Report of the Attorney General of South Carolina to the General Assembly for the Fiscal Year 1915*. Columbia, SC: Gonzales and Bryan, 1916.

———. *Report of the Attorney General to the General Assembly of South Carolina for the Fiscal Year 1916*. Columbia, SC: Gonzales and Bryan, 1917.

South Carolina Commissioner of Agriculture, Commerce and Industries. *Year Book and Seventeenth Annual Report of the Commissioner of Agriculture, Commerce and Industries of the State of South Carolina: 1920*. Columbia, SC: Gonzales and Bryan, 1921.

South Carolina Department of Agriculture, Commerce and Immigration. *Handbook of South Carolina: Resources, Institutions and Industries of the State*. 2nd ed. Columbia, SC: State Company, 1908.

South Carolina Department of Archives and History. State Historic Preservation Office. *African American Historic Places in South Carolina*. June 2009. http://shpo.sc.gov/pubs/Documents/aframerhisplinsc.pdf.

South Carolina General Assembly. *Acts and Joint Resolutions of the General Assembly of the State of South Carolina Passed at the Regular Session of 1902*. Columbia, SC: State Company, 1902.

———. *Acts and Joint Resolutions of the General Assembly of the State of South Carolina Passed at the Regular Session of 1904*. Columbia, SC: State Company, 1904.

———. *Constitution of the State of South Carolina Ratified in Convention, December 4, 1895*. Abbeville, SC: Hugh Wilson, 1900.

———. *Reports and Resolutions of the General Assembly of the State of South Carolina, Regular Session Commencing January 12, 1909*. Vol. 2. Columbia, SC: Gonzales and Bryan, 1909.

———. *Reports and Resolutions of the General Assembly of the State of South Carolina, Regular Session Commencing January 9, 1912*. Vol. 1. Columbia, SC: Gonzales and Bryan, 1912.

———. *Reports and Resolutions of South Carolina to the General Assembly, Regular Session Commencing January 11, 1916*. Vol. 4. Columbia, SC: Gonzales and Bryan, 1916.

———. *Report of State Officers, Board and Committees to the General Assembly of South Carolina for the Fiscal Year 1910*. Columbia, SC: Gonzales and Bryan, 1910.

———. *Report of State Officers, Board and Committees to the General Assembly of South Carolina: 1911*. Columbia, SC: Gonzales and Bryan, 1912.

———. *Report of State Officers, Board and Committees to the General Assembly of South Carolina for the Fiscal Year 1915*. Columbia, SC: Gonzales and Bryan, 1916.
———. *Reports of State Officers Boards and Committees to the General Assembly of the State of South Carolina, Regular Session Commencing January 8, 1918*. Vol. 2. Columbia, SC: Gonzales and Bryan, 1918.
———. *Reports of State Officers, Boards and Committees to the General Assembly of the State of South Carolina, Regular Session Commencing January 14, 1919*. Vol. 1. Columbia, SC: Gonzales and Bryan, 1919.
———. *Report of State Officers, Board and Committees to the General Assembly of the State of South Carolina, Regular Session Commencing January 13, 1920*. 2 vols. Columbia, SC: Gonzales and Bryan, 1920.
———. *Reports of State Officers, Boards and Committees to the General Assembly of the State of South Carolina, Regular Session Commencing January 11, 1921*. Vol. 2. Columbia, SC: Gonzales and Bryan, 1921.
———. *Special Joint Legislative Committee to Investigate Conditions in the State Penitentiary: Transcript of Testimony Taken by Witnesses at the Investigation before the Above Committee*. Columbia, SC: Gonzales and Bryan, 1923. Available from South Caroliniana Library, University of South Carolina, Columbia, SC.
South Carolina General Assembly. House of Representatives. *Journal of the House of Representatives of the General Assembly of the State of South Carolina, Being the Regular Session, Beginning Tuesday, January 12, 1909*. Columbia, SC: Gonzales and Bryan, 1909.
South Carolina General Assembly. Senate. *Journal of the Senate of the General Assembly of the State of South Carolina, Being the Regular Session Beginning Tuesday, January 13, 1913*. Columbia, SC: Gonzales and Bryan, 1914.
———. *Journal of the Senate of the General Assembly of the State of South Carolina, Being the Regular Session Beginning Tuesday, January 12, 1915*. Columbia, SC: Gonzales and Bryan, 1915–1916.
South Carolina Governor's Office. *Statement of Pardons, Paroles and Commutations Granted by Richard I. Manning, Governor of South Carolina: 1918*. Columbia, SC: Gonzales and Bryan, 1919.
———. *Statement of Pardons, Paroles and Commutations Granted by Robert A. Cooper, Governor of South Carolina: 1920*. Columbia, SC: Gonzales and Bryan, 1921.
———. *Statement of Pardons, Paroles and Commutations Granted by Robert A. Cooper, Governor of South Carolina: 1921*. Columbia, SC: Gonzales and Bryan, 1922.
South Carolina Penitentiary Superintendent's Office. *Annual Report of the Board of Directors and Superintendent of the South Carolina Penitentiary for the Fiscal Year 1921*. Columbia, SC: Gonzales and Bryan, 1922.
South Carolina Railroad Commission. *Forty-Third Annual Report of the Railroad Commission of South Carolina: 1921*. Columbia, SC: Gonzales and Bryan, 1922.
South Carolina Secretary of State. *Report of the Secretary of State to the General Assembly of South Carolina for the Fiscal Year Beginning January 1, 1920 and Ending December 31, 1920: Part Two*. Columbia, SC: Gonzales and Bryan, 1921.
South Carolina State Board of Charities and Corrections. *First Annual Report of the State Board of Charities and Corrections of South Carolina to the Governor*. Columbia, SC: Gonzales and Bryan, 1915.

South Carolina State Board of Public Welfare. *First Annual Report of the State Board of Public Welfare of South Carolina, 1920*. Columbia, SC: Gonzales and Bryan, 1920–1921.

———. *Second Annual Report of the State Board of Public Welfare of South Carolina, 1921*. Columbia, SC: Gonzales and Bryan, 1922.

———. *Third Annual Report of the State Board of Public Welfare of South Carolina, 1922*. Vol. 3, no. 4. Columbia, SC: Gonzales and Bryan, 1923.

South Carolina Superintendent of Education. *Forty-First Annual Report of the State Superintendent of Education of the State of South Carolina: 1909*. Columbia, SC: Gonzales and Bryan, 1910.

———. *Forty-Third Annual Report of the State Superintendent of Education of the State of South Carolina: 1911*. Columbia, SC: Gonzales and Bryan, 1912.

South Carolina Supreme Court. *Reports of Cases Heard and Determined by the Supreme Court of South Carolina*. Vol. 79. Columbia, SC: R. L. Bryan, 1908.

———. *Reports of Cases Heard and Determined by the Supreme Court of South Carolina*. Vol. 121. Columbia, SC: R. L. Bryan, 1928.

State Agricultural and Mechanical Society of South Carolina. *History of the State Agricultural Society of South Carolina from 1869 to 1916*. Columbia, SC: R. L. Bryan, 1916.

United States Bureau of the Census. *Fifteenth Census of the United States: 1930*. Vol. 3, pt. 2, *Population*. Washington, DC: Government Printing Office, 1931.

———. *Fourteenth Census of the United States Taken in the Year 1920*. Vol. 1, *Population 1920, Number and Distribution of Inhabitants*. Washington, DC: Government Printing Office, 1921.

———. *Fourteenth Census of the United States Taken in the Year 1920*. Vol. 3, *Population*. Washington, DC: Government Printing Office, 1922.

———. *Negro Population in the United States, 1790–1915*. Washington, DC: Government Printing Office, 1918.

———. *Prisoners and Juvenile Delinquents, 1910*. Bulletin 121. Washington, DC: Government Printing Office, 1911.

United States Congress. House of Representatives. *The Ku-Klux Klan: Hearings before the Committee on Rules, House of Representatives, Sixty-Seventh Congress, First Session*. Washington, DC: Government Printing Office, 1921.

United States Congress. Senate. *Brewing and Liquor Interests and German and Bolshevik Propaganda: Hearings before a Subcommittee on the Judiciary, United States Senate, Sixty-Fifth Congress*. Vol. 2. Washington, DC: Government Printing Office, 1919.

———. *Nomination of Frank A. Linney: Hearings before a Subcommittee of the Committee on the Judiciary, United States Senate, Sixty-Seventh Congress, First Session*. Washington, DC: Government Printing Office, 1921.

———. *Testimony Taken by the Joint Select Committee to Inquire into the Condition of Affairs in the Late Insurrectionary States*. Vol. 2, *North Carolina*. Washington, DC: Government Printing Office, 1872

United States Department of Labor. *Wages and Hours of Labor in the Hosiery and Underwear Industry, 1907 to 1914*. Washington, DC: Government Printing Office, 1915.

United States Provost Marshal General's Bureau. *Final Report of the Provost Marshal General to the Secretary of War on the Operations of the Selective Service System to July 15, 1919.* Washington, DC: Government Printing Office, 1920.

Wolfe, S. M., et al. *Code of Laws of South Carolina, 1922.* Vol. 2. Columbia, SC: R. L. Bryan, 1922.

Womack, Thomas B., Needham Y. Gulley, and William B. Rodman, eds. *Revisal of 1905 of North Carolina, Prepared under Chapter Three Hundred and Fourteen of the Laws of One Thousand Nine Hundred and Three.* Vol. 1. Raleigh, NC: E. M. Uzzell, 1906.

Published Primary Documents

America's Textile Reporter: For the Combined Textile Industries 36, no. 7 (1922).

"Bears Are Fat in North Carolina." *Forest and Stream*, November 1, 1913, 555.

British and Foreign Anti-Slavery Society. *Slavery and the Internal Slave Trade in the United States of North America.* London: Thomas Ward, 1841.

Bowditch, William Ingersoll. *Slavery and the Constitution.* Boston: Robert F. Wallcut, 1849.

Brooks, U. R. "Judge George E. Prince." *South Carolina Bench and Bar.* Vol. 1. Columbia, SC: State Company, 1908.

Brooks, V. L. *History of the First Baptist Church.* Austin, TX: n.p., 1923.

Campbell, John P. *Southern Business Directory, and General Commercial Advertiser.* Charleston, SC: Walker and James, 1854.

Catawba River Baptist Association. *Minutes of the Ninety-Eighth Annual Session of the Catawba River Baptist Association, October 20 and 21, 1927.* Morganton, NC: News-Herald Print, 1927.

Evans, Hiram W. "Preserving the American Home." *Kourier Magazine* 3, no. 4 (March 1927): 3–10.

Faison, W. E. *The Dignity, Power and Responsibility of Organized Labor: Labor Day Address, Greensboro, N.C., September 4, 1905.* Raleigh, NC: Allied Printing Trades Council, [1905?].

Grady, B. F. *The South's Burden.* Goldsboro, NC: Nash Brothers, 1906.

Grady, Henry A. "The Klan and the Negro." *The Searchlight*, April 19, 1924.

Holsclaw, Henry D., and Harry Lee Pennell. "The Murder of Gladys Kincaid." Lenoir, NC; privately published, 1927.

Ku Klux Klan. *Constitution and Laws of the Knights of the Ku Klux Klan.* Atlanta: Knights of the Ku Klux Klan, 1921.

———. *Papers Read at the Meeting of Grand Dragons Knights of the Ku Klux Klan.* New York: Arno Press, 1977.

Lewis, J. O. "The Costliest Railroad in America: A New Railroad That Cost More than Thirty Million Dollars." Supplement, *Scientific American* 1752, July 31, 1900.

"A 'Lynch-Law' Governor." *Literary Digest*, November 25, 1911, 964–965.

McGhee, Zach. "Tillman, Smasher of Traditions." *World's Work* 12, no. 5 (September 1906): 8013–8020.

"Miss Beatrice Cobb." *Editor and Publisher* 53 (April 30, 1921): 6.

"The Sportsman Abroad." *Gentleman's Magazine and Historical Review*, January 1867, 36–46.

Stowe, Harriet Beecher. *A Key to Uncle Tom's Cabin*. Boston: John P. Jewett, 1853.

Secondary Sources

Abbeville County Historical Society. *Abbeville County*. Charleston, SC: Arcadia, 2004.

Abbott, Lynn, and Doug Seroff. *Out of Sight: The Rise of African American Popular Music, 1889-1895*. Jackson: University Press of Mississippi, 2002.

Abrams, William H., Jr. "The Western North Carolina Railroad, 1855-1894." MA thesis, Western Carolina University, 1976.

Ames, Jessie Daniel. *The Changing Character of Lynching: Review of Lynching, 1931-1941*. 1942. Reprint, New York: AMS Press, 1973.

Arthur, John Preston. *Western North Carolina: A History*. Raleigh, NC: Edwards and Broughton, 1914.

Ayers, Edward L. *The Promise of the New South: Life after Reconstruction*. New York: Oxford University Press, 1992.

Bailey, Anna. "How Scuffletown Became Indian Country: Political Change and Transformation in Indian Identity in Robeson County, North Carolina, 1865-1956." PhD diss., University of Washington, 2008.

Baker, Bruce Edward. "Lynching Ballads in North Carolina." MA thesis, University of North Carolina at Chapel Hill, 1995.

———. "North Carolina Lynching Ballads." In *Under Sentence of Death: Lynching in the South*, edited by W. Fitzhugh Brundage, 219–246. Chapel Hill: University of North Carolina Press, 1997.

Baker, Ray Stannard. *Following the Color Line: An Account of Negro Citizenship in the American Democracy*. New York: Doubleday, Page, 1908.

Banner, Stuart. *The Death Penalty: An American History*. Cambridge, MA: Harvard University Press, 2002.

Beaney, William M. *The Right to Counsel in American Courts*. Ann Arbor: University of Michigan Press, 1955.

Beardsley, Edward H. *A History of Neglect: Health Care for Blacks and Mill Workers in the Twentieth-Century South*. Knoxville: University of Tennessee Press, 1987.

Beeby, James M. *Revolt of the Tar Heels: The North Carolina Populist Movement, 1890-1901*. Jackson: University Press of Mississippi, 2008.

Bennett, David H. *The Party of Fear: From Nativist Movements to the New Right in American History*. Chapel Hill: University of North Carolina Press, 1988.

Bethel, Elizabeth Rauh. *Promiseland: A Century of Life in a Negro Community*. Philadelphia: Temple University Press, 1981.

Betts, Otis A. *The North Carolina School for the Deaf at Morganton, 1894-1944*. Morganton, NC: North Carolina School for the Deaf, 1945.

Blackmon, Douglas A. *Slavery by Another Name: The Re-enslavement of Black Americans from the Civil War to World War II*. New York: Anchor Books, 2009.

Blu, Karen I. *The Lumbee Problem: The Making of an American Indian People*. New York: Cambridge University Press, 1980.

Booth, Edgar Allen. *The Mad Mullah of America*. Columbus, OH: Boyd Ellison, 1927.
Bowen, Ann Herd. *Greenwood County: A History*. Greenwood, SC: The Museum, 1992.
Brearley, Harrington C. "A Study of Homicides in South Carolina, 1920-1926." PhD diss., University of North Carolina at Chapel Hill, 1928.
Briggs, Vernon M., Jr. *Immigration and American Unionism*. Ithaca, NY: Cornell University Press, 2001.
Brooks, C. P. *Cotton: Its Uses, Varieties, Fibre Structure, Cultivation, and Preparation for the Market and as an Article of Commerce*. New York: Spon and Chamberlain, 1898.
Brown, Cecil Kenneth. *A State Movement in Railroad Development: The Story of North Carolina's First Effort to Establish an East and West Trunk Line Railroad*. Chapel Hill: University of North Carolina Press, 1928.
Brown, Leslie. *Upbuilding Black Durham: Gender, Class, and Black Community Development in the Jim Crow South*. Chapel Hill: University of North Carolina Press, 2008.
Burke, W. Lewis. "Pink Franklin v. South Carolina: The NAACP's First Case." *American Journal of Legal History* 54, no. 3 (July 2014): 265-302.
Burke County. "Burke County Sheriffs-1777 to Present." Burke County Sheriff's Office. Archived May 26, 2022. http://web.archive.org/web/20120725081253/http://burkesheriff.org/pastsheriffs.htm.
Burke County Historical Society. *The Heritage of Burke County*. 2 vols. Morganton, NC: Burke County Historical Society, 1981, 2001.
Butterfield, Fox. *All God's Children: The Bosket Family and the American Tradition of Violence*. New York: Vintage Books, 2008.
Byerly, Victoria. *Hard Times Cotton Mill Girls: Personal Histories of Womanhood and Poverty in the South*. Ithaca, NY: ILR Press, 1986.
Caldwell, A. B., ed. *History of the American Negro: South Carolina Edition*. Atlanta: A. B. Caldwell, 1919.
Campbell, Karl E. *Senator Sam Ervin, Last of the Founding Fathers*. Chapel Hill: University of North Carolina Press, 2007.
Carlton, David L. *Mill and Town in South Carolina, 1880-1920*. Baton Rouge: Louisiana State University Press, 1982.
Carper, Gordon. "Martin Tabert, Martyr of an Era." *Florida Historical Quarterly* 52, no. 2 (October 1973): 115-131.
Cash, W. J. "The Paladin of the Drys." *American Mercury* (October 1934): 139-147.
Cecelski, David, and Timothy B. Tyson, eds. *Democracy Betrayed: The Wilmington Race Riot of 1898 and Its Legacy*. Chapel Hill: University of North Carolina Press, 1998.
Chalmers, David M. *Hooded Americanism: The First Century of the Ku Klux Klan*. Garden City, NY: Doubleday, 1965.
Chase, Nan K. *Asheville: A History*. Jefferson, NC: McFarland, 2007.
Chong, Jane Y. "Targeting the Twenty-First Century Outlaw." *Yale Law Journal* 122, no. 3 (December 2012): 724-780.
Christensen, Niels, Jr. "The State Dispensaries of South Carolina." *Annals of the American Academy of Political and Social Science* 32 (November 1908): 75-85.

Christensen, Rob. *Paradox of Tar Heel Politics: The Personalities, Elections, and Events That Shaped Modern North Carolina*. Chapel Hill: University of North Carolina Press, 2008.

Clawson, Mary Ann. *Constructing Brotherhood: Class, Gender, and Fraternalism*. Princeton, NJ: Princeton University Press, 1989.

Cleve, George William Van. *A Slaveholders' Union: Slavery, Politics, and the Constitution in the Early American Republic*. Chicago: University of Chicago Press, 2010.

Clodfelter, Frank. "Saluda." *Trains*, November 1984, 26-39.

Cohen, Andrew. "South Carolina Is Still Defending Its Neglectful Prisons." *The Atlantic*, January 23, 2014. http://www.theatlantic.com/national/archive/2014/01/south-carolina-is-still-defending-its-neglectful-prisons/283260/.

———. "When Good People Do Nothing: The Appalling Story of South Carolina's Prisons." *The Atlantic*, January 10, 2014. http://www.theatlantic.com/national/archive/2014/01/when-good-people-do-nothing-the-appalling-story-of-south-carolinas-prisons/282938/.

Cohen, William. "Negro Involuntary Servitude in the South, 1865-1940: A Preliminary Analysis." *Journal of Southern History* 42, no. 1 (February 1976): 31-60.

Cooper, William J. *The Conservative Regime: South Carolina, 1877-1890*. Columbia: University of South Carolina Press, 2005.

Cooper, William J., Jr., and Thomas E. Terrill. *The American South: A History*. Vol. 2. Lanham, MD: Rowman and Littlefield, 2009.

Corbitt, David Leroy. *The Formation of the North Carolina Counties, 1663-1943*. Raleigh, NC: State Department of Archives and History, 1950.

Cottrol, Robert J., and Raymond T. Diamond. "The Second Amendment: Toward an Afro-Americanist Reconsideration." *Georgetown Law Journal* 80 (1991): 309-361.

Cox, Jim. *Rails across Dixie: A History of Passenger Trains in the American South*. Jefferson, NC: McFarland, 2010.

Craig, Lee A. *Josephus Daniels: His Life and Times*. Chapel Hill: University of North Carolina Press, 2013.

Crawford, Geddings Harry, ed. *Who's Who in South Carolina: A Dictionary of Contemporaries Containing Biographical Notices of Eminent Men in South Carolina*. Columbia, SC: McCaw, 1921.

Daniels, Jonathan. *Tar Heels: A Portrait of North Carolina*. New York: Dodd, Mead, 1941.

Davis, Marianna White. *The Enduring Dream: History of Benedict College, 1870-1995*. Columbia SC: Benedict College, 1995.

Dial, Adolph L., and David K. Eliades. *The Only Land I Know: A History of the Lumbee Indians*. Syracuse, NY: Syracuse University Press, 1996.

Dickson, Frank A. *Journeys into the Past: The Anderson Region's Heritage*. Anderson, SC: Anderson County Bicentennial Committee, 1975.

Dollard, John. *Caste and Class in a Southern Town*. 2nd ed. New York: Harper, 1949.

Donald, David Herbert. *Look Homeward: A Life of Thomas Wolfe*. Boston: Little, Brown, 1987.

Downs, Winfield Scott, ed. *Encyclopedia of American Biography*. 8 vols. New York: American Historical Society, 1938.

Dray, Philip. *At the Hands of Persons Unknown: The Lynching of Black America*. New York: Random House, 2002.
Du Bois, W. E. B. *Black Reconstruction in America*. New York: Harcourt, Brace, 1935.
———. *Some Notes on Negro Crime, Particularly in Georgia*. Atlanta: Atlanta University Press, 1904.
———. *The Souls of Black Folk*. Chicago: A. C. McClurg, 1903.
Duncan, Dayton, and Ken Burns. *The National Parks: America's Best Idea*. New York: Random House, 2009.
Eckberg, Douglas Lee. "Estimates of Early Twentieth-Century U.S. Homicide Rates: An Econometric Forecasting Approach." *Demography* 32, no. 1 (February 1995): 1–16.
Edgar, Walter. *South Carolina: A History*. Columbia: University of South Carolina Press, 1998.
Eelman, Bruce W. *Entrepreneurs in the Southern Upcountry: Commercial Culture in Spartanburg, South Carolina, 1845–1880*. Athens: University of Georgia Press, 2008.
Eichholz, Alice, ed. *Red Book: American State, County, and Town Sources*. Provo, UT: Ancestry, 2004.
1898 Wilmington Race Riot Commission. *1898 Wilmington Race Riot Final Report*. May 2006. http://www.ah.dcr.state.nc.us/1898-wrrc/report/report.htm.
Ellenberg, George B. *Mule South to Tractor South: Mules, Machines, and the Transformation of the Cotton South*. Tuscaloosa: University of Alabama Press, 2007.
Espy, M. Watt, and John Ortiz Smykla. *Executions in the United States, 1608–2002: The ESPY File*. 4th ICPSR ed. Ann Arbor, MI: Inter-university Consortium for Political and Social Research, 2004. Accessed December 20, 2014. http://doi.org/10.3886/ICPSR08451.v4.
Evans, Clement Anselm. *Confederate Military History: A Library of Confederate States History*. Vol. 4. Atlanta: Confederate Publishing, 1899.
Evans, William McKee. "Native Americans in the Civil War: Three Experiences." In *Civil War Citizens: Race, Ethnicity, and Identity in America's Bloodiest Conflict*, edited by Susannah J. Ural, 187–212. New York: New York University Press, 2010.
———. *To Die Game: The Story of the Lowry Band, Indian Guerrillas of Reconstruction*. Syracuse, NY: Syracuse University Press, 1995.
Farris, James J. "The Lowrie Gang: An Episode in the History of Robeson County, N.C., 1864–1874." In *Historical Papers Published by the Trinity College Historical Society*, Series 15, 55–93. Durham, NC: Duke University Press, 1925.
Feldman, Glenn. *The Disfranchisement Myth: Poor Whites and Suffrage Restriction in Alabama*. Athens: University of Georgia Press, 2004.
Finkelman, Paul. *Encyclopedia of African American History, 1896 to the Present*. Vol. 1. New York: Oxford University Press, 2009.
Finnegan, Terence. *A Deed So Accursed: Lynching in Mississippi and South Carolina, 1881–1940*. Charlottesville: University of Virginia Press, 2013.
Fleming, John E. *A Summer Remembered: A Memoir*. Yellow Springs, OH: Silver Maple, 2005.
Flink, James J. *America Adopts the Automobile, 1895–1910*. Cambridge, MA: MIT Press, 1970.

Ford, Lacy K., Jr. *Origins of Southern Radicalism: The South Carolina Upcountry, 1800–1860*. New York: Oxford University Press, 1988.
Fosdick, Raymond B. *American Police Systems*. New York: Century, 1920.
Frankenberg, Dirk. *Exploring North Carolina's Natural Areas: Parks, Nature Preserves, and Hiking Trails*. Chapel Hill: University of North Carolina Press, 2000.
Fulbright, Lucille M., ed. *The Heritage of Catawba County, North Carolina*. Vol. 1. Winston-Salem, NC: Hunter, 1986.
Fuller, Edgar I. *The Visible of the Invisible Empire: "The Maelstrom."* Denver, CO: Maelstrom, 1925.
Gardner, Miles. *Further Tales of Murder and Mayhem in Lancaster, Kershaw and Chesterfield Counties*. Spartanburg, SC: Reprint Co., 2006.
"Gen. Julian S. Carr." *Confederate Veteran* 32, no. 6 (June 1924): 204.
Gerth, H. H., and C. Wright Mills, eds. *From Max Weber: Essays in Sociology*. New York: Oxford University Press, 1946.
Giesen, James C. *Boll Weevil Blues: Cotton, Myth, and Power in the American South*. Chicago: University of Chicago Press, 2011.
Gillis, James M. *The Ku-Klux Klan*. New York: Paulist Press, 1922.
Gilman, Daniel Coit, Harry Thurston Peck, and Frank Moore Colby, eds. *The New International Encyclopaedia*. Vol. 14. New York: Dodd, Mead, 1907.
Gilmore, Glenda Elizabeth. "False Friends and Avowed Enemies: Southern African Americans and Party Allegiances in the 1920s." In *Jumpin' Jim Crow: Southern Politics from Civil War to Civil Rights*, edited by Jane Elizabeth Dailey, Glenda Elizabeth Gilmore, and Bryant Simon, 219–238. Princeton, NJ: Princeton University Press, 2000.
———. *Gender and Jim Crow: Women and the Politics of White Supremacy in North Carolina, 1896–1920*. Chapel Hill: University of North Carolina Press, 1996.
Goings, Kenneth W. *"NAACP Comes of Age": The Defeat of Judge John J. Parker*. Bloomington: Indiana University Press, 1990.
Gordon, Asa H. *Sketches of Negro Life and History in South Carolina*. 2nd ed. Columbia: University of South Carolina Press, 1971.
Gottlieb, Peter. "Rethinking the Great Migration: The Perspective from Pittsburg." In *The Great Migration in Historical Perspective: New Dimensions of Race, Class, and Gender*, edited by Joe William Trotter Jr., 68–82. Bloomington: Indiana University Press, 1991.
Gould, Claudia. "Fear and Truth in America." PhD diss., University of Birmingham, 2006.
———. *Jesus in America*. Logan: Utah State University Press, 2009.
Haley, John H. *Charles N. Hunter and Race Relations in North Carolina*. Chapel Hill: University of North Carolina Press, 1987.
Hall, Jacquelyn Dowd, et al. *Like a Family: The Making of a Southern Cotton Mill World*. Chapel Hill: University of North Carolina Press, 1987.
———. *Revolt against Chivalry: Jessie Daniel Ames and the Women's Campaign against Lynching*. New York: Columbia University Press, 1979.
Hamilton, Joseph Grégoire de Roulhac. *Reconstruction in North Carolina*. New York: Columbia University, 1914.

Hapgood, Norman. "The New Threat of the Ku Klux Klan, Part II." *Hearst's International* 43, no. 2 (February 1923): 58–61, 110.
Hart, Albert Bushnell. *The Southern South*. New York: Appleton, 1910.
Hart, Hastings H. *Social Progress of Alabama: A Second Study of the Social Institutions and Agencies of the State of Alabama*. Montgomery, AL: Brown, 1922.
Hearn, Daniel Allen. *Legal Executions in New England: A Comprehensive Reference, 1623–1960*. Jefferson, NC: McFarland, 1999.
———. *Legal Executions in North Carolina and South Carolina: A Comprehensive Registry, 1866–1962*. Jefferson, NC: McFarland, 2015.
Heath, Frederick M., and Harriett H. Kinard. "Prohibition in South Carolina, 1880–1940: An Overview." *Proceedings of the South Carolina Historical Association* (1980): 118–132.
Henderson, Walter P. *Death by Suicidal Means: The Killing of Wardell Burge*. Trenton, NC: Inheritance Press, 1994.
Henry, Mellinger Edward. *Songs Sung in the Southern Appalachians (Many of Them Illustrating Ballads in the Making)*. London: Mitre Press, 1934.
Hesse, Hermann. *Demian*. New York: HarperCollins, 1995.
Higham, John. *Strangers in the Land: Patterns of American Nativism 1860–1925*. New York: Atheneum, 1970.
Higgs, Robert. "The Boll Weevil, the Cotton Economy, and Black Migration 1910–1930." *Agricultural History* 50, no. 2 (April 1976): 335–350.
Hill, Rebecca. *Men, Mobs, and Law: Anti-lynching and Labor Defense in U.S. Radical History*. Durham, NC: Duke University Press, 2008.
Hilton, George W., and John Fitzgerald Due. *The Electric Interurban Railways in America*. Stanford, CA: Stanford University Press, 1960.
Holm, John James. *Holm's Race Assimilation: Or, The Fading Leopard's Spots*. Atlanta: J. L. Nichols, 1910.
Holt, Anne Haw. "Men, Women and Children in the Stockade: How the People, the Press, and the Elected Officials of Florida Built a Prison System." PhD diss., Florida State University, Tallahassee, 2005.
Hood, John. "The Tale of Crooked Neck John." *Carolina Journal*, October 3, 2011. https://www.carolinajournal.com/opinion/the-tale-of-crooked-neck-john/.
Hoyt, James A. *The Phoenix Riot*. Greenwood, SC: Index Journal, 1938.
Hudson, Janet G. *Entangled by White Supremacy: Reform in World War I–Era South Carolina*. Lexington: University Press of Kentucky, 2009.
Hurt, R. Douglass, ed. *African American Life in the Rural South, 1900–1950*. Columbia: University of Missouri Press, 2003.
Ifill, Sherrilyn A. *On the Courthouse Lawn: Confronting the Legacy of Lynching in the Twenty-First Century*. Boston: Beacon Press, 2007.
Inscoe, John C. *Mountain Masters: Slavery and the Sectional Crisis in Western North Carolina*. Knoxville: University of Tennessee Press, 1989.
Jackson, Henry Theodore. "Prison Labor." *Journal of the American Institute of Criminal Law and Criminology* 18, no. 2 (August 1927): 218–268.
Jackson, Kenneth. *The Ku Klux Klan in the City, 1915–1930*. New York: Oxford University Press, 1967.

Jaspin, Elliot. *Buried in the Bitter Waters: The Hidden History of Racial Cleansing in America*. New York: Basic Books, 2008.

Jeffrey, Thomas E. "An Unclean Vessel: Thomas Lanier Clingman and the 'Railroad Ring.'" *North Carolina Historical Review* 74, no. 4 (October 1997): 389–431.

Johnson, Daniel, and Rex Campbell. *Black Migration in America: A Social Demographic History*. Durham, NC: Duke University Press, 1981.

Johnson, Guy B. "The Negro and Crime." *Annals of the American Academy of Political and Social Science*. Vol. 217, *Crime in the United States*. September 1941, 93–104.

Kane, Sharyn, and Richard Keeton. *In Those Days: African-American Life near the Savannah River*. Atlanta: National Park Service, 1994.

Kantrowitz, Stephen. *Ben Tillman and the Reconstruction of White Supremacy*. Chapel Hill: University of North Carolina Press, 2000.

Kaufman-Osborn, Timothy V. "Capital Punishment as Legal Lynching?" In *From Lynch Mobs to the Killing State: Race and the Death Penalty in America*, edited by Charles Ogletree Jr. and Austin Sarat, 21–54. New York: New York University Press, 2006.

Kay, Marvin L. Michael, and Lorin Lee Cary. *Slavery in North Carolina, 1748–1775*. Chapel Hill: University of North Carolina Press, 1995.

Keever, Homer M. *Iredell: Piedmont County*. Statesville, NC: Iredell County Bicentennial Commission, 1976.

Kemp, Verbon Eric, ed. *Alumni Directory and Service Record of Washington and Lee University*. Lexington, VA: Alumni, 1926.

Kennedy, Richard S. *The Window of Memory: The Literary Career of Thomas Wolfe*. Chapel Hill: University of North Carolina Press, 1962.

Kephart, Horace. *The Book of Camping and Woodcraft: A Guidebook for Those Who Travel in the Wilderness*. New York: Outing, 1906.

Key, V. O. *Southern Politics in State and Nation*. New York: Knopf, 1949.

Kirby, Jack Temple. *Darkness at the Dawning: Race and Reform in the Progressive South*. Philadelphia: Lippincott, 1972.

———. *Rural Worlds Lost: The American South, 1920–1960*. Baton Rouge: Louisiana State University Press, 1987.

Kirchwey, George W. "The Prison's Place in the Penal System." *Annals of the American Academy of Political and Social Science* 157 (September 1931): 13–22.

Kleinshmidt, Bruce Lee. "The Phoenix Riot." *Furman Review* 5 (Spring 1974): 27–31.

Klosky, Beth Ann. *Daring Venture: A Biography of Anne Austin Young, Pioneer Woman Doctor*. Columbia, SC: R. L. Bryan, 1978.

Kluger, Richard. "The Story of John Johnston Parker: The First Demonstration of Negro Political Power since Reconstruction." *Journal of Blacks in Higher Education* 46 (2004–2005): 124–125.

Kohn, August. *The Cotton Mills of South Carolina*. Columbia, SC: South Carolina Department of Agriculture, 1907.

Kotch, Seth. *Lethal State: A History of the Death Penalty in North Carolina*. Chapel Hill: University of North Carolina Press, 2019.

———. "Unduly Harsh and Unworkably Rigid: The Death Penalty in North Carolina, 1910–1961." PhD diss., University of North Carolina at Chapel Hill, 2008.

Kousser, J. Morgan. *The Shaping of Southern Politics: Suffrage Restriction and the Establishment of the One-Party South, 1880-1910*. New Haven, CT: Yale University Press, 1974.

Lange, Fabian, Alan L. Olmstead, and Paul W. Rhode. "The Impact of the Boll Weevil, 1892-1932." *Journal of Economic History* 69, no. 3 (September 2009): 685-718.

Lau, Peter F. *Democracy Rising: South Carolina and the Fight for Black Equality since 1865*. Lexington: University Press of Kentucky, 2006.

Lee, Susanna Michele. *Claiming the Union: Citizenship in the Post-Civil War South*. New York: Cambridge University Press, 2014.

Let the Dead Speak: The Saga of Gladys Kincaid. Videocassette. Directed by Terry Helton. No distributor. 1997.

Lewis, Nell Battle. "North Carolina." *American Mercury* 8, no. 1 (May 1926): 36-43.

Lichliter, M. D. *History of the Junior Order United American Mechanics of the United States of North America*. Philadelphia: J. B Lipincott, 1908.

Lowery, Malinda Maynor. *Lumbee Indians in the Jim Crow South: Race, Identity, and the Making of a Nation*. Chapel Hill: University of North Carolina Press, 2010.

MacLean, Nancy. *Behind the Mask of Chivalry: The Making of the Second Ku Klux Klan*. New York: Oxford University Press, 1994.

Mancini, Matthew J. *One Dies, Get Another: Convict Leasing in the American South, 1866-1928*. Columbia: University of South Carolina Press, 1996.

Marks, Carole. *Farewell—We're Good and Gone: The Great Black Migration*. Bloomington: Indiana University Press, 1989.

Mauldin, Joanne Marshall. *Thomas Wolfe: When Do the Atrocities Begin?* Knoxville: University of Tennessee Press, 2007.

Mays, Benjamin E. *Born to Rebel: An Autobiography*. Athens: University of Georgia Press, 2003.

Mays, Harry R. *The History of Main Street United Methodist Church, Greenwood, South Carolina*. Franklin, TN: Providence House, 1992.

McAninch, William S. "Criminal Procedure and the SC Jury Act of 1731." In *South Carolina Legal History: Proceedings of the Reynolds Conference, University of South Carolina, December 2-3, 1977*, edited by Herbert A. Johnson, 179-198. Columbia: University of South Carolina, 1980.

McGregor, Clarence H. *The Hosiery Manufacturing Industry in North Carolina and Its Marketing Problems*. Chapel Hill: Graduate School of Business Administration, Research Paper Series, 1965.

McKissick, James Rion. *Men and Women of Carolina*. Columbia: University of South Carolina Press, 1948.

Mecklin, John Moffatt. *The Ku Klux Klan: A Study of the American Mind*. New York: Harcourt, Brace, 1924.

Megginson, W. J. *African American Life in South Carolina's Upper Piedmont, 1780-1900*. Columbia: University of South Carolina Press, 2006.

Mencken, H. L. *The American Language: An Inquiry into the Development of English in the United States*. New York: Knopf, 1937.

Minchin, Timothy J. *Hiring the Black Worker: The Racial Integration of the Southern Textile Industry, 1960-1980*. Chapel Hill: University of North Carolina, 1999.

Moore, John Hammond. *Carnival of Blood: Dueling, Lynching, and Murder in South Carolina, 1880-1920*. Columbia: University of South Carolina Press, 2006.
Moore, W. Stanley, and Samuel W. Freeman. *A History of First Baptist Church Morganton, North Carolina, 1879-1900*. N.p., n.d.
Morris, Margaret W. "The Completion of the Western North Carolina Railroad: Politics of Concealment." *North Carolina Historical Review* 52, no. 3 (July 1975): 256-282.
Morris, Thomas D. *Southern Slavery and the Law, 1619-1860*. Chapel Hill: University of North Carolina Press, 1996.
Mull, J. Alex. *Tales of Old Burke*. Morganton: News Herald Press, 1975.
Myers, Lois E., and Rebecca Sharpless. "'Of the Least and the Most': The African American Rural Church." In *African American Life in the Rural South, 1900-1950*, edited by R. Douglass Hurt, 54-80. Columbia: University of Missouri Press, 2003.
National Association for the Advancement of Colored People. *Thirty Years of Lynching in the United States, 1889-1918*. New York: Arno Press, 1969.
National Digital Library Program, Library of Congress. *American Life Histories: Manuscripts from the Federal Writers' Project, 1936-1940*. Accessed February 1, 2014. https://www.loc.gov/collections/federal-writers-project/about-this-collection/.
Newby, I. A. *Black Carolinians: A History of Blacks in South Carolina from 1895 to 1968*. Columbia: University of South Carolina Press, 1973.
———. *Plain Folk in the New South: Social Change and Cultural Persistence, 1880-1915*. Baton Rouge: Louisiana State University Press, 1989.
Newkirk, Vann R. *Lynching in North Carolina: A History, 1865-1941*. Jefferson, NC: McFarland, 2009.
Norment, Mary C. *The Lowrie History*. Lumberton, NC: Lumbee, 1909.
"Notable Visitors." *Confederate Veteran* 31, no. 5 (May 1923): 165.
Oliphant, Albert D. *The Evolution of the Penal System of South Carolina from 1866 to 1916*. Columbia, SC: State Company, 1916.
Olson, Eric J. "Race Relations in Asheville, North Carolina: Three Incidents, 1868-1906." In *The Appalachian Experience: Proceedings of the Sixth Annual Appalachian Studies Conference*, edited by Barry M. Buxton et al., 153-166. Boone, NC: Appalachian Consortium Press, 1983.
Ownby, Ted. *Subduing Satan: Religion, Recreation, and Manhood in the Rural South, 1865-1920*. Chapel Hill: University of North Carolina Press, 1990.
Parker, Roy, Jr. "Beatrice Cobb." North Carolina Press Association, 1998.
Payne, Wyatt. "Outlawry." *American Lawyer* 11, no. 6 (1903): 252.
Pegram, Thomas R. *One Hundred Percent American: The Rebirth and Decline of the Ku Klux Klan in the 1920s*. Lanham, MD: Ivan R. Dee, 2011.
Perman, Michael. *Struggle for Mastery: Disfranchisement in the South, 1888-1908*. Chapel Hill: University of North Carolina Press, 2001.
Phifer, Edward W., Jr. *Burke: The History of a North Carolina County*. Morganton, NC: Burke County Historical Society, 1977.
Phillips, Charles D. "Exploring Relations among Forms of Social Control: The Lynching and Execution of Blacks in North Carolina, 1889-1918." *Law and Society Review* 21, no. 3 (1987): 361-374.

Pleasants, Julian M. *Buncombe Bob: The Life and Times of Robert Rice Reynolds*. Chapel Hill: University of North Carolina Press, 2000.
Pollard, Frederick, and Frederic William Maitland. *The History of English Law Before the Time of Edward I*. Boston: Little, Brown, and Company, 1895.
Pope, Thomas H. *The History of Newberry County, South Carolina*. Vol. 2, 1860–1990. Columbia: University of South Carolina Press, 1992.
Powell, William S., ed. *Dictionary of North Carolina Biography*. 5 vols. Chapel Hill: University of North Carolina Press, 1988–1997.
Prassel, Frank Richard. *The Great American Outlaw: A Legacy of Fact and Fiction*. Norman: University of Oklahoma Press, 1993.
Prather, H. Leon. "The Red Shirt Movement in North Carolina 1898–1900." *Journal of Negro History* 62, no. 2 (April 1977): 174–184.
Preuss, Arthur A. *Dictionary of Secret and Other Societies*. St. Louis, MO: B. Herder, 1924.
Puckett, Martha Mizell. *Memories of a Georgia Teacher: Fifty Years in the Classroom*. Athens: University of Georgia Press, 2002.
Rable, George C. "The South and the Politics of Antilynching Legislation, 1920–1940." *Journal of Southern History* 51, no. 2 (1985): 201–220.
Ransom, Roger, and Richard Sutch. *One Kind of Freedom: The Economic Consequences of Emancipation*. New York: Cambridge University Press, 1977.
Raper, Arthur Franklin. *The Tragedy of Lynching*. Chapel Hill: University of North Carolina Press, 1933.
Rice, Arnold S. *The Ku Klux Klan in American Politics*. Washington, DC: Public Affairs Press, 1962.
Richards, H. Erle. "Is Outlawry Obsolete?" *Law Quarterly Review* 18, no. 3 (1902): 297–304.
Richardson, William H. "No More Lynchings! How North Carolina Has Solved the Problem." *American Review of Reviews* 69 (April 1924): 401–404.
Robeson, Elizabeth. "An 'Ominous Defiance': The Lowman Lynchings of 1926." In *Toward the Meeting of the Waters: Currents in the Civil Rights Movement of South Carolina during the Twentieth Century*, edited by Winfred B. Moore Jr. and Orville Vernon Burton, 65–92. Columbia: University of South Carolina Press, 2008.
Rusher, Tom. *Until He Is Dead: Capital Punishment in Western North Carolina History*. Boone, NC: Parkway, 2003.
Sakowski, Carolyn. *Touring the Western North Carolina Backroads*. Winston Salem, NC: John Blair, 1990.
Schneider, Mark Robert. *"We Return Fighting": The Civil Rights Movement in the Jazz Age*. Boston: Northeastern University Press, 2002.
Scott, Emmett Jay. *Scott's Official History of the American Negro in the World War*. Chicago: Homewood Press, 1919.
Sherman, Richard B. *The Republican Party and Black America from McKinley to Hoover, 1896–1933*. Charlottesville: University Press of Virginia, 1973.
Shotwell, John M. "Crystallizing Public Hatred: Ku Klux Klan Public Relations in the Early 1920s." MA thesis, University of Wisconsin, 1974.
Sider, Gerald M. *Living Indian Histories: Lumbee and Tuscarora People in North Carolina*. Chapel Hill: University of North Carolina Press, 2003.

Simkins, Francis Butler. *Pitchfork Ben Tillman: South Carolinian*. Columbia: University of South Carolina Press, 2002.

———. *The Tillman Movement in South Carolina*. Durham, NC: Duke University Press, 1926.

Simmons, Charles A. *The African American Press: A History of News Coverage during National Crises, with Special Reference to Four Black Newspapers, 1827-1965*. Jefferson, NC: McFarland, 1998.

Simon, Bryant. *A Fabric of Defeat: The Politics of South Carolina Millhands, 1910-1948*. Chapel Hill: University of North Carolina Press, 1998.

Smith, Mika. "Hooded Crusaders: The Ku Klux Klan in the Panhandle and South Plains, 1921-1925." MA thesis, Texas Tech University, 2008.

Snowden, Yates, and Harry Gardner Cutler, eds. *History of South Carolina*. Vol. 3. New York: Lewis, 1920.

Starnes, Richard D. *Creating the Land of the Sky: Tourism and Society in Western North Carolina*. Tuscaloosa: University of Alabama Press, 2005.

Steiner, Jesse F., and Roy M. Brown. *The North Carolina Chain Gang: A Study of County Convict Road Work*. Chapel Hill: University of North Carolina Press, 1927.

Stewart, Bruce E., ed. *Blood in the Hills: A History of Violence in Appalachia*. Lexington: University Press of Kentucky, 2012.

Summers, Mark Wahlgren. *Railroads, Reconstruction, and the Gospel of Prosperity: Aid under the Radical Republicans, 1865-1877*. Princeton, NJ: Princeton University Press, 1984.

Sweeney, Charles P. "The Great Bigotry Merger." *The Nation* 115, no. 2974 (July 5, 1922).

Tannenbaum, Frank. *Darker Phases of the South*. New York: G. P. Putnam's Sons, 1924.

———. *Wall Shadows: A Study in American Prisons*. New York: G. P. Putnam's Sons, 1922.

Terrell, Bob. *The Will Harris Murders*. Alexander, NC: WorldComm, 1997.

Tessier, Mitzi Schaden. *Asheville: A Pictorial History*. Virginia Beach, VA: Donning, 1982.

Thompson, Holland. *From the Cotton Field to the Cotton Mill: A Study of the Industrial Transition in North Carolina*. New York: Macmillan, 1906.

Tindall, George Brown. *The Emergence of the New South, 1913-1945*. Baton Rouge: Louisiana State University Press, 1967.

———. *South Carolina Negroes, 1877-1900*. Columbia: University of South Carolina Press, 2003.

Tolnay, Stewart E., and E. M. Beck. *A Festival of Violence: An Analysis of Southern Lynchings, 1882-1930*. Chicago: University of Illinois Press, 1995.

Tomkovicz, James J. *The Right to the Assistance of Counsel: A Reference Guide to the United States Constitution*. Westport, CT: Greenwood Press, 2002.

Town of Ware Shoals. *From Hill to Dale to Hollow: Ware Shoals, South Carolina*. Ware Shoals, SC: R. L. Bryan, 1983.

Trealease, Allen W. *White Terror: The Ku Klux Klan Conspiracy and Southern Reconstruction*. New York: Harper and Row, 1971.

Trinkley, Michael, and Debi Hacker. *The Penitentiary Cemetery, Columbia, South Carolina*. Columbia, SC: Chicora Foundation, 2009.
Trotter, Joe William, Jr. *The Great Migration in Historical Perspective: New Dimensions of Race, Class, and Gender*. Bloomington: Indiana University Press, 1991.
Trotti, Michael Ayers. "What Counts: Trends in Racial Violence in the Postbellum South." *Journal of American History* 100, no. 2 (September 2013): 375–400.
Turnbull, Andrew. *Thomas Wolfe*. New York: Scribner, 1967.
Underwood, Mary Evelyn. *The Scotsman from Lumber River: Farmer, Industrialist, Banker, Public Servant*. Raleigh, NC: Pentland Press, 1996.
"United Confederate Veterans." *Confederate Veteran* 31, no. 4 (April 1923): 123.
Vandiver, Louise Ayer. *Traditions and History of Anderson County*. Atlanta: Ruralist Press, 1928.
Wade, James H., Jr. *Greenwood County and Its Railroads, 1852–1993*. Greenwood, SC: The Museum, 1993.
Waldrep, Christopher. "National Policing, Lynching, and Constitutional Change." *Journal of Southern History* 74, no. 3 (2008): 589–626.
——— . "War of Words: The Controversy over the Definition of Lynching, 1899–1940." *Journal of Southern History* 66, no. 1 (2000): 75–100.
Waronker, Cecile Cohen. "Dillon's Ohav Shalom: A Small Town's Dream Come True." *Jewish Historical Society of South Carolina* 18, no. 2 (Fall 2012): 17.
Waters, Darin J. "Life beneath the Veneer: The Black Community in Asheville, North Carolina from 1793 to 1900." PhD diss., University of North Carolina at Chapel Hill, 2011.
Watson, Alan D. *Wilmington, North Carolina, to 1861*. Jefferson, NC: McFarland, 2003.
Watson, Margaret. *Greenwood County Sketches: Old Roads and Early Families*. Greenwood, SC: Attic Press, 1970.
Webb, Mena. *Jule Carr: General without an Army*. Chapel Hill: University of North Carolina Press, 1987.
Wells, Tom Henderson. "The Phoenix Election Riot." *Phylon* 31, no. 1 (1970): 58–69.
West, Stephen A. *From Yeoman to Redneck in the South Carolina Upcountry, 1850–1915*. Charlottesville: University of Virginia Press, 2008.
White, Newman Ivey, ed. *The Frank C. Brown Collection of North Carolina Folklore*. Vol. 2. Durham, NC: Duke University Press, 1952.
Wideman, John Edgar. *Fatheralong: A Meditation on Fathers and Sons, Race and Society*. New York: Pantheon, 1994.
Wilk, Daniel Levinson. "The Phoenix Riot and the Memories of Greenwood County." *Southern Cultures*, Winter 2002, 29–55.
Williams, Chad L. *Torchbearers of Democracy: African American Soldiers in the World War I Era*. Chapel Hill: University of North Carolina Press, 2010.
Williams, G. Croft. "Crime and Its Treatment in South Carolina." *Quarterly Bulletin of the State Board of Public Welfare* 8, no. 2 (1922).
Williamson, Joel. *The Crucible of Race: Black-White Relations in the American South since Emancipation*. New York: Oxford University Press, 1984.
Wilson, Harry L., Jr. *Lazarus Bros, the Early Years: The Story of Their Store and Their Times 1893–1993*. (Morganton, NC?): n.p., n.d.

Wilson, Leonard, ed. *Makers of America: Biographies of Leading Men of Thought and Action*. Vol. 2. Washington, DC: B. F. Johnson, 1916.
Wise, Bill M. *The Wisdom of Sam Ervin*. New York: Ballantine Books, 1973.
Witherspoon, Pauline. "Social Legislation in South Carolina." *Journal of Social Forces* 2, no. 2 (1924): 232–233.
Wolfe, Thomas. *The Complete Short Stories of Thomas Wolfe*. Edited by Francis E. Skipp. New York: Simon and Schuster, 1987.
———. *Look Homeward, Angel*. New York: Charles Scribner's Sons, 1957.
———. *Welcome to Our City: A Play in Ten Scenes*. Edited by Richard S. Kennedy. Baton Rouge: Louisiana State University Press, 1983.
Wood, Amy Louise. *Lynching and Spectacle: Witnessing Racial Violence in America, 1890–1940*. Chapel Hill: University of North Carolina Press, 2009.
Woodward, C. Vann. *Origins of the New South, 1877–1913*. Baton Rouge: Louisiana State University Press, 1951.
———. *The Strange Career of Jim Crow*. 3rd ed. New York: Oxford University Press, 1974.
Woody, Howard. *South Carolina Postcards*. Vol. 9, *Anderson County*. Charleston, SC: Arcadia, 2003.
Wright, Gavin. *Old South, New South: Revolutions in the Southern Economy since the Civil War*. New York: Basic Books, 1986.
Young, Kevin Wayne, "The World of Broadus Miller: Homicide, Lynching, and Outlawry in Early Twentieth-Century North and South Carolina" (PhD diss., University of Georgia, Athens, 2016), 366–377.

Index

Page numbers in italics refer to illustrations.

Abbeville, SC, 7, 16, 18, 34–38, 49, 56
Abbeville County, SC, 6, 7, 14, 21, 23, 37–38, 74, 171n1, 184n9
Abbeville Opera House, 174n9
Abbeville *Press and Banner*, 23, 30, 38
Abernethy, Rev. Arthur T., 82–83
Acker, Dr. Halbert H., Jr., 48
Adako, NC, 126, 127, 128, 130
Adam's Knob (NC), 126
African Americans: churches, 10, 16–17, 122, 155; disfranchisement of, 12, 14–15, 20, 77, 79, 81, 185n1; home invasions, by law enforcement, 20, 37, 174n7; housing, 1, 8, 43, 75–76, 166n4; intraracial homicides among, 17, 21–24, 43–45, 51, 54–58, 170–171n17; labor of, 13, 36–37, 43, 75, 78–79, 103, 104, 107 (*see also* convict labor); racial violence against, 14–15, 25–41, 52, 54, 77–78 (*see also* lynching); relationship between native Black residents and Black newcomers, 88, 105, 107, 123; schools, 10–12, 39, 40, 41, 167n9; self-defense by, 4, 20, 27–28, 30, 37, 51–52, 174n7. *See also* hot suppers; segregation
Agnew, Clarence, 48–49
Agnew, James, 9
Agnew, Larkin, 31
Agnew, Orlena, 10
Agnew, William E., 9
alcohol: prohibition of, 18, 60, 103, 197n12; role in fueling violence, 17, 18–19, 21, 25, 27–28, 29, 53, 104–105, 118, 119, 140, 147, 174n9, 197n12

Algary, SC, 9–11, 14, 167n9
Algary, W. E., 9, 48–49
American Civil Liberties Union, 155
Anderson, SC, 7, 29, 31, 42–45, 47, 48–50, 55; African American community, 43; homicides in, 44; South Main Street, 44; West Market Street, 43
Anderson County, SC, 7, 29, 44–47, 49, 50, 53, 54, 171n1, 176n5
Anderson Daily Mail, 30
Asheville, NC, 94, 127, 128, 133, 138, 140, 150, 155; First Christian Church, 82; immigration of Black South Carolinians, 75–76, 85, 86, 88; Ku Klux Klan in, 82–85, *84*, 86–87; Pack Square, 75, 76, 84, 85; rape allegations of 1925, 86–91; segregation in, 85; South Beaumont Street, 75, 76, 94; Sunset Mountain, 86; Valley Street, 76, 91, 118; West Asheville, 87; Will Harris case, 117–118; Young Men's Institute, 75, 88. *See also* Wolfe, Thomas
Asheville High School, 83–84
Asheville Times, 85
Ashford, NC, 127, 133–134, 135, 146
Ashley, Ernest, 55–56, 179n11
Ashley, John Marion, 27–29, 179n11
Ashley, Joshua ("Citizen Josh"), 26–27, 29–33, 34, 51
Augusta, GA, 18
Autry, Gerald, 155
Avery, Daisy Moore, 107
Avery, Isaac T., 104
Avery, Louise, 104
Avery County, NC, 127, 130, 133, 152

231

Aycock, Charles, 77, 185n1
Ayden, NC, 119
Ayers, Edward, 175n11

Baker, Ray Stannard, 149
ballads, 152
Bamberg Herald, 32
Banks, Hugh, 132–133
baseball, 62, 110
Battle, George, 113
Baxley, J. Michael, 156
bears, 117, 131–132, *132*, 139, 200–201n2
Belser, Morgan, 142
Benedict Institute, 39
Berry, Annie, 1
Berry, Will, 1–4, 109, 121, 123, 126, 151, 158
Bicknell, Frank W., 131
Big Rock Creek (NC), 121
Birthright, The (play), 106
Black Codes, 115
Blackshear, GA, 103
Blease, Coleman, 12, 31, 32, 34, 52–53, 58, 67
bloodhounds, use of, 118, 119, 126, 128–130, 134, 199n9
Blowing Rock, NC, *127*, 129
Blue Ridge Mountains, 126, 129
boll weevil, 71–75, 88, 149, 183n2
Borglum, Gutzon, 81
Boston, MA, 144
Bowditch, William Ingersoll, 115
Bradshaw, Rev. Rufus, 112, 137
Bradshaw, Tom, 145–146
Bridges, Edwin, 131, 132, 135, 138, 139, 141
Bridgewater, NC, 4–5
Brisbane, Arthur, 144
British and Foreign Anti-Slavery Society, 115
Broad River (SC), 59
broadside poems, 151–152
Brown, Robert, 114
Brown, Roy, 92
Brown Mountain (NC), 126

Buncombe County, NC, 75, 82, 85, 86, 89, 90–91, 102, *127*, 132, 133
Burke County, NC, 1, 95, 99, 100–102, 106, 108, 113, 119, 121, 123, *127*, 128, 132, 138, 145, 151–152, 157, 160; African Americans in, 96, 104; courthouse, 1, 97, *98*, 156. *See also* Cobb, Beatrice
Burke Tannery, 3, 107
Burleson, Charles, 158–159
Burleson, Commodore Vanderbilt, 131–136, *132*, 138–141, *140*, 142–143, 145, 146–148, 152–153, 157, 158–159
Burleson, Gillam, 136
Burleson, Margaret, 136
Burnett, John C., 133
Burnsville, NC, *127*, 133

Caldwell County, NC, 3, 126, *127*, 128–130, 134, 146, 200n15
Campbell, Charles, 52
Cann, Lester, 37–38, 174n9
Cann, McKinney, 34–36
Cann, Will, 35
capital punishment: in North Carolina, 148–149; in South Carolina, 53, 56–58, 179n14. *See also* electrocution; hanging
Carr, Julian, 80, 108
Cash, W. J., 79
Catawba County, NC, 3, 103, 124, *127*, 128, 151
Catawba River (NC), 1, 4, 109, *127*, 160
Catawba Valley Baptist Church, 112, 159, 160
Catholics, 100, 142, 191–192n9
chain gangs, 8, 21, 51, 60, 65, 67, 74, 78, 92, *93*, 189n15; conditions on, 92–94; escapees from, 78, 117, 118–119, 199n10; individuals sentenced to, 22, 25, 64, 83, 87, 91, 117, 124; legislation concerning, 8, 60
Charlestown State Prison, Boston, MA, 144
Charlotte, NC, 74, 82, 87, 124, 131, 141, 142, 191n7

232   *Index*

Charlotte Observer, 36, 110, 122, 126, 128, 129, 130, 136, 143, 146, 200n15
Chesterfield, NC, 109, 112, 125–126, 127
Chicago Defender, 203n5
"The Child by Tiger" (Wolfe), 118
Chiquola Mills, 27
churches, 10, 16–17, 112, 122, 155, 160; importance for landless tenant farmers, 10, 112
Clarendon County, SC, 46
class divisions: among white North Carolinians, 96, 185n1; among white South Carolinians, 26–30, 36–37, 54
Cleveland Star, 144
Cobb, Beatrice, 100–103, *101*, 120, 138, 143, 144, 146, 148, 153, 156, 194n5; attitude toward lynching, 103, 105, 123, 198n6; as defender of local Blacks, 102–103, 107, 123, 151; idealized portrayal of Morganton by, 102, 122, 141; racially inflammatory reporting by, 103, 105, 110, 148. *See also* Morganton *News-Herald*
Cobb, T. G., 100, 123
Cobb, William, 115
Cold Water Creek (NC), 129
Collettsville, NC, 126, *127*, 128, 129, 130
Columbia, SC, 39, 56, 59, 62, 69, 155
Columbia Canal, 59
Columbia Hosiery, 67, 182n19
Columbia *State*, 25, 38, 53, 54
Concord United Methodist Church, 133–134
Confederacy, 36, 78, 80, 95, 116, 137; monument to, 80, 97, *98*, 137, 144–145, 156
Congaree River (SC), 59
Conley, Elizabeth Kincaid, 160
convict labor: convict lease, 66–67; in penitentiary, 67–68; on prison farms, 65–66; on railroads, 66, 74, 96, 190n3. *See also* chain gangs; peonage

Cooper, Robert, 19, 20, 51–52, 60
corporal punishment. *See* capital punishment; chain gangs; flogging; solitary confinement
Costin, Miles, 115
cotton, 12–14, 16, 17, 36, 37, 42, 44, 66, 71–72, 74, 155, 183n2. *See also* boll weevil; textile mills
Crawford, Anthony, 34–37, *35*, 171n1
Crisis, The (NAACP magazine), 40
Cuthbertson, Roscoe, 151

Daniels, Josephus, 77, 80
Darker Phases of the South (Tannenbaum), 94
Davis, Bob "Snowball," 34, 171n1
Davis, Jefferson, 36
Democratic Party, 21, 77, 81, 95, 102, 156
DeSaussure prison farm, 65
disfranchisement. *See* African Americans: disfranchisement of
Dollard, John, 49, 102
Donalds, SC, 7, 18, 31
"The Dreadful Fate of Gladys Kincaid" (ballad), 152
Du Bois, W. E. B., 24, 68
Duckworth, Fons, 133–135, 152, 153
Dula, Clyde, 146–147
Duncan, John, 21
Duncan, Walter E., 55
Dunn Creek Baptist Church, 7, 10, 11, 16, 39, 41, 49, 155
Duplin County, NC, 80
Durham, NC, 79, 80, 117, 154
Durham Daily Globe, 117
Durham Hosiery Mill Company, 108
Dyer, Leonidas, 80

Eastes, Rev. George, 99
Edgefield Advertiser, 17, 20
Edgefield County, SC, 6, 7, 17, 23, 72
Editor and Publisher, 100
electrocution, executions by, 56–58, 59, 106, 144, 148–149

Index   233

Ervin, Sam, Jr., 89, 100–101, 113, 128, 131, 135, 138–139, 147, 153, 156–157, 199n9
Erwin, Jones, 102
Evans, Dave, 118–119
Evans, Hiram, 142

Fant, Foster, 48
Felton, Rebecca Latimer, 103
Ferree, H. Clay, 157
feudal protectoral relationship, of whites to African Americans, 26, 49, 74, 102–103
Fiber Craft Chair Company, 61, 67, 68–69
Fleming, Mae, 112
Fleming, Marjorie, 158
flogging, 63–64, 65, 68, 70, 79, 94, 118
Forsyth County, NC, 149
Fox, Virgil, and Fox family, 1–2
Frank, "Jew," 68–69
Franklin, Pink, 20
Franklin Pierce Tate House, 95, 97, 156
Froneberger, Lawrence, 82–84, 99
fugitive slaves, 114–115
furniture factories, 1, 61, 67, 97, 108, 114, 153

Gaffney, SC, 124
Gardner, Max, 91
Garrou, Francis, 108
Garrou Knitting Mill, 1, 108–109, *109*, 156
Gaston Chapel AME Church, 122
Gaston County, NC, 82
Gastonia, NC, 124, 144
"Gladys Kincaid" (ballad), 152
Globe, NC, 130
Goggans, Will, 52
Goldsboro, NC, 147–148
Gordon, Asa, 71
Goss, John, 78, 185n4
Gould, Claudia, 158
Grady, Henry Alexander, 80–82, 84, 142, 147–148, 153–154, 186n9, 191–192n9, 204n17
Gragg, H. W., 146–147

Grand Army of the Republic, 186n8
Grandfather Mountain (NC), 126, *127*, 134
Great Migration, 43, 71, 74, 176n3, 183n2
Great Smoky Mountains National Park, 83
Greene, Walter, 139
Greensboro, NC, 87
Greensboro Daily News, 143, 145
Greenville, NC, 119
Greenville, SC, 31–32, 39
Greenville County, SC, 7, 30, 58, 59, 94, 178n6
Greenwood, SC, 6, 7, 21, 72, 92
Greenwood and Augusta Railroad, 66
Greenwood County, SC, 6, 7, 17, 18, 47, 91–92, 149, 155, 166n1, 166n5; agriculture, 12, 72, 74; boll weevil, 72–73; bootlegging, 18; chain gangs, 21, 92–94; election of 1898, 14–15; executions, 56; gun violence, 19; homicides, 21–24, 170n14, 170n17; lynching, 14–15, 25, 34, 171n1; railroads, 6, 42, 66, 74; schools, 9–10; textile industry, 16, 74
Greenwood *Daily Journal*, *Index*, and *Index-Journal*, 14, 15, 18, 32, 39, 40
Guilford County, NC, 154
gun violence. *See* pistol ban
Gwynn, Tom, 103, 192n13

Hale, Kenneth, 149
Hallyburton, Julius "Jules," 2, 5, 113, 121, 122, 124, 131, 135, 138, 139, 151
Hallyburton, William, 113
Hamlett, William, 143
Hampton, Wade, 66
Handy, Frederick Chaillé, 80, 186n7
hanging, executions by, 56–58
Harris, Leon W., 48, 54
Harris, Will: in Asheville, 118, 119; in Mecklenburg County, 117
Hart, Albert Bushnell, 48, 68
Harvey, Wilson, 66
Henry, Mellinger, 152
Hertford County, NC, 153–154

Heyward, Duncan, 28, 34
Hickory, NC, 3, 121, 124, 126, *127*, 128, 141, 151
Hickory Daily Record, 110, 119, 124, 144
Holsclaw, Henry D., 151–152
home invasion, by law enforcement, 20, 37, 174n7
homicide, role of alcohol in, 17–19; distinction between murder and manslaughter, 51; punishment for, in South Carolina, 51–58; in upstate South Carolina, 21–24, 44, 170–171n17
Honea Path, SC, 7, 26–29, 31–32, 55
Hoover, J. Edgar, 80
hosiery mills, 1, 108
hot suppers, 17–18, 22, 44, 168n4
Humphries, Lula, 170n14

India, individual from, targeted by posse, 124
Ingram, Charlie, 129, 200n15
Iredell County, NC, *127*, 143

Jackson, Willis, 31–33, 34, 171n1
Jeter, David, 22
Jim Crow, 20
Johnson, Guy B., 47, 100
Johns River (NC), 4, 126, *127*, 129, 134
Johnston, Olin, 178n5
Johnston, Tom, 117
Jones, Sloan, 55
Jones County, NC, 115, 154
Junior Order of United American Mechanics, 100, 133, 191–192n9

Keelan, Tom, 64
Kershaw County, SC, 65
Kincaid, Cecil, 111, 160
Kincaid, Gladys, 1–2, 108–112, *111*, 159–160, *159*, 194n5
Kincaid, Harvey, 2
Kincaid, James, 109, 111
Kincaid, Mary Jane, 1–2, 109, 111, 112, 140, 159–160

Kincaid, Willie, 3
King, Martin Luther, Jr., 9
Ku Klux Klan, 79–85, 98–100, 142–143, 186nn7–8, 191n7, 191n9; anti-Catholicism, 142; anti-miscegenation, 82–83; in Asheville, 82–85, 84, 86–87; in Morganton, 98–100, 106, 132, 153; opposition to lynching, 81–82, 86–87, 99; political activity, 90; prominent Klansmen, 80–81; Reconstruction-era Klan, 79; relationship with law enforcement, 79, 82–84, 86–87, 99–100, 143; state rally in Statesville, 142–143. *See also* Grady, Henry Alexander; white supremacy

Lake James (NC), 4
Lancaster, SC, 56, 87
Lander College, 47
Laurens County, SC, 7, 25, 39, 53, 56, 149, 178n5
Leak, John, 149
Lenoir, NC, 121, 124, *127*, 128
Lentz, Eugene, 126, 199n10
Lewis, Nell Battle, 101
Lexington, NC, 149
Lexington County, SC, 62
Linville Falls, NC, *127*, 131–134, *132*
Linville Gorge (NC), 130, *131*
Linville River (NC), *127*, 130
Little Switzerland, NC, 135
Lomax, Will, 58
Long Cane Creek (SC), 8
Look Homeward, Angel (Wolfe), 76
Louisiana, 80
Lowry, Henry Berry, 116
Lowry, Stephen, 116–117
Lowry, Tom, 116–117
Lowry Gang, 116
Lumbee, 116
Lumberton, NC, 116
Lynchburg, VA, 124
lynching: anti-lynching legislation, 46, 80; compared to legal hangings, 58; compared to other racially motivated

Index 235

lynching (cont.)
   homicides, 41; definition of, 28, 145-146, 151, 186-187n11, 203nn9-10; evidence against persons lynched, 199n9; kinship among lynch mob members, 26, 32, 35; Klan's attitude toward, 81-82, 86-87, 99; in North Carolina, 77-79, 90-91, 123, 131, 198n6; opposition to, 28, 34, 36, 37, 46, 77-79, 91; similarity to hunting trophy photographs, 131-132, 139, 202n14; support for, 31, 32-33, 103, 105, 123, 198n6; threatened lynchings, 3, 5, 29, 83, 86-87, 105, 121-122, 124, 147-148; in upstate South Carolina, 14-15, 25-26, 27-29, 31-33, 34-38, 171n1. *See also names of specific victims*

Mace, Charles, 119
MacNeill, Ben Dixon, 135, 137, 143, 147-148
Maddox, James Selden, 10, *11*, 41, 49, 155, 167n8
Manning, Richard, 53
Mansel, Alvin, 86-91, *87*, 98, 149
Marion, NC, 124, *127*, 133
marriage, Catholic, 142
Martin, Dante, 94-95, 149
Martin, Eugene, 124
Masa, George, 83
Masonic Order, 80
Mattison, James, 44-45, 48
Mays, Benjamin, 9, 12, 17, 19, 39
McCarty, Pope, 39-41, 53, 175n13
McCormick County, SC, 17
McDowell County, NC, *127*, 133, 134
McGaha, John T., 29-30, 51
McLaurin, John, 21, 169n12
McLean, Angus, 90-91, 113, 121, 122, 131
McLeod, Thomas, 73
Mecklenburg County, NC, 117
mental illness and impairment, 34, 47, 50, 58, 147, 154; in South Carolina prisons, 60-61, 156, 181n5
Metts, John Van Bokkelen, 78, 89, 121

Miller, Broadus: in Anderson, SC, 42, 44-45; in Asheville, NC, 75-76, 91, 94; attack on Gladys Kincaid, 2-3, 109-110; attempted burglary by, 91-92; burial, 141; on chain gang, 92, 94; corpse on public display, 136-141, 143, 145; death of, 134-135, 146-147; early years, 8, 10, 12, 13; manhunt for, 5, 123-130, 133-134; marriage, 75; mental condition, 47, 50; in Morganton, NC, 2-3, 95, 96-97; outlawing of, 113; parents, 8, 75; physical description, 59, 124; rewards offered for, 113-114, 125-126, *125*, 133, 137-138, 152-153; in South Carolina State Penitentiary, 59, 70; on trial for murder, 49-50
miscegenation, 46-47, 81, 82-83
Mitchell, E. M., 86, 87
Mitchell County, NC, 78, 98, 121, *127*, 199n10
Montague, Arthur, 103-106, 107, 132, 148, 149
Moore, Jim, 27-28, 179n11
Morehouse College, 9
Morganton, NC, 1-5, 89, 95-106, 107-112, 113-114, 119-120, 121-124, 131-133, 135-141, 143-145, 148-150, 151-153, 156-160; Bouchelle Street, 1-2, 4, 109, 158; Concord Street, 104; East Baptist Church, 99; East Union Street, 1, 108, 156; First Methodist Church, 99, 103, 132, 136, 152; Grace Hospital, 2; Ku Klux Klan in, 98-100, 106, 132, 153; National Guard company, 3, 89, 98, 105, 121, 131; School for the Deaf, 95, 104-106, 107, 193n1
Morganton *News-Herald*, 95, 98, 99, 100, 102, 105, 107, 110, 122, 123, 126, 141, 151, 152, 153, 156, 159. *See also* Cobb, Beatrice
Morganton Star, 123
Morrison, Cameron, 64, 77-79, 90, 98, 182n12

Mortimer, NC, 127, 129, 130, 133, 134
Mulberry Creek (NC), 126, 127
Mull, John, 152
Mull, John Alex, 157–158
"The Murder of Gladys Kincaid" (broadside poem), 151–152

Nash County, NC, 77, 145
National Association for the Advancement of Colored People (NAACP), 20, 25, 40, 43, 145, 186n10, 198n6, 203n9
National Guard, in North Carolina: Company B of the 105th Engineers, 3, 89, 98, 105, 121, 131; deployed against mob violence, 77–79, 89–90, 98, 105, 121–122, 148
Nebo, NC, 4–5
Neely, John Alexander, Jr., 48
Neely, Preston, 87–90, 98, 149
Negro Methodist Church, 16
Newberry *Herald and News*, 28, 33
New Hanover County, NC, 114
Newsome, Larry, 147–148, 204n17
New York Herald, 54
Ninety Six, SC, 7, 20, 22, 23, 73
Northampton County, NC, 155
North Carolina: capital punishment in, 148–149; class divisions among white residents, 96, 185n1; disfranchisement of African Americans in, 77, 79, 81, 185n1; judicial system, 1, 77–78, 81, 86–87, 89, 91, 123, 148–149, 156; lynching in, 77–79, 90–91, 123, 131, 198n6; outlawry statute, 113, 115–116, 154–155, 196n8, 206n11; racial segregation in, 81, 85; textile industry in, 1, 95, 97, 107–108. *See also* Ku Klux Klan; National Guard, in North Carolina
North Carolina Judicial Council, 154
North Carolina Press Association, 102
North Carolina School for the Deaf, 95, 104–106, 107, 193n1
North Cove (NC), 133

Oliphant, Albert, 68
Olivette, NC, 128
Orangeburg County, SC, 20
outlawry, 113–120, 154–155; of Broadus Miller, 113, 119–120, 146; in Buncombe County, 117–118; in Burke County, 113, 119, 121, 145; in Craven County, 195n5; in Durham County, 117, 154; of fugitive slaves, 114–115, 195nn5–6; in Guilford County, 154; in Jones County, 115, 154; of the "Lowry Gang," 116–117, 196n9; in New Hanover County, 114, 115, 117; in Northampton County, 155; North Carolina outlawry statute, 113, 115–116, 154–155, 196n8, 206n11; in Pitt County, 118–119; racial demographics of, 117, 197n12; in Robeson County, 116

Pacolet Creek, 74
Parker, John, 81, 186n10
Parrish, Arthur, 154–155, 206n10
Pendleton, Allen, 27–29, 33, 171n1, 179n11
Pennell, Harry Lee Pennell, 151–152
peonage (involuntary servitude), 8, 25, 30
Phifer, Edward, Jr., 157
Philadelphia, PA, 74, 100
Phoenix, SC, 7, 14–15, 25
Pickens County, SC, 86
Piedmont & Northern Railway, 6, 42, 74
Piedmont region, 1, 74, 95, 108
Pierce County, GA, 103
pistol ban: in Florida, 19–20; in South Carolina, 19–20, 169n7
Pitt County, NC, 118–119
Pittsburgh, PA, 74, 184n9
poet laureate, of North Carolina, 82
Populist Party, 77
Poteat, Britt, 152
Poteat, Tim, 152
Premier Hosiery, 156
Prince, George E., 45–48, 46, 50, 52–53, 55–56, 176n8
prison farms, 65–67, 182n15

Index 237

Pritchard, Harrison, 133–134
prohibition, in South Carolina, 18–19; in North Carolina, 197n12

railroads, 6, 16, 18, 42, 66–67, 74–75, 96, 124, 150. *See also* Greenwood and Augusta Railroad; Piedmont & Northern Railway; Southern Railway; Western North Carolina Railroad
Raleigh, NC, 1, 77, 79–80, 95, 101, 105, 124, 142
Raleigh *News and Observer*, 3, 77, 101, 102, 117, 129, 135, 143
Raleigh Times, 143
Raper, Arthur, 42, 107, 199n9
Rasor, Ezekiel, 9–10
Rasor, Harrison "Lat", 9–10, 14, 31, 48–49, 73
Reconstruction era, 59, 66, 79, 80, 106, 116, 117
Red Shirts, 7
Reed, Wallace Putnam, 15
Reed prison farm, 65
Republican Party, 77, 81
rewards, 199n10; for Broadus Miller, 113–114, 125–126, 125, 133, 137–138, 152–153; for the "Lowry Gang," 116–117; for outlaws, 117–118; for runaway slaves, 114, 115, 196n7
Reynolds, Nathaniel Augustus "Gus", 82–83
Reynolds, Robert "Buncombe Bob", 82
Richardson, William, 79
Richland County, SC, 69
Roberts, Clay, 62–63, 68–70, 183n24
Robeson County, NC, 116, 196n9
Robinson, George, 22
Robinson, Howard, 155
Rogers, Doc, 203
Rogers, Henry, 117
Rowan County, NC, 124
Russell, Bob, 59, 61

Salisbury, NC, 124, 128
Saluda, NC, 83
Saluda Mountain, 74
Saluda River (SC), 6, 25, 59
Sanders, Arthur K., 62–66, 69, 71
Sanders, James, 51–52
Savannah, GA, 104
Savannah River, 6, 7, 38
schools, 10–12, 39, 40, 41, 46, 81, 83–84, 100, 109, 167n9. *See also* North Carolina School for the Deaf
segregation, 21, 61, 81; on chain gangs, 60, 93; in prison mess hall, 61; on railways, 6, 42; of schools, 10–11; in textile industry, 16, 107–108; of water fountains, 85
sharecropping, 8, 13–14, 73, 109, 147
Shaw, Thomas A., 83
Shoals Junction, SC, 6, 7, 9, 16, 18, 42, 49, 73, 74, 150, 155; nearby lynchings, 25, 171n1
Sisney, Louis, 83
Slade, Magnus, 117
slavery, 6, 9, 10, 13, 59, 66, 68, 81, 95, 96, 104, 106, 108, 114–115, 129, 195nn5–6, 196n7. *See also* fugitive slaves; peonage
Smith, Mark, 37–39, 171n1
solitary confinement, 63, 156
Songs Sung in the Southern Appalachians (Henry), 152
South Carolina: capital punishment in, 53, 56–58, 179n14; class divisions among white residents, 26–30, 36–37, 54; concealed weapons ban, 19; constitution of 1895, 14, 37, 46; disfranchisement of African Americans in, 12, 14–15, 20; 1897 labor law, 8, 20; election of 1898, 14–15; judicial system, 21, 47–48, 51–58; lynching in, 14–15, 25–26, 27–29, 31–33, 34–38, 171n1; pistol ban, 19–20, 169n7; prohibition of alcohol, 18; racial segregation in, 6, 10–11, 16, 60, 61, 93; regulation of automobiles, 16; textile industry in, 6, 16, 27, 30, 42, 43, 46, 74. *See also* lynching: in upstate

South Carolina (cont.)
  South Carolina; town people, in South Carolina
South Carolina Department of Corrections, 156
South Carolina State Board of Public Welfare, 63
South Carolina State Penitentiary, 59–70, 155. *See also* chain gangs; convict labor; prison farms
Southern Railway, 6, 74, 102
South Mountains (NC), 104, 119
Spartanburg, SC, 32, 56, 74
Spartanburg County, SC, 64, 72, 93
Spencer, NC, 124
Spruce Pine, NC, 78–79, 98, 127, 199n10
Stark, James S., 36, 37
State Hospital for the Insane (North Carolina), 95, 104, 107
State Hospital for the Insane (South Carolina), 47, 61
Statesville, NC, 127, 141, 142–143, 150
Statesville *Landmark*, 153
Steiner, Jesse, 92
Stowe, Harriet Beecher, 114–115
Strong, Andrew, 116–117
Stuart, James "Babe," 25, 171n1
Sumter County, SC, 65
Sunday, Rev. Billy, 191n7
Swearingen, J. E., 11, 12

Tabert, Martin, 64
Tales of Old Burke (Mull), 157
Tannenbaum, Frank, 65, 94
Tate, Franklin Pierce, 95, 97, 108, 149, 156
Tate, Martha "Pattie" Thomason, 95
Tate, Samuel McDowell, 95–97
Taylor, Sam, 113
Teague, Ernest, 23
textile mills and industry, 1, 6, 16, 27, 30, 42, 43, 46, 74, 95, 97; hosiery mills, 1, 108, 109; segregation of, 16, 107–108
Thompson, Holland, 108
Tiede, Tom, 154

Tillman, Ben, 12, 26, 46, 48, 169n12
Tinkham, George, 80
town people, in South Carolina, 26–27, 28, 29, 30, 33, 54, 72. *See also* Prince, George E.; Stark, James S.
"The Tragedy of Gladys Kincaid" (ballad), 152
Trebark, 153
Triplett, Rev. Oney Williams, 99
Turkey Creek (SC), 8
Turkey Creek Baptist Church, 10, 49
Tuskegee Institute, 82, 145

United Confederate Veterans (UCV), 80, 186n8
US Department of Justice, 64, 80, 186n7

Valdese, NC, 3, 108

Wadlington, Mamie, 75
Wake County, NC, 117, 199n9
Waldensians, 108
Walker, Alpha Williams, 6, 8, 9, 31, 55, 71, 73, 75, 76, 84, 155, 184n6
Walker, Emma Mouldin, 39, 40, 41, 155
Walker, Essie, 43–45, 47–48, 51, 56, 58, 176n4
Walker, Frank, 43
Walker, Rev. James H., 39–41, 40, 155, 175n11
Walker, Tom, 6, 8, 9, 10, 14, 31, 49, 71, 73, 75, 76, 84, 184n6
Walnut Grove township (Greenwood County, SC), 6, 8, 74, 167n9
Ware Shoals, SC, 6, 7, 16, 22, 74; Briar Hollow neighborhood, 23, 39; killing of Rev. James Walker in, 39–41
Washington Post, 121
Wayne County, NC, 147–148
Webb, Lloyd, 139
Webb, Thomas, 50
Weber, Max, 117
Welcome to Our City (Wolfe), 76
Western North Carolina Railroad, 95–96

Whisenant, Ida, and Whisenant family, 1–2
white supremacy, 15, 16, 20, 21, 25, 26, 32, 37, 53, 77, 79, 81, 145. *See also* Ku Klux Klan; lynching
Wilmington, NC, 115; 1898 massacre, 77, 78
Wilmington Journal, 115
Wilmington Morning Star, 117
Wilmington Sun, 117
Wilson, Harry, Jr., 158

Wilson Creek (NC), 126, 127, 130
Winston-Salem, NC, 140, 149
Winston-Salem Journal, 5, 121
Winston-Salem *Twin City Sentinel*, 110
Wiseman, John, 133
Wolfe, Thomas, 76, 118, 149
World War I, 20, 42, 44, 60, 83, 98, 186n7

Yancey County, NC, 127, 132, 133
Young, Dr. Anne, 47, 50, 177n11
Young Men's Institute, 75, 88

www.ingramcontent.com/pod-product-compliance
Lightning Source LLC
Chambersburg PA
CBHW021854230426
43671CB00006B/385